T0113876

THE RETURN
OF CHRIST

✠ ✠ ✠

A description of events at the end of
the age as prophesied in the Bible

ROBIN CORNER

WESTBOW
PRESS®
A DIVISION OF THOMAS NELSON
& ZONDERVAN

WestBow Press books may be ordered through booksellers or by contacting:

WestBow Press
A Division of Thomas Nelson & Zondervan
1663 Liberty Drive
Bloomington, IN 47403
www.westbowpress.com
844-714-3454

Scripture taken from the New King James Version® Copyright © 1982 by Thomas Nelson. Used by permission. All rights reserved.

ISBN: 978-1-6642-4876-2 (sc)
ISBN: 978-1-6642-4877-9 (e)

Print information available on the last page.

WestBow Press rev. date: 02/03/2022

To my wife Margaret

without whose help this book would
never have been written

CONTENTS

✠ ✠ ✠

ACKNOWLEDGEMENTS

✠ ✠ ✠

I would like to thank all those who have helped me with their encouragement in the four-year project of study for this book. In particular, I would like to thank Jack Guerin, Geoff Willmott, Dave Mann, Drs Tony and Felicity Dale, Dr Victor Choudhrie, David Hall, Gloria Adagi, Dr Fritz Cobrado, Dr Mary Okelo, and the late Ken Kissling in this regard. Thank you all for your positivity and enthusiasm.

I would also like to acknowledge the great work of other authors in the field of eschatology, who have helped me understand the teaching of the Bible on this topic, especially the teaching on the Book of Revelation. Two notable scholars I would mention in this regard are Geoff Beale and Dean Davis. Their painstaking attention to detail, and thorough grasp of the subject, have really helped cement what I have felt God was showing me, and given me a satisfying clarity on a number of details.

Most of all, I would like to thank my wife Margaret. Many times, I have spent time studying or writing, which otherwise would have been time with her, or family time with our adult children and grandchildren, and she has generously accepted that time away. While I have been absorbed in the project, she has been a great encouragement, and in many ways has "gone the extra mile" in helping in all sorts of ways. Not only all this, but as a trained professional editor, she has edited this text, and has made it easier to read. This book is therefore dedicated to her.

Finally, the acknowledgements would not be complete if I did not publicly thank God, who created me and the universe, and provided the keys outlined in this book to gain some understanding of it, and my Lord Jesus Christ, who delivered me from darkness and daily leads me into the Heavenly Father's ways.

FOREWORD BY JOHN REA, SM

✠ ✠ ✠

Thank you, Robin Corner, for this work, the fruit of four years of close study of "End Times."

The backbone of "The Return of Christ" is the New Testament and the detailed examination the author has made of Scripture verses that refer to the Christ's Second Coming. However, he has not limited his research to the Bible. He has also made use of the Church Fathers, the major Creeds, biblical commentaries and the writings of theologians.

Robin Corner gives us an in-depth presentation of St Matthew's statements on the last things and concludes that the prophetic words they contain were fulfilled partly in the year 70 of our era and continue to be fulfilled in our own time. He doesn't mind if readers choose to disagree with him.

In the chapters that follow his exposition of the relevant passages in St Matthew's Gospel, the author outlines the major views about the End Times that have emerged through the centuries. He is concise and accurate in defining the words used to explain the different stances. He outlines the strengths and weakness of the major positions. He encourages his readers to study the pertinent Scriptures for themselves and draw their own conclusions.

Corner then returns to his theme and sums up what the whole of the New Testament has to say about the End. Within this section of the work, before he begins his comments on the Book of Revelation, he usefully reminds the reader of basic generally accepted principles for interpreting the Bible.

But it is not only the New Testament that deals with the Day of the Lord. The Hebrew Scriptures also expound it and that's the content of chapter 17. Chapter 18 is about the Seventy-week prophecy in the Book of Daniel. The chapters that follow look at the final Judgment and the New Heavens and the New Earth. In the final chapter and in the epilogue the author lays down challenges to all who read his book.

A pleasing feature of the "Day of the Lord" is Corner's respect for the people whose views differ from his own. Nor does he try to force his conclusions on others. He is courteous throughout.

"The Return of Christ" is an excellent book for anyone interested in the big Biblical themes.

John Rea, SM

PROLOGUE BY GEOFF WILLMOTT, EVANGELIST

✛ ✛ ✛

Inspired by the Holy Spirit to present a fresh understanding of what scripture says, Robin embarked on four years of research to present an emphatic answer to an age-long topic in Christian thought.

I grew up as a teenager in the 1960's when The Second Coming was a popular teaching. My dad, Roy, was a keen student and teacher who sowed this reality into my heart. I have vivid memories of evangelist George Curle presenting his Faithfinder Film Crusade to our church in Hamilton. He even had an estimated time, based on his understanding, of when Jesus was coming back. Needless to say, many people came to faith at these meetings. Probably a better known End Time evangelist that I knew in the 1980's was Barry Smith who wrote eight books on Christian eschatology. He spoke worldwide on the New World Order and New Zealand being chosen as the first test of this new governance. (Wikipedia - Barry Smith - preacher)

I guess, because of this predictive type of End Times preaching, a lot of Christians have been turned off. All these types of events have happened over the centuries and Jesus has not returned. A warning came from Jesus: "Therefore you also be ready, for the Son of Man is coming at an hour you do not expect" (Matthew 24:44). As followers of Jesus, we cannot be ignorant of His command. Robin brings fresh revelation to engage a new generation with a subject that has been totally ignored by most preachers over the last twenty years.

Robin is a trained Bible scholar, evangelist, disciple maker and movement initiator (in Kenya). In 2009, he organised the first World House Church Summit in Delhi for Victor Choudhrie who has, probably, one of the largest movements of house churches in the world created by disciples who make disciples. I, personally, know of occasions when Robin has led people of peace to faith in Jesus. He is not just a theorist but lives out what he believes. His wife, Margaret, is an entrepreneur in education and actively moves in the power of Holy Spirit in tandem with Robin's ministry.

Robin has written a book which will satisfy the 'detail' person and the 'overview' person. He covers the historical background and the different understandings that scholars have had. He introduces a very simple understanding mainly with conclusions from Jesus' Olivet Discourse. Robin uses the Old Testament as a backdrop to the New Testament. He says Jesus and the Apostles build on the Old Testament with a greater clarity and authority. I agree with his conclusion that The End of Time and The Last Day is the culmination of everything on earth when Jesus returns, once and for all, to complete the work that He started.

As a former pastor and now evangelist and disciple maker, I find the coming of Jesus again is an exciting part of my Gospel message. For example, the current Corona virus outbreak can be compared to an even worse virus the Bible calls "sin". This is a sign of Jesus' return (Mt.24:7). As always, the antidote to sin is Jesus who can heal us from all our sicknesses and diseases and deliver us from our sinful nature, death, and Satan. I have found students are more willing to talk about the supernatural, the future and judgment, than believers. People are looking for answers to what is happening. We should not let Hollywood film makers and 'fake news' readers usurp that role.

You will be blessed by reading 'The Return of Christ' written by Robin. I pray for open hearts to receive this 'now' word from the throne room of heaven. I believe it will be used by God to raise an army of young people (and older ones!!) to evangelise the world with a new boldness to fulfill the Great Commission.

AUTHOR'S INTRODUCTION

✚ ✚ ✚

Hi! I'm Robin Corner. I'm married to Margaret, with two adult children, and I became a follower of Jesus Christ some years ago. Did you know that you can actually get to know God? I started following Jesus 35 years ago, and soon found that He wanted me to get to know Him. How do you get to know a person? You talk to them, but more importantly you listen to them. I found that I started getting to know God as soon as I asked Him into my life. It wasn't that He shouted at me from the sky. And it wasn't that I heard with my ears an audible voice. I would just get impressions in my mind that He was saying something. And as I acted on these impressions, I found out that His guidance was very real. Many Christians will speak about the same experience. In fact, I believe that every Christian "hears from God", but some do not recognise the experience for what it is. Being a Christian is not just a matter of attending a church. We need a personal relationship with Jesus.

I was brought up as an Anglican and became a Catholic after marrying Margaret. We have both participated in Pentecostal / charismatic / evangelical churches. Nowadays, we both worship at our local Catholic church, and have connections with several home-based churches.

There is no more stimulating topic than The Return of Christ. My prayer is that this book will shake people up and get us all talking about the soon return to planet Earth of the Lord Jesus Christ. I urge you to check out the passages I quote and find other passages which either confirm or question my conclusions. Come to your own conclusions and become an expert in eschatology ("The study of the last things"). To me, the Christian experience is the most exciting thing in the world. God has shown me that He is real in so many ways. More than that, He has shown me that He has a plan for my life.

The "Day of the Lord" was the most exciting prospect to Christians in the first century. They believed a day was coming when Jesus would come back to earth in glory. They had another term for this event as well. They called it "the *parousia*"[1] – which means "the appearing" in Greek. The appearing of Jesus Christ would also signal the end of this present age, and the beginning of the age to come.

Today there are many different ideas amongst sincere Christians on what the Return of Christ will look like. Some say there will be a seven-year "tribulation" – time of deep suffering and trouble on earth before Jesus comes. Some think that before this seven-year period, Jesus will come and "rapture" all the Christians off the earth and take them to a place of safety in heaven. And what will happen when He does finally come to earth? What does the "Day of the Lord lead into? Many Bible believers think that He will reign on earth for 1000 years before His rule is transferred to heaven, but others think "the new heavens and the new earth" will start immediately following His return.

I love a debate! So we'll look at the main ideas on the way through, and consider some points for and against. We'll look at the history and find out how it came about that there is such difference of opinion. We will be studying a lot of scripture on our way. I began this search for truth several years ago, and intensified it just four years ago, when I resolved to gather together all the scripture I could find about Jesus' return. My own views will quickly become obvious – but let's dialogue if you don't agree. For me it's been a fascinating journey, and I hope it will be for you also.

Finally, what difference does it all make? I will share some ideas on how we can apply this knowledge to our lives in the here and now. I've

---

[1] Or the "epiphania" or "apokalupsis" – see page 131

written this book to interest not only Christians of all ages and stages, but also people who may not have made a decision to follow Jesus. This book is for you if you have no knowledge of the topic! But if you have extensive prior knowledge, I think what I have written here will be thought provoking. If you are a believer in Jesus and look to His return, we are in 90% agreement anyway, regardless of your view of the end times. If you are not yet a believer in Jesus, I pray this book helps to complete the jigsaw just a little!

I pray you understand the implications of the coming "Day of the Lord".

Sincere best wishes
Robin Corner

Chapter One

EXPECTATIONS

✠ ✠ ✠

BABY BOOMER GENERATION EXPECTATION

Many Christians today have an expectancy about Jesus Christ coming again. This is not a new phenomenon – it was the expectation of Christians in the first century. They talked about the coming "Day of the Lord". As I mentioned in the introduction, expecting the Day of the Lord is associated with expecting the end of the age, and a new age to begin. I think this expectancy is not limited to Christians. For myself personally, even before I became a Christian, I had the idea that some sort of new age was about to start. As a boy and later as a teenager in the 1960's and early 70's, I was part of the Beetles, Bob Dylan, and Baby Boomers' generation. Young people were in many cases idealistic, more so than now I think. There was a general perception held by many that the old order was coming to an end.

A NEW AGE COMING?

The Bob Dylan song reflected this feeling:

"The order is
Rapidly fadin'

And the first one now
Will later be last
For the times they are a-changin'".

MY SEARCH FOR MEANING

When I was 18, at university, I was looking for some sort of meaning to life. As a child growing up in the UK, my parents had encouraged my brother and me to attend our local Anglican church, where we were choirboys. I had stopped attending at age 13, concluding that it was all very boring. The idea that there could be any kind of deep truth related to church or Christianity never crossed my mind. I decided that "the yogis from the east" must have the secret. So I learned transcendental meditation as taught by the Hindu monk, Maharishi Mahesh Yogi. He taught that we were at the start of an "Age of Enlightenment". I practiced meditation, yoga, and read the Hindu text the "Rig Veda" every day, seeking to attain the knowledge of "enlightenment".

Others in my generation in the 60's and 70's took on a similar kind of mindset. The Beetles famously went on a retreat with the Maharishi in India. Other entertainment icons took on other "new age" ideas. Dr Timothy Leary talked about psychedelic drugs giving a "consciousness expanding" experience, and prescribed LSD to subjects as young as seven. People sang about the "age of Aquarius" – a new age according to astrology. Half a million young people attended the legendary Woodstock music festival in 1969. Many of us thought the old order was coming to an end and a new, kinder age would begin. We had picked up on something. A new age was coming! But we didn't understand how or what it would be like. We had an utterly mistaken concept of the new age. No new, kinder age has been established. The only obvious carry-over from those heady days of the 60's and 70's is a proliferation of ageing rock-stars giving concerts. The "free love" of those days proved to be just licentious sexual behaviour, and for the most part idealism turned to materialism. Among the more mystically inclined, no "Age of Enlightenment" or "Age of Aquarius" ever started.

But what sort of expectations of change did the Christians have?

CHRISTIAN EXPECTATIONS

I knew one guy at school, Phil, who had such a strong commitment to Christ he talked about his faith to school friends and became known at school as a Christian. Despite having attended church and been a choirboy, I really had no idea why anybody would want to talk about Christ to school mates and face possible mockery and exclusion from the "cool" set. Of course, I knew that in general the UK was considered a "Christian country", and that people who went to church were at least loosely "Christian", but this was another dimension altogether, which I thought was very strange. I discovered years later that there were such people as what some term as "born-again" Christians in the 1960's and 1970's, to whom commitment to Christ was a serious, life-impacting way of living, and who believed in such things as heaven and eternal punishment, and the Bible. I never met any apart from Phil, and two friends of my mother's, Geoff and John, both of whom were obviously genuinely caring guys. Geoff, an Anglican vicar who did a lot of volunteer social work, talked about his "call from the Lord", which I considered puzzling but only slightly intriguing. John was a student counsellor at the local polytechnic and exuded care for the students and indeed for anyone who crossed his path. I never talked to Phil about his convictions, but he seemed very comfortable with them. I did know that some Christians thought the end of the world was near. Some believed in what they called "the rapture" but I was not aware of that.

"LEFT BEHIND"

The idea of being "left behind" really caught on in the culture, in some cases to be mocked, and in some to be believed. The "Left Behind" films came out in 2000 and again in 2014. In the 2014 version, the heroine, Chloe Steele, is hugging her little brother, when the "rapture" comes, and instantaneously she is left holding a set of empty clothes. Every child in the world, and millions of adults, suddenly vanish (to meet with Jesus in the air) and we see the empty children's ward in the hospital with neat little piles of clothes in the cots, as well as piles of clothes on the ground where adults have disappeared. All is chaos in the shopping mall, with mothers and child minders screaming and wondering where their children have gone. A car comes hurtling through the plate glass windows because the driver has been "raptured". This is followed by a small plane ploughing into the car park, looters breaking into shops, and fires starting where cars have crashed.

Meanwhile Chloe's father, Rayford, is an airline pilot, and he is flying an airliner on a New York to London flight. He was visiting the cabin crew area at the rear of the plane when there was a jolt and the "rapture" happened. Sudden screams erupt from the mothers as they realise their children and some of the other passengers have vanished. Rayford dashes to the pilot's seat when he feels the plane lurch, noticing on the way that one of the flight attendants has disappeared. When he gets back to the pilots' cockpit, he finds his co-pilot gone, just leaving his clothes on the co-pilot's seat. He manages to wrestle with the joystick to bring the plane back under control. But then another airliner enters his airspace and comes screaming towards his plane. As it shoots past, just clipping his plane on the way through, he notices that there is no-one piloting it. The pilot must have been "raptured"! He sends out a mayday radio message about this other plane crashing but gets no response.

Threads of the rest of the movie include Chloe looking for her mother, who was a believer and had unsuccessfully tried to persuade all the family to follow Jesus. Of course she can't be found – she has been "raptured"; Rayford nursing his plane back to New York; Chloe meeting the pastor of the church the family attended (he missed out on the "rapture" because though he preached about Jesus he didn't really believe); and all the various characters gradually coming to the realisation that this was what many of them had been taught at Sunday school, or by a friend, or in Rayford's case by his believer-wife. To varying degrees, they had been taught that all believers in Jesus would one day be taken out of the world to meet Jesus in the air ("the rapture"). This event would come completely unexpectedly, and after it, there would be a time of great suffering and struggle on earth, for those "left behind". The movie ends with the plane landing precariously. Amidst a scene of great devastation one of the characters says "This looks like the end of the world". Chloe closes ominously with "No. I'm afraid this is only the beginning."

The "Left Behind" series of books on which the "Left Behind" movies were based started with the novel "Left Behind" in 1995, by Tim LaHay. Originally intended as a one-off novel, it grew into a series of 16 books, which sold a massive 80 million copies, and influenced the thinking of a generation, particularly in the USA (Wikipedia). The 2001 movie grossed over US$4 million, all in the US, and the 2014 movie grossed over US$14 million in the US, plus over $5 million internationally.

LATE, GREAT, PLANET EARTH AND OTHER THEORIES

Non-fiction books sprung up to back up this interpretation of Bible prophecy, one of the best known being Hal Lindsay's book "The Late Great Planet Earth", published in 1970, (Lindsey, 1970) which the New York Times called the "number 1 non-fiction bestseller of the decade." A whole industry of books, videos, seminars, and movies developed, including such titles as "88 Reasons the Rapture will be in 1988" by Edgar Whisenant which sold 4.5 million copies. Whisenant's subsequent book on why the Rapture would take place in 1989 was less popular! Lindsay also picked 1988 as the year of the rapture. I remember the otherwise notable New Zealand evangelist Barry Smith, who was absolutely convinced in the 1990's that we had entered the "seven-year" tribulation period at the end of the age (I think he believed in a "mid-tribulation rapture"). So the Christians by and large unfortunately were not any more successful in visualising the future than my Transcendental Meditation friends and me. Nevertheless, eventually I became convinced of the truth of Christ and the Bible for other reasons, and "jumped ship", giving up TM and being baptised a Christian in 1985. It was the best and most important decision of my life.

Chapter Two

THE TIME OF THE END – SO MANY DIFFERENT THEORIES

✠ ✠ ✠

When I began my Christian adventure, somebody gave me "The Late Great Planet Earth", and I didn't think to question it, assuming it taught what the Bible taught. Most Bible-believing Christians I knew didn't know that any alternative view about "the rapture" and the "7-year tribulation" existed. And this is still true in some churches today, though there is widespread disillusionment with talk about the second coming. Many Christians have concluded that end-time doctrine is just too confusing or divisive to discuss. Others believe in these end-time events with the same fervency as the virgin birth, or eternal life for the believer. Read, for example, this article from a 2017 issue of Charisma Magazine:

"Jesus said, "Not everyone who says to Me, 'Lord, Lord,' shall enter the kingdom of heaven, but he who does the will of My Father who is in heaven" (Matt. 7:21-23). If you are reading this after the rapture has occurred, it's because you weren't ready. Jesus said in Matthew 25:10 that "those who were ready went in ... And the door was shut." Let me give you 20 pieces of counsel to survive this terrible time if you miss God's first roundup, the rapture.

"1. Do not believe the explanations given by the secular media. Christians have not been beamed to some interplanetary spaceship to be reprogrammed. We have not been taken by aliens, and we're not in Buenos Aires, Togo or Europe. We have left the earth on a cloud of glory to be with Jesus forever.

"2. Get rid of your cell phone. If you do not agree with the government of the final shabua and the charming world leader, you will be hunted. Your cell phone can be tracked. Throw it in a river or lake far from where you are going to be."

The article goes on to make another 15 points on what to do if you miss the rapture (Williams, 2017)

I was somewhat surprised to receive the article, from which the above extract has been taken, from a friend. I wondered if it was a spoof for a moment, but quickly realised that it was penned by a perfectly serious author in a reputable Christian magazine. Many of my friends would take it very seriously. But in the article, though written by an academic, there is absolutely no suggestion that the events outlined are anything other than undisputed fact. The advice is given in the same factual tone as if the author was explaining how to get from New York to Washington. All practical tips, such as throwing away a cell phone, and later how to recognise the "Antichrist", are given as if the rapture and seven-year tribulation were a universally accepted sequence of events to start some time soon. The article does not even hint at the following:

- The Biblical presuppositions assumed in the article were only formulated from 1830 or thereabouts;
- These pre-suppositions are part of a system of Biblical interpretation known as Dispensationalism;
- That the so-called "7-year tribulation" is nowhere found plainly stated in the Bible but is based on an interpretation of Daniel 9:27 by a Catholic Jesuit priest in the 17th century.

- There are at least 8 different theological positions in relation to eschatology[2] taken by reputable sections of the Church over the centuries, and all these positions still have advocates today!

Another tenet of Dispensationalism is the 1000-year reign of Jesus from Jerusalem when He returns, again a firm belief of many evangelical Christians who are unaware of any contrary opinion, not realising that over history by far the majority of Christians have rejected this idea. Also, all the early church creeds, and the classical reformers rejected the idea of the "millennial reign". The idea that there is no literal millennial reign became known as "Amillennialism" in the 20th century. That is far too long a word! I refer to it as "Amil" throughout this book.

Over the years I became aware of alternatives and became more and more doubtful especially about the "pre-tribulation rapture theory". It seemed to me that there was little Biblical evidence supporting it, even though it is taught by many reputable and popular Bible teachers. In 2016 I determined to do a thorough study on the end of the age. As there are so many conflicting theories, I decided to identify every scripture passage I could find on the topic, and let the Bible tell its own story. My collection of passages grew and grew; I stopped copying them when I had collected over 380 passages, but the collection still grew.

Now I want to state at the outset that my intention in this book is not to cause division or confusion. The first and major issue which everyone needs to settle in their own minds is whether Jesus is coming again at all. If you believe He is coming, we are 99% in agreement. I don't mind if you have a different view of the sequence of events and have the utmost respect for all sincere Christ followers, whatever their opinion on this topic. As you read through the book, you will become aware of my view! But if I become over-polemical in my writing style, please forgive me and put it down to an excess of zeal. I am passionate about this because I have found that when all the scriptures are laid out next to each other, the conclusion is not difficult, but simple! And the result is an end to confusion. This book will particularly be of interest

---

[2] Eschatology is the technical term for the branch of theology which deals with the return of Jesus and the end of the age

to people who like to read the scriptures for themselves and make their own minds up, while not getting lost in the territory of the cults.

So let us explore the scriptures together and see what they actually say in regard to this greatest climax in all of history. During my intensive study of scripture, I realised that the coming "Day of the Lord" referred to by many of the Bible authors is synonymous with Jesus coming in glory to earth a second time (though the Old Testament authors did not understand this) and is also referred to by such terms as the "day of doom", "day of wrath", "day of Jesus Christ" and others. It is a central theme of the Bible. This was a new revelation for me, and it came not through consulting theologians, but through pondering the scriptures and asking God to open them to my understanding. I also found some theological authors very helpful, but this was very much a secondary aid to understanding. Another thing I did not know at the beginning of my quest was that even today the Catholic and Orthodox churches have a quite different view from the Dispensationalist teaching which is so familiar to many, and their teachings greatly encouraged me at the end of the project.

Matthew's Gospel, especially in the "Olivet Discourse" of Mat 24-25, which is supported by similar passages in Mark 13 and Luke 18 and 21, is the definitive view of Jesus on the matter and is written in a plain, non-symbolic manner. Matthew of all the New Testament writers had most to say about the second coming of Jesus, apart from Revelation, which is symbolic and much more open to interpretation than Matthew. So, we will take a section of Matthew to give an initial foundation, then we will survey the history of the Church and track the emergence of each of the main systems of interpretation. I find that most Christians know that there are different teachings on Bible prophecy, but few are aware of the full range of different interpretations over history. It will be helpful to gain some perspective on the different views across the centuries. After that we will look at the Bible as a whole and let the scripture speak for itself. Thankfully, there is much teaching about the Return of Christ in the Bible which we can all agree on, whatever system of Biblical interpretation we prefer. I also summarise the positions of some of the major churches in the epilogue.

Some may ask, "Can we base our study predominantly on the Bible? In our day, shouldn't we go to science with our questions on the future of the world and universe?" At the outset, I would like to say that I believe that there is nothing in the Bible which contradicts science. Of course, as we shall see, the books of the Bible are written in various genres, a fact which is often missed by popular commentators. But fundamentally I believe we can trust sacred scripture. There is not space at present for a full discussion on its reliability. But, confining this topic for the present to my own impressions, I was surprised to find what I thought was the most articulate and inspiring statement on the reliability of scripture in the Catechism of the Catholic Church, which I quote below. Of the 2.3 billion professing Christians in the world today, 1.2 billion (52%) are Catholic (Lim, 2018), which suggests to me we should take the Catholic view seriously. The Catechism was promulgated by Pope John Paul II in 1992, as a summary of Catholic belief.

(Catechism in *italics*, with my comments in ordinary type):

CATHOLIC POSITION ON THE VALUE OF SCRIPTURE

The Catechism begins its section on scripture with a beautiful statement of its precious nature as the Word of God. This includes clauses 103 and 104:

103 For this reason, the Church has always venerated the Scriptures as she venerates the Lord's Body. She never ceases to present to the faithful the bread of life, taken from the one table of God's Word and Christ's Body.

104 In Sacred Scripture, the Church constantly finds her nourishment and her strength, for she welcomes it not as a human word, "but as what it really is, the word of God". "In the sacred books, the Father who is in heaven comes lovingly to meet his children, and talks with them."

The Catechism affirms the belief that scripture is inspired by the Holy Spirit and therefore cannot teach error:

107 The inspired books teach the truth. "Since therefore all that the inspired authors or sacred writers affirm should be regarded as affirmed by the Holy Spirit, we must acknowledge that the books of Scripture firmly, faithfully, and without error teach that truth which God, for the sake of our salvation, wished to see confided to the Sacred Scriptures."

The Catholic Church holds that scripture should be understood within the framework of received tradition. Protestant churches disagree with this, maintaining that scripture alone should determine faith and Christian living. But surely in practice, each church has developed its own traditions for interpreting scripture?

113 2. Read the Scripture within "the living Tradition of the whole Church". According to a saying of the Fathers, Sacred Scripture is written principally in the Church's heart rather than in documents and records, for the Church carries in her Tradition the living memorial of God's Word, and it is the Holy Spirit who gives her the spiritual interpretation of the Scripture (". . . according to the spiritual meaning which the Spirit grants to the Church").

We will have much to say on the difference between didactic teaching and metaphorical writing in scripture as this book progresses. Clauses 115 and 116 draw attention to the difference between literal and spiritual understandings, and mention the necessity of sound exegesis. "Exegesis" is the analysis of what was the intent of the original author when writing a given passage:

115 According to an ancient tradition, one can distinguish between two senses of Scripture: the literal and the spiritual, the latter being subdivided into the allegorical, moral and anagogical senses. the profound concordance of the four senses guarantees all its richness to the living reading of Scripture in the Church.

116 The literal sense is the meaning conveyed by the words of Scripture and discovered by exegesis, following the rules of sound interpretation: "All other senses of Sacred Scripture are based on the literal."

So we can be confident that it is through the Bible that we will learn the true picture of the shape of events to come.

Chapter Three

THE END OF THE AGE ACCORDING TO MATTHEW'S GOSPEL

✠ ✠ ✠

THE WHEAT AND THE TARES GROW TOGETHER UNTIL THE HARVEST

In Matthew 13, Jesus told a very succinct parable about the time of the end. It describes very simply and clearly the destinations of the "sons of the Kingdom" ie the "righteous", and of the "sons of the wicked one", alias "those who practice lawlessness".

THE PARABLE OF THE TARES

Jesus contrasts the fate of the righteous and the unrepentant wicked in this parable and explanation:

Note there is no ambivalence at all in the chronology, or meaning, of this parable. Jesus says twice that the time portrayed is the "end of the age", then makes clear that this coincides with the start of the kingdom of God. We will discuss who are the "sons of the kingdom" and the "sons of the wicked one" after we have read the passage.

Mat 13:24-30 Another parable He put forth to them, saying: "The kingdom of heaven is like a man who sowed good seed in his field; [25] but while men slept, his enemy came and sowed tares among the wheat and went his way. [26] But when the grain had sprouted and produced a crop, then the tares also appeared. [27] So the servants of the owner came and said to him, 'Sir, did you not sow good seed in your field? How then does it have tares?' [28] He said to them, 'An enemy has done this.' The servants said to him, 'Do you want us then to go and gather them up?' [29] But he said, 'No, lest while you gather up the tares you also uproot the wheat with them. [30] Let both grow together until the harvest, and at the time of harvest I will say to the reapers, "First gather together the tares and bind them in bundles to burn them, but gather the wheat into my barn."

THE PARABLE OF THE TARES EXPLAINED

Matthew records Jesus explanation to the disciples of this parable later in the chapter:

Then Jesus sent the multitude away and went into the house. And His disciples came to Him, saying, "Explain to us the parable of the tares of the field."

[37] He answered and said to them: "He who sows the good seed is the Son of Man. [38] The field is the world, the good seeds are the sons of the kingdom, but the tares are the sons of the wicked *one*. [39] The enemy who sowed them is the devil, the harvest is the end of the age, and the reapers are the angels. [40] Therefore as the tares are gathered and burned in the fire, so it will be at the end of this age. [41] The Son of Man will send out His angels, and they will gather out of His kingdom all things that offend, and those who practice lawlessness, [42] and will cast them into the furnace of fire. There will be wailing and gnashing of teeth. [43] Then the righteous will shine forth as the sun in the kingdom of their Father. He who has ears to hear, let him hear!"

SONS OF THE KINGDOM VS SONS
OF THE WICKED ONE

It is important to realise that we all start off as "those who practice lawlessness" on account of the fact that we have all fallen short of God's standard in some way. I have never met anyone who could look me in the eye and say, "I have never sinned", nor could I ever say such a thing myself. Our sin has alienated us from God, who must punish sin, because He is God, and justice must be seen in the universe. Even if we are reasonably well behaved and have not committed any crimes, it is still the case that we have fallen short of God's standard. In Biblical thought, and in reality, everyone starts off as needing forgiveness.

Christians believe that God offers every one of us the opportunity to be forgiven for our sins completely, no matter what they have been. Jesus was the only person who ever lived who was completely free from sin. Because He did not sin, He had no penalty to pay for Himself so He could pay our penalty. There is a two-step process to becoming a "son or daughter of the kingdom". 1. We must be willing to repent, which means we must accept that we have sinned, being sorry for our sins and be willing to change. 2. We must trust in this sacrifice of Jesus and believe in Him. We then receive full remission of penalties immediately. We are completely forgiven, freed from the bondage of sin and empowered to live a life of holiness and righteousness in the eyes of God. If we live out our life in relationship with the Lord, and are obedient to Him, He transforms us so that our character embodies true righteousness.

It is important to realise that we are not talking about an odious self-righteousness which makes us think we are better than other people. We are talking about the righteousness of Christ, which is a gift from God when we put our trust in Him. From that point on, if we have genuinely believed, He works on us so that our character becomes more like His character.

Throughout this book, when I refer to "righteous" (adjective), "the righteous" (righteous people), and/or "righteousness" (the abstract noun), I am always referring to those made righteous in God's eyes through faith in Jesus Christ. I am never referring to some supposedly superior, moral being claiming to be better than anyone else. This type of "righteousness" is immediately available to anyone who is willing to 1. Admit that they have fallen short of God's standards and have "sinned"; 2. Are willing to trust Jesus Christ for forgiveness and 3. Are willing to cooperate with God's work in their life to improve their moral character. Anyone requiring clarification of this and assistance with beginning or deepening a life of relationship with Jesus Christ should write to me at the email address at the back of the book.

COMPARISON OF THE PARABLE OF THE TARES WITH THE POPULAR VIEW

The pattern of events we have seen in the movie, "Left Behind" in chapter 1, assume a pattern of events including

1. The "rapture" – all the Christians are snatched secretly away to meet Jesus in the air (this is known as the pre-tribulation rapture theory which has been extensively taught in many evangelical churches).
2. The rest of humanity is "left behind" to endure seven years of intense "tribulation".

I have no desire to "attack" brothers and sisters in Christ who hold this view. Love is the most important thing between followers in Christ. But surely we can examine the Bible and discuss our observations with a view to establishing what the Bible actually teaches? This theory conflicts with the parable of the Tares, which quite categorically states "let both (the believers and the non-believers) grow together until the harvest", which happens at "the end of the age". The good seeds (wheat) are the "sons of the kingdom" – so from this parable we know that the believers will only be separated at the time of the harvest from the "sons of the wicked one". The reapers are told FIRST to gather the tares, i.e., the wicked, and throw them into the fire. THEN the believers will shine forth like the sun, even as they are being taken to Jesus' barn, in the metaphor. This passage surely poses a difficulty for the "pre-tribulation rapture" theory because (1) they both grow together until the harvest and (2) at the time of the harvest, the wicked are gathered first.

MATTHEW ON THE SECOND COMING OF JESUS

So let's continue looking at the light Matthew can shed on the issue. As previously mentioned, Matthew, of all the New Testament writers has the most extensive and detailed description of Jesus' future coming, as described by Jesus Himself. This description is found as a continuous discourse from Matthew 24:3 to Matthew 25:46, in response to a question from His disciples. It comprises of a chronological description of events, with explanations and three succinct parables, and so makes an easy to study foundation for understanding of the events. To set the context for Jesus' response, we will start discussion at Matthew 21, the last visit of Jesus to Jerusalem during His earthly ministry.

JESUS COMES TO JERUSALEM

Matthew's Gospel verses 21:1 through 24:2 describe this last visit, around 31 AD. He arrives on a donkey (fulfilling Zechariah 14) amidst rapturous greetings from the crowd. He makes His way to the temple, clears out the money-changers in a glorious torrent of righteous indignation, and miraculously heals the blind and the lame there. The scribes and Pharisees, the religious professionals of that time, react with anger and Jesus rebukes them, saying

(Mat 21:43) ... the kingdom of God will be taken from you and given to a nation bearing the fruits of it...................

This is a key point, and we shall return to it. Jesus powerfully confronted those who thought they were very virtuous and religious, but in fact were not.

TRYING TO TRAP HIM

They carried on trying to trap Him in His words, wanting Him to incriminate himself, but they were no match against His powerful parables and wisdom. After they had exhausted their fruitless attempts to bring Him down, He then gave a prolonged discourse containing the strongest language He had yet used against them:

Mat 23:27-28, 33 "Woe to you, scribes and Pharisees, hypocrites! For you are like whitewashed tombs which indeed appear beautiful outwardly, but inside are full of dead men's bones and all uncleanness. Even so you also outwardly appear righteous to men, but inside you are full of hypocrisy and lawlessness...Serpents, brood of vipers! How can you escape the condemnation of hell?"

While they should have been rejoicing at the miraculous healings in the temple and appreciating the boldness of Jesus in clearing the temple of the corrupt money changers, they were full of jealousy and hate. They were plotting to have Him killed. It was the ultimate rejection of an incredible blessing from God. Rejection of something which is genuinely from God is a perilous thing. Jesus knew what was happening. He prophesied the complete destruction of the temple:

Mat 24:2 "Do you see all these things?" he asked. "I tell you the truth, not one stone here will be left on another, every one will be thrown down."

THE DISCIPLES' QUESTION

It was in this context that His disciples approached Him, as He sat on the Mount of Olives, and asked Him to answer the question that lay on their hearts:

Mat 24:3 "Tell us, when will these things be? And what will be the sign of Your coming, and of the end of the age?"

They were first century Jewish men. They believed that the end of the age was close and the "Day of the Lord" was at hand. They had been with Jesus for three years. They vacillated, but at least in their clearer moments, they realised that Jesus was the Messiah, the chosen One of God. They expected Him to come in glory at the end of the age. The full answer He gave takes up the rest of Matthew chapter 24 and the whole of Matthew chapter 25. It forms the most comprehensive and clear answer to their question in the Bible. We will examine His answer in detail.

We must be aware that His comments were directed to His followers at that time and very accurately predicted what would happen to them. He said "…. this generation will by no means pass away till all these things take place." We will look at some of the events as recorded in history and we will find indeed that the prophetic discourses in Matthew were remarkably fulfilled in many ways in Jesus' own generation.

But He was not just speaking to his disciples at that time. He was speaking to His disciples of all times, and especially to us as some of the prophecies are being fulfilled in a way today that they could never have been in the past. This is a very common feature of Biblical prophecy. The prophets often spoke about a situation in their own time, but as they considered the local contemporary scenes, the Holy Spirit gave revelation also about the future, sometimes the distant future. Jesus Himself was the same. As well as speaking to His disciples of that time, He gave us in our generation clues to alert us to watch for His coming, perhaps in our own time. So, as we look at the prophetic discourse, we will also consider how the prophecy may apply to our world today. The reader may judge whether the events and conditions of the past and present outlined here are convincing fulfilments of Jesus' prophecies. We will also consider the events still future. Can we expect the final end of the era to unfold as Jesus described?

Chapter Four

SIGNS OF JESUS' RETURN IN MATTHEW'S GOSPEL

✛ ✛ ✛

WIDESPREAD DECEPTION

Mat 24:4-5 And Jesus answered and said to them: "Take heed that no one deceives you. For many will come in My name, saying, 'I am the Christ,' and will deceive many.

HISTORICAL FULFILMENT (MAT 24:4-5) SHORTLY AFTER JESUS' DEATH AND RESURRECTION

We will start with historical fulfilment. As the early church grew, Rome declined in morality. This reached a new low point when Nero became emperor (date of reign: 54 -68 AD). During the time of Nero and after, worse and worse cults sprang up and the old virtues ceased to exert their moderating influence. He told the people he was a god and was completely unrestrained in sin. He murdered his brother with the help of his mother, then murdered her, then his wife. He then "married" a young man who looked like his wife, and then murdered him. He organised the most depraved orgies and started viciously persecuting

Christians. In this environment all sorts of pagan cults thrived, and deception was widespread.

MODERN-DAY FULFILMENT (MAT 24:4-5)

Turning our attention to our own era, one sign prior to the events leading to His return is deception – which abounds everywhere today. European countries which once had Christian culture at the root, are now "multi-religious". Hindu gurus and Buddhist monks with what Christians believe to be deceptive philosophies flood into the once-Christian West and attract adherents. Celebrities publicise new-age worldviews, again deceptive according to the Bible. Few are even aware that the truths of the Bible, which once undergirded our society, are being turned upside-down by these philosophies.

THE SIGNS OF HIS RETURN – WARS, FAMINES, PESTILENCES, AND EARTHQUAKES

(Jesus continued:) Mat 24:6-8 And you will hear of wars and rumours of wars. See that you are not troubled; for all these things must come to pass, but the end is not yet. For nation will rise against nation, and kingdom against kingdom. And there will be famines, pestilences, and earthquakes in various places. All these are the beginning of sorrows.

HISTORICAL FULFILMENT (24:6-8)

Wars: the Roman Empire was at peace since Augustus inaugurated an Age of Peace in 17BC. But when Nero came to power, this all changed. A series of events began which fulfilled Jesus' prophecies made about 36 years earlier to the letter. There was war with Parthia, war in Britain, and the Jewish rebellion against Rome which started in 66AD.

Famines: Immediately preceding Nero's reign many died in a huge famine affecting the whole Roman Empire.

Pestilences: we know that many diseases ravaged the Roman world.

Earthquakes: During Nero's reign there were earthquakes in Laodicea, Crete, Smyrna, Miletus, Chios, Samos, Hierapolis, Colossae, Campania, Judea itself, and Rome. (Josephus)

MODERN-DAY FULFILMENT (24:6-8)

Wars: it may seem the world has been largely at peace since WWII but research shows that the number of conflicts between pairs of states rose steadily from 6 per year on average between 1870 and 1913 to 17 per year in the period of the two World Wars, 31 per year in the Cold War, and 36 per year in the 1990s (Harrison). So in fact there are ever-increasing wars and rumours of wars today.

Famines: many of us in the developed world could think there is no need to worry about hunger in today's modern, technological world but we would be mistaken. World grain stocks are at their lowest levels for many years. Experts believe food surpluses will soon be a thing of the past. Here are four factors:

1. Population explosion: world population is expected to increase from 7 billion today to 8 billion by 2025 and 9 billion by 2050 (UN estimates).
2. Biofuels: many farmers now sell corn to ethanol producers rather than to food producers.
3. Even economic growth can threaten food production: emerging middle classes in India and China now prefer to eat dairy foods, eggs or chicken than the plain grain foods of the past. Grain which is fed to cattle or poultry, and thereby transformed into more sophisticated food products (chicken, beef and eggs), produces less actual food than if the grain is just consumed as grain. World grain stocks were expected in 2018 to fall to their lowest ever level.
4. Wayward weather patterns and climate change are a major threat to food production. (Sheeran, 2017)

Diseases: Humanity is locked in a millennia-old battle to the death with diseases. Covid-19 has already changed the world. It reminds us that the growth of cities with huge populations, and ever-increasing international travel, lead to the risk of even worse pandemics.

Earthquakes: "The USGS report found that earthquake activity has increased drastically from 2000 to 2009 in 17 states, which include Alabama, Arkansas, Colorado, Kansas, New Mexico, Ohio, Oklahoma and Texas — all states with increased oil and gas drilling operations......."These earthquakes are occurring at a higher rate than ever before and pose a much greater risk to people living nearby," said Mark Petersen, chief of the USGS National Seismic Hazard Modelling Project. (Hendee, 2015)

PERSECUTION, HATRED, FALSE PROPHETS, LAWLESSNESS, ENDURANCE

Mat 24:9-13 "Then they will deliver you up to tribulation and kill you, and you will be hated by all nations for My name's sake. And then many will be offended, will betray one another, and will hate one another. Then many false prophets will rise up and deceive many. And because lawlessness will abound, the love of many will grow cold. But he who endures to the end shall be saved."

HISTORICAL FULFILMENT (24:9-13)

Persecution and betrayal: the Book of Acts gives the early history of persecution of Christians. Confirming the Acts account, the early church historian, Eusebius, wrote "First they [the Jews] stoned Stephen to death; then James the son of Zebedee and the brother of John was beheaded." He continued the history, "… James, the first after our Saviour's Ascension to be raised to the bishop's throne there, lost his life … while the remaining apostles, in constant danger from murderous plots, were driven out of Judaea." (Eusebius).

Fresh persecution broke out in Rome in A.D. 64. Some Christians were arrested, and in the words of the contemporary Roman historian, Tacitus, "then on their information a very large multitude was convicted." (Tacitus). Grant Jeffrey writes, "Nearly all the original apostles and many other early Christians were imprisoned and/or killed during the persecution. These Christians who were betrayed by their brethren were draped in animal skins and ripped apart by dogs or crucified in a major public spectacle. And at night, these people were burned as torches to light the streets of Rome. According to church tradition, it was during this massacre that Peter was crucified and Paul beheaded. Tradition also has it that nearly all the disciples were martyred. Matthew was killed by a sword in Ethiopia. Mark was dragged by horses through the streets of Alexandria. Luke was hanged in Greece. Bartholomew was flogged to death. Andrew was crucified. Thomas was stabbed with a spear in India. Jude was pierced with arrows. Matthias was stoned then beheaded, and Barnabas was stoned in Salonica." (Jeffrey, 1998)

False Prophets: according to Josephus, the Zealots (revolutionary Jewish leaders) bribed or forced a number of people to claim falsely to be prophets and tell the people that God would defend them. This was to give the people hope and dissuade the rebels from deserting. These prophecies of course were completely wrong. Jerusalem was destroyed, and most Jews killed.

Lawlessness: The Jews of Jesus' day had largely turned away from following God. Jesus called them a "wicked and adulterous generation". Josephus said of the Jews of that generation, "...nor did any age ever breed a generation more fruitful in wickedness than this was, from the beginning of the world." (Josephus)

Endurance: There are many accounts of incredible endurance in the early church. Perhaps one of the most remarkable would be the apostle Paul who carried on travelling and founding new churches despite imprisonment, floggings, shipwreck, hunger, fatigue, betrayal and many obstacles (see 2 Corinthians 11:22-33).

MODERN-DAY FULFILMENT (24:9-13)

Persecution: In our time, which is considered by many as an age of religious toleration, many are being persecuted for their Christian faith. Christians are being persecuted or killed in 68 countries today (Global report, 2017) according to data from Voice of the Martyrs, an advocacy organisation for persecuted Christians. For example, in India Christians have been murdered by extremist Hindus. On average, more than 15

Christians were physically attacked every week in India in 2016 (Open Doors UK, 2016).

"Since the Hindu nationalist Bharatiya Janata Party (BJP) came into power in 2014, radical Hinduism has increased steadily. There are anti-conversion laws to prevent people from leaving Hinduism in five states, and there have been efforts to impose such a law at a national level. Some of those who have left Hinduism to follow Jesus have been attacked and even killed by their own parents". - Open Doors report

The Middle East has been a hotspot for persecution of Christians recently. Many of us will remember the TV footage of 20 Egyptian nationals in red jumpsuits lined up to be executed by black hooded jihadists, who killed them by slitting their throats. The final moments were not shown on our TV screens, but videos including the final barbaric end were obtained by Egyptian Christians. These Christians told us what the world's press did not: all 20 died proclaiming the name of Jesus and expressing confidence in His eternal salvation. Persecution and killing of Christians is alive and well in the 21st century.

Offences: Many people today, while they may be loosely in favour of what they see to be "Christian values", are offended by radical Christian discipleship. Many others, especially in the West, will not tolerate Christianity at all, considering it "homophobic", "judgmental", "narrow minded" etc.

Hatred: Of course, there has been hatred in every age, but of note is the history of war between supposedly "Christian" nations. Think for example of World War II, the event that shaped our modern world. How must people of other religions see Christianity when the UK, USA and Germany, all leading nations of the Reformation, were locked in war with one another?

False prophets: False prophets abound today. Some are obvious. The "Eastern Lightening" cult in China follow a woman who claims to be Jesus returned to earth, and the cult grows mainly by threats of violence, and the female cult devotees attracting male members by sex. We might wonder how anyone could be taken in by this, but in the West, we have public discussion, freely available books on all kinds of doctrines, and a heritage of Christian theology. In China, the Christian faith is comparatively new, and it is impossible to get the breadth of public knowledge of theology to eliminate extreme cults such as Eastern Lightening.

Most false prophets are much subtler and more believable than Eastern Lightning. Many cult leaders embrace the idea that all religions are the same. My wife Margaret's and my own cult leader from our pre-Christian days, Maharishi Mahesh Yogi, taught that all religions were branches growing from the pure trunk of the Indian *Vedas* and we were encouraged to read these Hindu holy books for half an hour a day as part of a programme of meditation, breathing exercises and yoga. We were told not to reflect on the meaning of the words, but just to read them aloud and let them affect us on the subconscious level. The first words of one reading were "I adore Agni (the Hindu god of fire) ......" The whole deceptive system was built on orthodox Hinduism, but this was subtly disguised. I gave my spiritual allegiance to the Maharishi for 13 years before I became convinced that Christ offered the only way to eternal life.

Lawlessness: That lawlessness is taking over the world need hardly be debated today. In New Zealand where I live, every day in the newspapers we read about horrific crimes which in my school days would be a rare occurrence. From television documentaries we learn that the prisons are now almost ruled by the prisoners, particularly those with gang connections.

Love gone cold: The love of many has gone cold in society today. My father fought in the Second World War to "defend Christianity and freedom", as would have most of his contemporaries. Even if they were not disciples of Jesus, they had a generally positive view of Christianity, and held the church and God in respect. But I am convinced that if there were another world war today, defending Christianity would not be the motivation of most young men going to fight. The average person in the street in much of the west at least no longer believes even that "Christianity is a good thing".

To every generalisation, there are exceptions. There are many enthusiastic and committed young Christians and Christian leaders. But overall, the current young generation is known as "generation Me". Young (and old) people in many cases have been deceived into thinking fulfilment will come from primarily looking after "me and my needs".

The catch cry is "you can be whatever you want to be if you believe in yourself." People are relentlessly told "nothing is impossible", "hold on to your dreams" and it is your responsibility to make your dreams come true. Napoleon Hill in 1937 popularised the idea that "whatever the mind can conceive and believe, the mind can achieve" (Hill, 1937). Ever since, "positive thinking" motivational speakers and intellectuals have promoted this kind of thinking so that now it is endemic in the West. Dr Jean Twenge, in her thoroughly researched book *Generation Me* (Twenge, 2014), extensively documents this change of attitude through surveys of students conducted from the 1970's to the present day. Google's N-gram Viewer can be used to examine the frequency of different phrases in all Google books. Phrases such as "be yourself" and "believe in yourself" capture the way of thinking. "Be yourself" was used 2 ½ times more often in 2005 than in 1960. "Believe in yourself" was used 10 times more often. Both the phrases have become a deep part of the culture of our time. We have made *ourselves* the measure of all things. The problem with this kind of thinking is that all too often, there is no place for God in it. I must think that, in the hearts of many, love has gone cold. I believe this indifference to the things of God is what Jesus meant by "love going cold".

Endurance: Everywhere we see the advance of darkness, we see heroic Christians endure and overcome. Richard Wurmbrand was one example. A Romanian pastor, he was jailed for 14 years by the communists, three of those years in solitary confinement, and tortured. Yet he preached the Gospel by tapping it to his fellow prisoners on the wall in Morse code, and kept himself sane by composing sermons. When he was released his ministry became well-known worldwide through his books and assistance to other persecuted believers.

Chapter Five

THE GOSPEL WILL
BE PREACHED IN ALL
THE WORLD

✠ ✠ ✠

Mat 24:14 And this Gospel of the kingdom will be preached in all the world as a witness to all the nations, and then the end will come.

HISTORICAL FULFILMENT (24:14) – RAPID
SPREAD OF THE GOSPEL – BOOK OF ACTS.

The Gospel quickly spread throughout the Roman Empire, which to contemporaries was the known "world" at that time. The Book of Acts documents this movement. After the time covered by Acts, the faith continued to grow explosively so that by a short time after 300 AD it was the dominant religion in the Roman empire.

Christianity.com poses the following question: "How did the early Christian church survive? Humanly speaking, the odds were all stacked against it. It was unthinkable that a small, despised movement from a corner of Palestine could move out to become the dominant faith of the Roman Empire, an empire steeped in fiercely defended traditional pagan religions. The spread of the Christian church in its earliest centuries is one of the most amazing phenomena in all of human history. The church was considered a *"religio prava"*, an illegal and depraved religion. Wave after wave of persecution was unleashed to squash it. At least two of the persecutions were empire-wide and intended to destroy the church. So how did this young fledgling movement make it?" (Christianity.com, 2020)

Of course, the ultimate answer is that the faith survived because of God's providence and purposes. But notwithstanding that, we can find reasons for the incredible growth. There were no church buildings, no public lectures, and no "big names" after the original apostles had gone. But early Christianity had more powerful ways to multiply than these, and we have today the writings of contemporaries to verify this. It was at that time what we would today call a grass roots movement. Despite at times ruthless persecution, all the believers participated and took responsibility for caring for not only each other but also neighbours and strangers. "Christianity really established a realm of mutual social support for the members that joined the church. And I think that this was probably in the long run an enormously important factor for the success of the Christian mission." (Koesta, Undated) New believers were taught how to be disciples of Jesus Christ. And so, hundreds of thousands if not millions were swept into the Kingdom. Obedience to this command of Jesus to take the Gospel to all the world is the foremost thing we can do to hasten His coming. And so, we will take time to examine it closely.

MODERN-DAY FULFILMENT (24:14) – SPREAD OF THE GOSPEL TO THE WHOLE WORLD

The incredible movement that Jesus started was a huge endorsement of His ministry and must have been exciting beyond measure to have been involved in, as well as challenging. But it was only as the world was discovered that the extent of the task of making disciples in all the world was realised. At the end of what is known as the Patristic period (around 800), Christianity had become established in the Roman empire, and started to expand to embrace lands beyond.

Some milestones in global mission (Wikipedia, Undated)

- 450 approx. St Patrick went to Ireland.
- 597 – Pope Gregory the Great (Wikipedia, undated) commissioned and sent missionaries, including Augustine of Canterbury, to England.
- 1253 William of Rubruck (Franciscan) sent to Mongols.
- 1289 John of Montecorvino (Franciscan) sent to China, India and Persia.
- 1316 approx. Friar Odoric of Poredenone went to Asia.
- 1321 French Dominican missionary, Fr Jordanus Catalani, went to India.
- 1498 Vasco da Gama took Portuguese missionaries to India.
- 1482 Portuguese explorer Diogo Cão started Portuguese missions to Africa.
- 16th – 19th centuries Spanish Catholic missions to North and South Americas.
- 1549 St Francis Xavier went to Japan.
- 1575, Pope Gregory XIII ruled that Japan should come under the Portuguese diocese of Macau.
- 1588 Japan got its own diocese, Funai (Nagasaki), still under the Portuguese.
- 1583 The Jesuit Matteo Ricci went to China.
- 1598 Missions were established in New Mexico by the Franciscans.
- 1626 – After entering Japan in disguise, Jesuit missionary Francis Pacheco is captured and executed at Nagasaki.
- 1642 – Catholic missionaries Isaac Jogues and Rene Goupil captured by Mohawk Indians. Goupil was tomahawked to death; Jogues made a slave. He was an active missionary while a slave.
- 1726 John Wright, a Quaker missionary to Native Americans, went to Pennsylvania
- 1731 Count Nicolaus Ludwig Zinzendorf attends the coronation of King Christian VI of Denmark and witnesses two Inuit converts. Zinzendorf founded the Moravian missionary movement.

- 1732 Redemptorist Fathers founded to conduct rural missions.
- 1743 David Brainerd started ministry to Native Americans.
- 1750 Jonathan Edwards, after banishment from his church, started mission to Native Americans.
- 1769 Franciscans established 21 missions in California to convert the Native Americans.
- 1787 William Carey was ordained in England by the Particular Baptists.
- 1791 120 Korean Christians, including Paul Yun Ji-Chung, tortured and killed for their faith.
- 1794 Eight Russian Orthodox missionaries win several thousand converts.
- 1795 Catholic missionary Zhou Wenmo celebrated first mass in Korea.
- 1843 Baptist John Taylor translated the New Testament into Thai.
- 1844 Johann Krapf of the Church Missionary Society (CMS) started work in Mombasa.
- 1845 Southern Baptist Convention mission organisation founded.
- 1854 Hudson Taylor arrived in China – later penetrated the Chinese interior.
- 1897 Russian Orthodox Church started mission in Korea.
- 1899 James Rodgers started Presbyterian mission in the Philippines.
- 1900 189 missionaries and their children killed in the Boxer rebellion in China.
- 1900 Andrew Murray, author of "The Key to the Missionary Problem", challenged the church to hold weeks of prayer for the world.
- 1905 Sadhu Sundar Singh, an Indian convert from Sikhism, starts preaching in North India and Tibet.
- 1907 Massive revival meetings in Korea.
- 1910 Edinburgh Missionary Conference led by John Mott, leading to more ecumenical cooperation between Protestant missions.

- 1913 CT Studd founded "Heart of Africa Mission", now known as WEC International.
- 1914-1918 war blunted enthusiasm for missions. Doubts about "cultural imperialism" surfaced.
- 1914 Large scale revival in Uganda.
- 1925 Daniel Fleming wrote "Whither Bound in Missions" – challenged emphasis on conversions and advocated emphasis on social and justice issues.
- 1931 Franciscan missionary the Venerable Gabriele Allegra started translating the Bible.
- 1931 Clarence Jones started first missionary radio station, HCJB, in Quito, Ecuador.
- 1932 William Ernest Hocking et al "Rethinking Missions: A Laymen's Inquiry After 100 Years" marked the turning away from conversion-centred mission by the mainstream Protestant denominations, and the predominance of evangelicals and fundamentalists.
- 1932 Assemblies of God started missions work in Colombia.
- 1934 Columbans (Catholic missionary society) entered Japan.
- 1939-1945 War – many missionaries expelled or detained.
- 1942 Wycliffe Bible Translators started with the object of translating the Bible into every language.
- 1946 Thomas Tien Ken-sin named first Chinese Cardinal by Pope Pius XII, exiled from 1951.
- 1951 Campus Crusade for Christ started by Bill and Vonette Bright – promoted small discipleship group strategy.
- 1954 Augustinians (Catholic missionary order) re-established in Japan.
- 1960 Lauren Cunningham founded Youth with a Mission – young people's missionary organisation.
- 1962 – 1965 Second Vatican Council brought extensive difference to Catholic missions. Social justice received a much stronger emphasis.
- 1970 onwards – Chinese leaders such as Xu Yong-ze and Zheng Rongliang established and multiplied into huge "underground"

networks of house churches. Several networks attracted over 10 million members.

- 1971 Basic Church Communities (BCC's) started in the Philippines and Brazil.
- 1973 Services by Billy Graham drew 4.5 million people in South Korea.
- 1974 Lausanne Congress on World Evangelisation – Ralph Winter introduced the concept of unreached people groups (UPG's).
- 1979 Production of Jesus film, widely used in mission.
- 1981 Project Pearl – one million Bibles were secretly delivered in one night to thousands of waiting believers in China.
- 1981 "Back to Jerusalem" movement started in Henan Province, China. Chinese believers prepare for world mission with Simon Zhou and Deborah Xu.
- 1989 Lausanne II Congress – concept of 10/40 window emerged (the majority of non-Christian religions are found in the "window" between latitudes 10 and 40 degrees).
- 1991 Basic Ecclesial Communities ("BEC's") started in the Philippines, out of Catholic Bishops' resolve to be "the church of the poor".
- 1992 Victor Choudhrie started church planting movements ("CPM's") in India
- 1997 International Mission Board formed by Southern Baptist Convention – development of church planting movement (CPM) strategy.
- 1999 Trans World Radio (Gospel radio) went on air from Moldova using a 1-million watt AM transmitter.
- 2000 and beyond – now that the whole extent of the world is known, and communication and travel to almost all parts of it are now possible, Jesus' words can be finally fulfilled in their complete meaning.
- Pope Francis papal visits (examples)– Brazil 2013; Israel, Jordan, Palestine 2014; Turkey 2014; Sri Lanka, Philippines 2015; Kenya, Uganda, Central African Republic, 2015; Armenia 2016; Poland 2016; Iraq 2021.

- Christian population in China estimated in 2021 at 100 million Protestants and 12 million Catholics (Balcombe, Dennis, 2021). Taking the true Christian population as those who are converted and intentionally living a life of Christian discipleship, it could be that the Chinese church is now the biggest in the world.

The Gospel going out to all the world is the most important sign that we are nearing the end of the age. It's important to realise that "nations" in this verse does not just mean modern political nations. The Greek word used is *ethne* which could better be translated as "people groups" or "tribes". For example, India has over 2000 "people groups" with their own ethnicity, language and culture. The progress of the Gospel is the most important sign in Matthew 24, because for the first time in history it is conceivably possible that the task of "preaching the Gospel in all the world" could be finished.

CHURCH PLANTING MOVEMENTS (CPM'S) – THE INDIAN EXPERIENCE

Perhaps the most effective method of reaching all the world for Christ in our time is the starting and maintenance of church planting movements ("CPM's"), which has been undertaken since the early 1990's. A CPM is a rapidly growing network of small house churches or church groups which multiply to impact an area or population segment in a short span of time. One of the most remarkable is the massive CPM in India facilitated by my friend Victor Choudhrie. He started training CPM workers in 1992, beginning in northern India, mainly with uneducated rural women, who proved to be extremely effective in starting small churches in villages when the teaching was kept simple, and non-biblical teaching avoided. The movement expanded and multiplied far beyond the expectations of any conventional missionary strategy. When I became involved in 2009, on the day of Pentecost of that year, the CPM workers baptised thousands of new believers in different parts of India in one day!

THE CHINESE HOUSE CHURCH MOVEMENT AND OTHER MOVES OF GOD

The CPM in India is reminiscent of another major church movement, the Chinese house church movement. In 1948 it is estimated that China had some 750,000 Christian believers. It was God's time for China. The communists took over, closed all churches and expelled all missionaries. What the communists did not realise was that this would enable the Chinese church to become a truly indigenous movement.

Initially many believers left the church. Some, for instance the well-known Dutch Christian writer, Corrie Ten Boom, accredit this to the Pretrib teaching of missionaries before the war. Because they were expecting the Christians to be "raptured" before the tribulation, and they believed they were living in the last days, they did not expect to experience any severe hardship. So, when the communists started forcibly closing churches, and humiliating, jailing and torturing Christians, they were totally unprepared. Many, tragically, lost their faith, and the incomparable gift of eternal life that goes with it. In my opinion, this illustrates the fact that it is important to teach new Christians (and many long-standing Christians who seem unaware of it) that all genuine Christian believers may face challenge and tribulation for their faith.

Following this, God raised up groups of indigenous believers in different parts of China. Their evangelising of the whole nation is one of the most inspiring accounts in all Christian history. For now, let it suffice to say that in the last 70 years, that the number of believers has grown from an estimated 750,000 believers in 1948 to an estimated one hundred million believers or more today.

Other moves of God that have swept millions or hundreds of thousands into the kingdom of God have taken place in Korea, Singapore, Taiwan and places in South America. There is no question that it is the time now for the Gospel to reach all the people groups of the world. We cannot see the complete fulfilment of the rest of the prophecy of Matthew 24 until the preaching of the Gospel of the Kingdom has reached the whole earth. God envisages at least some representatives from every people group receiving the incomparable gift of everlasting life, as shown by these verses of Revelation:

Rev 7:9-10 After these things I looked, and behold, a great multitude which no one could number, of all nations, tribes, peoples, and tongues, standing before the throne and before the Lamb, clothed with white robes, with palm branches in their hands and crying out with a loud voice, saying, "Salvation *belongs* to our God who sits on the throne, and to the Lamb!"

THE GREAT COMMISSION (MAT 24:14; 28:18-20): SUMMARY OF PROGRESS (MANDRYK, 2016)

Christians living in the west could perhaps be forgiven for thinking that the church is struggling severely. But a little research would show them that worldwide this is not at all the case. The following summary was delivered at the Third Lausanne Younger Leaders Gathering, 2016. Christianity is the most globally dispersed and culturally diverse religion of all the religions. There are 2.3 billion people identifying as Christian in 38,000 denominations. In every single country there are groups of believers meeting. There are expressions of Christianity in more languages, more geographical places and more ethnicities than ever before. For the last 100 years approximately one person out of three in the world identifies as a Christian.

Christians living in Asia, Africa, or Latin America, as a percentage of all Christians:
1960 – 29%
2017 – 78%
2020 – 80% estimated

Proportion of the world's population evangelical or charismatic Christian:
1960 – 3%
2017 - 8% - This is a huge change.

Proportion of the World's population who have never heard the Gospel
1960 – 50%
2017 – 29% This is real progress.

Proportion of Christians evangelical or charismatic:
2017 – 1 in 4

RESEARCH GIVES AN ACCURATE PICTURE

Only in 1990's did an accurate picture of the Great Commission task ahead emerge through research. Complete views of all ethnic and language groups, together with their progress in evangelisation, their existing religion, and to what degree they have been exposed to the Gospel, have been compiled in the new resources. Patrick Johnstone started Operation World, and David Barrett researched the World Christian Encyclopaedia. This information allowed the Joshua Project, which aims to engage all Christians in the Great Commission, to be launched. We know where the church is, where it needs to go, and what it needs to do. This information is fuel for prayer and planning effective strategy.

More planning and collaboration is happening across the many missions organisations than ever before. The complexity of the task requires it, but also there is more willingness and desire to collaborate amongst missionaries and missions agencies. More prayer movements and prayer initiatives are starting all the time across the global church. For example, a monthly "one million strong" gathering meets monthly in Nigeria.

MORE NEW BELIEVERS THAN EVER BEFORE IN THE LAST 25 YEARS

During the last 25 years more people have become Christians than at any time in history. Much growth has happened in the context of suffering and persecution. Of the 16000 ethno-linguistic people-groups in the world, only 600-650 are unreached or have no group focussed on them with a mission strategy.

MISSIONARIES SENT FROM ALL NATIONS

Missionaries are no longer all from the UK or the US, or other Western countries. It used to be said that missionaries were "from the West to the Rest". But now missionaries are being sent "from everywhere to everywhere"; A modern term is "polycentric mission" – there are multiple centres of mission sending and receiving missionaries. Many places that were served by former generations of missionaries are now sending their own missionaries out. Nations in this bracket include India, Nigeria, China, Brazil, Philippines, Ethiopia and others. Some are now sending missionaries to the places that originally sent missionaries to them. For example, the Miso people of North-East India have sent missionaries to Wales. Over 100 years ago, it was Wales that sent the original missionaries that led many Miso people to Jesus. Now it is Wales where there are few believers and the people need the Gospel. The Miso people, at their own initiative, are sending missionaries to Wales!

At this stage in world evangelism, missions planners are seeking God for strategy to reach the remaining people groups to spread the good news of the Gospel, believing the promise of the Bible: Isa 11:9 For the earth shall be full of the knowledge of the Lord as the waters cover the sea.

We have many difficulties to overcome, and many issues to think through. For instance, what difference does urbanisation make to our plans? To what extent do we need to adjust our plans to take account of an ageing population, another widespread trend? We are urged on by the hugely successful house church networks in India to have a "completion mentality" towards the Great Commission. For the first time in history, it is actually feasible to reach the whole world for Christ. Much more needs to be done but Matthew 24:14 is coming to pass in our time. Jesus, through Matthew, is telling us that when this commission is finished, the end shall come.

FULFILLING THE GREAT COMMISSION IN CATHOLIC CULTURES

Out of the nearly 2.5 billion Christians in the world, 1,231,050,000 (52%) are Catholics. The five countries with the largest number of Catholics are, in decreasing order of Catholic population, Brazil, Mexico, the Philippines, the United States, and Italy. If we take the

Philippines as an example, in spite of all the evangelisation of the country by Protestant missions, and pressure from Communism and Islam in the south, 82% of the population are still Catholic. Surely this suggests that there is vital, internal spirituality in Catholic Christianity in the Philippines. Is there, then, a need at all for a great commission strategy in this population?

We must be mindful of the nature of the commission Jesus gave us. In the wording of Matthew 28:19-20, we must "make disciples of all the nations, baptizing them in the name of the Father and of the Son and of the Holy Spirit, [20] teaching them to observe all things that I have commanded you". We are commanded to make disciples who do all the things Jesus' immediate disciples did. The perennial problem of the Catholic and indeed most churches is nominalism. Many people have been ignorant or indifferent about their faith. In the Philippines, this has applied especially to the poor, who, because of long working hours and low pay, often have no time or money to attend religious meetings. Only a living, robust faith will do! This is recognised by the Catholic Bishops Conference of the Philippines, who have called for the "re-evangelisation of the people", recognising the need to help them find satisfying encounters with the living God, and become intentional disciples of Jesus Christ.

RENEWAL MOVEMENTS

There have been at least three renewal movements in the Philippines, which have attempted to teach Filipinos to practice pro-active lives of discipleship, learning in small groups to have a personal relationship with God, and to live a lifestyle of mutual support, making life much more tolerable for the poor. The first of these, centring on "Basic Church Communities" or "BCC's", developed in the early 1970's. This movement had some success but remained on the fringe of Filipino society because of its flirtation with communism. Secondly, "Basic Ecclesial Communities" or "BEC's", grew out of the pledge of the Catholic Bishops in 1991 to become "the church of the poor".

Finally, the Catholic charismatic movement in the Philippines has been much more prolific in results than either of these two movements. According to Lim (Lim, 2018)[3] many surveys show that 88% of Catholics and 94% of non-Catholic Christians consider they have had "charismatic experiences". This equates to 90% of the Filipino population. Many have been impacted by "Life in the Spirit seminars". There has been a lot of teaching on love and mutual support between the believers, practical cooperation, for instance in the formation of micro-finance cooperatives, every member participation in meetings, and every member participation in low-key, friendship evangelism. Many lay leaders have emerged with support of Catholic clergy and much ecumenical activity has taken place. The net result has been not at all unlike the church planting movements in India, China and Africa. The Lord is clearly at work on His Matthew 24:14 agenda!

---

[3] David Lim's paper cited has been the source of much of this discussion on the Philippines, as well as my own observations during my seven ministry visits there.

Chapter Six

THE GREAT TRIBULATION

✛ ✛ ✛

Matthew 24:15-21 "Therefore when you see the 'abomination of desolation,' spoken of by Daniel the prophet, standing in the holy place" (whoever reads, let him understand), ¹⁶ "then let those who are in Judea flee to the mountains. ¹⁷ Let him who is on the housetop not go down to take anything out of his house. ¹⁸ And let him who is in the field not go back to get his clothes. ¹⁹ But woe to those who are pregnant and to those who are nursing babies in those days! ²⁰ And pray that your flight may not be in winter or on the Sabbath. ²¹ For then there will be great tribulation, such as has not been since the beginning of the world until this time, no, nor ever shall be.

HISTORICAL FULFILMENT (24:15-21)

In 70AD, the Roman general, subsequently emperor, Titus, determined to annihilate the Jewish rebels once and for all. He and his army marched to Jerusalem and, after a bitter siege, destroyed the city, mercilessly killing most of the inhabitants. There can be no absolute way the modern commentator can know what the "abomination of desolation" referred to in Jesus' discourse. One credible theory is that the fulfilment of this prophecy was the worship of the Roman army standards by the Roman soldiers at Jerusalem and at the site of the temple. The standards were not just like regimental colours in today's armies. They bore images of the Roman and Greek gods, and so were associated with serious idolatry. The wording of Luke when reporting the same discourse adds support to this theory:

Luke 21:20 "But when you see Jerusalem surrounded by armies, then know that its desolation is near. 21 Then let those who are in Judea flee to the mountains, let those who are in the midst of her depart, and let not those who are in the country enter her. 22 For these are the days of vengeance, that all things which are written may be fulfilled.

Verse 15 of Matthew "when you see…the abomination of desolation" is equivalent to Luke's verse 20, "when you see Jerusalem surrounded by armies." So, it does seem quite likely that the two are connected and the "abomination" was indeed the idolatrous standards.

The Christians, forewarned by Jesus' remarkable prophecy, stayed away from the city, and escaped as a result. Jesus' words about the destruction of the temple, with not one stone being left on another, were clearly fulfilled at that time. Enraged by the fierce fighting of the Jews, the Roman army demolished it. After burning it, molten gold and silver flowed into the joins between the stone and the soldiers prised apart the stones to get the precious metals. So quite literally "not one stone was left on another".

MODERN-DAY FULFILMENT (24:15-21)

We are seeing massive growth in idolatry all over the world. All the Old and New Testament prophecies of the end of the age point to a time when God will remove from among His people those that worship idols. And the idolaters will be severely dealt with by God. So surely the main point of this section for those of us who don't live in Jerusalem is to warn us to "flee" when we see gross idol-worship, and when we see the signs of the end spoken of in this passage intensify. "Flee" may mean different things according to our context. But especially we should not have anything to do with idol-worship.

Jesus indicates that there is going to be a time of extreme tribulation on earth leading to His coming again. Will this be the worst tribulation ever in the history of mankind? Think of the Second World War; think of the holocaust; the Russian front; mediaeval battles fought by hand-to-hand combat; the nuclear bombs dropped on Japan; times of extreme sickness such as the plague or the black death. If we see this prophecy in Matthew as relevant to our time, it seems the coming time could be worse than all these. The Gospel of Mark confirms this:

Mar 13:19 For in those days there will be tribulation, such as has not been since the beginning of the creation which God created until this time, nor ever shall be.

It is obvious that Matthew and Mark are talking about the same event previously described by Daniel:

"At that time Michael shall stand up,
The great prince who stands watch over the sons of your people;
And there shall be a time of trouble,
Such as never was since there was a nation,
Even to that time.
And at that time your people shall be delivered,
Everyone who is found written in the book.
2 And many of those who sleep in the dust of the earth shall awake,
Some to everlasting life,
Some to shame and everlasting contempt.
3 Those who are wise shall shine
Like the brightness of the firmament,
And those who turn many to righteousness
Like the stars forever and ever. Daniel 12:1-3

This time of trouble can only be the same time of trouble in Matthew and Mark. There can only be one time of trouble such as never was and never shall be again.

In all three books:

1. The tribulation is the worst ever.
2. It will usher in the judgment of all mankind.
3. The righteous and wicked will appear in the judgement.

4. All the righteous shall be delivered
5. Their names are in the Book of Life
6. The wicked shall go to eternal "shame and contempt"

It is obvious that three descriptions sharing these 6 features must, of necessity, be describing the same scene. We shall refer again to this point and learn a lot more about these cataclysmic events as we continue with this book. The mention of the "abomination of desolation" is another important link to Daniel (see 11:31, 12:11)

TRIBULATION CUT SHORT FOR THE SAKE OF THE ELECT (24:22-26)

Matthew 24:22-26 "If those days had not been cut short, no one would survive, but for the sake of the elect those days will be shortened. 23 At that time if anyone says to you, 'Look, here is the Messiah!' or, 'There he is!' do not believe it. 24 For false messiahs and false prophets will appear and perform great signs and wonders to deceive, if possible, even the elect. 25 See, I have told you ahead of time. 26 "So if anyone tells you, 'There he is, out in the wilderness,' do not go out; or, 'Here he is, in the inner rooms,' do not believe it."

WHO ARE THE "ELECT"?

Let's start by settling, if we can, this issue.

Hebrew: bachiyr (pronounced baw-kheer) – choose, chosen one, elect

Greek: eklektos – chosen, elect, (by implication "favourite"); (from "eklegomai" – select)

In Matthew 24:31 Jesus sends His angels to gather the elect "from the four winds". Who are the elect? In the New Testament, every reference to the elect obviously refers to those of us who have been "sanctified" (made holy) by faith in Jesus Christ. An example is:

To the pilgrims of the Dispersion in Pontus, Galatia, Cappadocia, Asia, and Bithynia, 2 elect according to the foreknowledge of God the Father, in sanctification of the Spirit, for obedience and sprinkling of the blood of Jesus Christ.......... 1Peter1:1-2

In Peter's letter here, these pilgrims are elect or chosen for the "sanctification" of the Holy Spirit and "the sprinkling of the blood of Jesus Christ", by which he means Christ's blood cleanses us of sin by faith.

How do we know if we are elect (chosen) according to God's foreknowledge, made holy by the Holy Spirit, and living a life of obedience to Jesus Christ?

Preachers over the centuries have talked about the "full assurance of faith". This is a faith which is available to every believer and comes primarily through the Word of God. When I had my conversion experience, I was so certain, and still am so certain, that the things we talk about in this book are not "cunningly devised fables" as sceptics both in our time and in the Bible time have charged, but they are realities which it would be perilous, and tragic, to ignore. Most likely anyone who can join with me in this conviction is part of the elect. And Jesus will shorten the troubles on the earth for the sake of the elect, if we should still be on the earth at the time of His coming!

HISTORICAL FULFILMENT

The days of the siege of Jerusalem were terrible beyond description. Josephus wrote that women were so hungry they ate their own children. As previously discussed, the rebels hired or forced people to give false prophecies saying that God would deliver Jerusalem. Of course, He didn't and people relying on these prophecies lost their lives.

MODERN-DAY FULFILMENT

Pre-tribulation rapture - in my view, Matthew 24:22 brings the pre-tribulation rapture theory into serious question. If the time of tribulation will be cut short for the sake of the elect, then surely they must be on earth during the tribulation. Also, if the possibility exists for them to be deceived (verse 24) this also shows they will be on earth during this time.

The inner rooms - when I was a teenager, some of my contemporaries took "the hippy trail" through Afghanistan to India. Some spent time on ashrams in India or found some "holy man" to follow. It all sounded very romantic, but I never met anyone who claimed to have found ultimate truth by that path. Margaret and I, when we were involved in Transcendental Meditation, were always involved with people who would say in effect, "Here He is, in the inner rooms". In other words, "Find the Christ within you"; "meditate"; "look deep within yourself". There is an element of truth in this. Jesus wants us to spend time getting to know Him by reading and meditating on His words in the Bible, seeking Him in prayer, and listening to His voice. However, Christians believe that searching "the inner rooms" of the mind or soul is not an end, but that the end is following and obeying Christ. And when He comes, He will make His coming known in an obvious way to all peoples, whether or not they are believers.

Chapter Seven

JESUS COMES IN GLORY; THE "DAY OF THE LORD"

✝ ✝ ✝

THE ACCOUNT OF HIS COMING 24:27-35

As we read the following passage, let's try to visualise what His coming will look like, and what is really going on in the heavens and the earth. It is the most intense true-life drama ever written, holding no fear for the sincere believer, but a drama of terror to the scorners and mockers of the world, and others who will not sincerely seek the Creator of the universe and His counsels.

Mat 24:27-35 For as the lightning comes from the east and flashes to the west, so also will the coming of the Son of Man be. [28] For wherever the carcass is, there the eagles will be gathered together. [29] "Immediately after the tribulation of those days the sun will be darkened, and the moon will not give its light; the stars will fall from heaven, and the powers of the heavens will be shaken. [30] Then the sign of the Son of Man will appear in heaven, and then all the tribes of the earth will mourn, and they will see the Son of Man coming on the clouds of heaven with power and great glory. [31] And He will send His angels with a great sound of a trumpet, and they will gather together His elect from the four winds, from one end of heaven to the other. Now learn this parable from the fig tree: When its branch has already become tender and puts forth leaves, you know that summer *is* near. ³³ So you also, when you see all these things, know that it is near—at the doors! ³⁴ Assuredly, I say to you, this generation will by no means pass away till all these things take place. ³⁵ Heaven and earth will pass away, but My words will by no means pass away.

HISTORICAL FULFILMENT (24:27-35)

It appears there was a historical fulfilment even of these verses. The ferocity with which the Roman Army over-ran Jerusalem has been well documented. But contemporary writers Josephus, Tacitus, and Dio Cassio also reported the sighting of supernatural events in the sky connected with the rebellion. Josephus recorded that, "On the 21st of the month Iyar [66 A.D.], there appeared a miraculous occurrence, beyond belief. Indeed, what I am about to relate would, I think, have been reckoned a fable, were it not for the statements of eyewitnesses . . .. before sunset throughout all areas of the country, there were seen in the air many chariots and armed battalions, coursing through the clouds, encircling the cities." Could it be that there was a visitation of Jesus at this time? On several occasions in the Old Testament, God is described as coming to earth. Some commentators have even regarded these supernatural signs in the sky as the complete fulfilment of Matthew 24: 27-35. What do you think? We will discuss this further in the section on Preterism (chapter 12).

MODERN-DAY FULFILMENT (24:27-35)

That the destruction of Jerusalem was a visitation of Jesus is quite possible, but impossible to prove either way. There will be no ambiguity about the final return of Jesus when it does happen. All the people who rejected Christ will mourn, suddenly aware of the disastrous choice they made. The cataclysmic nature of the events – sun and moon darkened, stars disappeared, the visible sky "rolled up like a scroll" – will emphasise the total powerlessness of man acting on his own volition, and the finality of the end of this age.

This will be an incredible moment for "the elect". The phraseology here, "from the four winds, from one end of the heavens to the other", is a poetic way of saying "from every part of the world". No words can capture the infinite privilege of being gathered by the angels to meet with our Lord. He is coming with power and great glory, so we will have a full revelation of His divinity and grace. We will be joyful in His presence for all eternity.

One important thing I noticed when studying these verses that what is described is the one, only, and final coming of Christ. Nowhere in the New Testament does anyone write about the second, third or fourth coming of Christ. It's only ever ONE appearing, though different Greek words are used, the most common of which is the "Parousia" (Greek for "appearing"). We will be looking at parallel passages in other books of the Bible in later chapters.

During our study of Matthew 24, we have noted that all the signs indicating the approaching end of the age are either actually or potentially present in our time. This is especially true of the key sign in verse 14, the preaching of the Gospel of the Kingdom in all the world. It does seem then that the appearance of Jesus Christ is close. Of course, it is best to hold to this at least somewhat lightly. In every generation there have lived Christians who thought they were the last generation before the return of Christ.

Mat 24:36-44 "But of that day and hour no one knows, not even the angels of heaven, but My Father only. 37 But as the days of Noah were, so also will the coming of the Son of Man be. 38 For as in the days before the flood, they were eating and drinking, marrying and giving in marriage, until the day that Noah entered the ark, 39 and did not know until the flood came and took them all away, so also will the coming of the Son of Man be. 40 Then two men will be in the field: one will be taken and the other left. 41 Two women will be grinding at the mill: one will be taken and the other left. 42 Watch therefore, for you do not know what hour your Lord is coming. 43 But know this, that if the master of the house had known what hour the thief would come, he would have watched and not allowed his house to be broken into. 44 Therefore you also be ready, for the Son of Man is coming at an hour you do not expect.

HISTORICAL FULFILMENT (24:36-44)

We have noted that many if not all of these signs spoken of by Jesus were fulfilled in the events of the 40 years following His resurrection. This observation applies especially to the destruction of Jerusalem and the temple in 70 AD. Jesus here compares His coming to the days of Noah. He points out that the flood came to take all the unbelievers away – they were swept to their destruction by the waters. From the Jewish point of view, even this was fulfilled at the time of the destruction of Jerusalem, with Titus and his legions taking the same role as the waters in the time of Noah. The Jews were either killed (the majority) or taken captive as slaves by the brutal Romans.

MODERN-DAY FULFILMENT (24:26-34)

However, it is obvious that not everything was fulfilled in 70 AD or before, by a long way. The Great Commission to go into all the world with the Gospel is being fulfilled in far greater measure in our day. Secondly, though the Jews came under earthly judgment in a devastating way, there was no judgment at that time which included the whole of humanity or eternity in its scope. For the first time in history, all the signs indicating the approaching end of the age are either actually or potentially present in our time. This is especially true of the key sign in verse 14, the preaching of the Gospel of the Kingdom in all the world.

COMPARISON WITH NOAH'S TIME –

The way in which Dispensationalist Bible commentators have used Jesus' comparison with Noah's time is questioned by Amillennial writers. Dispensationalists take this passage to mean that of the two men in the field, the one who "is taken" will be taken to meet Jesus in the clouds at the "rapture". The same is thought regarding the two women. This teaching has given rise to the well-known exhortation "don't be left behind", meaning "don't be left behind when Jesus comes for His church".

However, the way Jesus tells the story, the ones who will be "taken" in the coming times of judgment are the ones who were "taken" in the flood – that is the evil ones were taken by the flood and destroyed! This agrees with the parable of the wheat and the tares in Matthew 13. At the time of the harvest the first to be gathered by the angels will be the tares or weeds, which will be burned. So rather than praying "please let me not be left behind", shouldn't we be praying "please let me be left behind"?!

This passage makes it clear that the timing of the Lord's return will not be known, even though the signs indicate that it is not far away. This is God's deliberate doing, because He wants to test the hearts of those that follow Him. Will they continue to be watchful, even if around them the world is in party mode like Noah's contemporaries? Some have stumbled at the description of life in Noah's day, as the time will be one of war and dreadful suffering (Matthew 24:21-22). But even during war-time, people eat and drink, and some get married. Jesus is emphasising that people will be doing the same things as they have always done right until the coming of the Return of Christ, and the appearance of His sign in the heavens – getting married, working, eating and drinking. If we are not serious in commitment to our faith we will be caught unawares.

"One taken and one left" equates to 50%. Some believe this indicates that 50% of the world's population will be saved at the final cataclysm.

Chapter Eight

THREE WARNINGS

✠ ✠ ✠

At this point in the discourse, Jesus digresses from the main narrative to tell us three parables, in order that we should properly prepare ourselves for His coming. The overall subject is still the same, however: the Lord's return.

WARNING PARABLE 1: THE FAITHFUL SERVANT AND THE EVIL SERVANT

The "watch and be ready" theme is very prevalent in the New Testament texts but is rarely preached in our churches today. Jesus spoke of two servants left by their master in charge of his household while he went away. One was faithful, but the other started to live a dissolute life and to beat his fellow servants, thinking the master would not return. The parable ends:

Mat 24:50-51 The master of that servant will come on a day when he is not looking for him and at an hour that he is not aware of, [51] and will cut him in two and appoint him his portion with the hypocrites. There shall be weeping and gnashing of teeth.

The master stands for Jesus Himself. Many do not realise that He will come as Judge at the end of the age, as is depicted here. Two types of servant are discussed in the parable. Both are servants of the master and therefore stand for two types of followers of the Lord. Both types are more than just servants, as the master puts them in charge of all his household. All believers are being warned here, but perhaps the message has a special application to all who are in some form of Christian leadership. The faithful servant is rewarded richly. But the evil servant will evidently lose his gift of eternal life.

Some Christians believe that, once a person has made a commitment to Jesus Christ, he or she cannot "lose their salvation", i.e. lose their gift of eternal life. But if loss of salvation through being careless of Jesus' command to be watchful were not a real possibility, then why would Jesus tell the parable, and why would Matthew record it? There are many other scriptures which support the viewpoint that one can lose salvation, and therefore at all times we should be watchful (see for example John 15:1-7; Gal 4:19-20; 2 Peter 1:8-9).

WARNING PARABLE 2: THE PARABLE OF THE WISE AND FOOLISH VIRGINS

The next parable also has a "watch and be ready" theme. One parable at such a crucial juncture of Matthew's Gospel should cause us to take heed, but two should really cause us to sit up. Both parables have contrasts: in the first a faithful servant vs. an evil servant; in the second wise vs. foolish bridesmaids. In the first parable Jesus is the master, the believer the servant; in the second, Jesus is the bridegroom, the believers the bridesmaids. Five were prepared, with oil in their lamps. The others had no oil. Suddenly the bridegroom arrived, and the five with no oil asked the others for some of their oil, to be told that there would not be enough. The five were locked out of the wedding.

This second parable speaks of intimacy with the Lord. The mature believer seeks intimacy with Jesus, the immature in many cases can only understand what it is to be a servant. But even the mature believer can wander off-track and lose out merely for being spiritually asleep. Let's hope we will never hear the fateful words "assuredly, I say to you, I do not know you." We must watch and be ready no matter how long we have walked with Christ, and no matter how many mighty works we have done with Him.

WARNING PARABLE 3: THE TALENTS. USE IT OR YOU LOSE IT!

The third parable (Mat 25:14-30) casts Jesus once again as the master, and the believers as servants. Once again, the topic is the final judgment. The Lord is showing us one criterion by which the final judgment will be made. The previous parables showed us that we need to watch and be ready. But what should we watch? One thing we should watch for is: "Are we using the gifts He has given us to promote His Kingdom?" The parable concerns a man who travelled to a far country, having given his three servants his wealth. Two of the servants traded the money (in one case five and in the other case two talents) given to them wisely and were richly rewarded when the man returned (an analogue for Jesus' own return). But the man who was given one talent was scared of losing money and so hid the money given to him.

Mat 25:29-30 But his lord answered and said to him, 'You wicked and lazy servant, you knew that I reap where I have not sown and gather where I have not scattered seed. So you ought to have deposited my money with the bankers, and at my coming I would have received back my own with interest. Therefore take the talent from him, and give it to him who has 10 talents. 'For to everyone who has, more will be given, and he will have abundance; but from him who does not have, even what he has will be taken away. [30] And cast the unprofitable servant into the outer darkness. There will be weeping and gnashing of teeth.'

As in the earlier two parables, Jesus knows He is about to leave this world, and is continuing to give criteria by which vital, obedient faith will be recognized at the judgment. Some points (Coffman, 1992):

- The goods given out correspond to the abilities of the servants. Their reward would depend on their faithfulness in using the gifts, not on the size of the gifts given out. To have given five talents to the two talent servant would not have been good for the servant – he would have been burdened by a responsibility that would have been too heavy for him.

- Exercising the gifts we are given improves them.
- We are expected to be carrying on in some work for God.
- It is vital to recognize that at the settling of accounts (the judgment) we will all be judged individually for our faithfulness. There is no group assessment!
- The faithful will be "set over many things" at the judgment – we do not know what these things will be.
- The folk wisdom "use it or you lose it" applies to gifts and talents given by God, and we are expected to use them.

Where did the sin of the unprofitable servant lie? He had a low opinion of God, and therefore had no confidence that God would be just (v24); he was lazy and unfaithful. Note that these faults are enough to keep him out of eternal joy with God, once again contrary to the "Once saved, always saved" school. This man represents a believer – he was a servant of Jesus, the King of Kings. He was not a murderer or a rebel. But he is cast into outer darkness. If words have meaning, he has gone to eternal punishment.

Jesus has demonstrated by telling these three parables that He is a master disciple-maker. The discussion started when Jesus and the disciples were looking around the temple buildings. He caught their attention by predicting the destruction of the temple. He pauses, and brings these three parables which are of extraordinary relevance to the disciples. The imagery and the stories must have captivated them and prepared all of them except Judas for the lives of service and sacrifice they were about to embark upon. Then He described for them and us the scene in the greatest court in the universe.

Chapter Nine

END OF THE OLIVET DISCOURSE: JESUS TO COME IN GLORY

✠ ✠ ✠

Mat 25:31 "When the Son of Man comes in His glory, and all the holy angels with Him, then He will sit on the throne of His glory.

Now Jesus is back to narrative style. Immediately, He establishes the connection with the Matthew 24:30 description of the appearance of Jesus. "…the Son of Man comes in His glory". Matthew 25:31 "….. they see the Son of Man coming on the clouds of heaven, with power and great glory." These two scriptures very obviously describe the same event (see further discussion in Chapter 14). Jesus digressed to give the three parables (on the same topic of the judgment at the end of the age), but now He is back to the main sequence of events.

Mat 25:32 All the nations will be gathered before Him, and He will separate them one from another, as a shepherd divides his sheep from the goats.

Immediately Jesus will proceed to the judgment. ALL the nations will be gathered before Him[4]. Later in this book, we will examine in

---

[4] This passage is a great problem for Dispensationalist commentators because it assumes everyone being judged at one time instead of some at the rapture, perhaps some at the

detail what will happen in this most solemn court hearing of all time. For now we will content ourselves to read the passage and drink in the awesome scene described:

Mat 25:33-46 And He will set the sheep on His right hand, but the goats on the left. 34 Then the King will say to those on His right hand, 'Come, you blessed of My Father, inherit the kingdom prepared for you from the foundation of the world: 35 for I was hungry and you gave Me food; I was thirsty and you gave Me drink; I was a stranger and you took Me in; 36 I was naked and you clothed Me; I was sick and you visited Me; I was in prison and you came to Me."

37 "Then the righteous will answer Him, saying, 'Lord, when did we see You hungry and feed You, or thirsty and give You drink? 38 When did we see You a stranger and take You in, or naked and clothe You? 39 Or when did we see You sick, or in prison, and come to You?' 40 And the King will answer and say to them, 'Assuredly, I say to you, inasmuch as you did it to one of the least of these My brethren, you did it to Me.'

41 "Then He will also say to those on the left hand, 'Depart from Me, you cursed, into the everlasting fire prepared for the devil and his angels: 42 for I was hungry and you gave Me no food; I was thirsty and you gave Me no drink; 43 I was a stranger and you did not take Me in, naked and you did not clothe Me, sick and in prison and you did not visit Me.'

---

end of the tribulation, some at the last judgment and some not judged at all. Some have theorised that this is only a judgment for gentile nations. The reason postulated is that *ethne,* the word translated as "nations", in some contexts means gentile (or non-Jewish) nations. But it is obvious that in this context it means literally all the world's people groups. It is used in Matthew 24:14 – and this Gospel shall be preached in all the world as a witness to all the nations; and Matthew 28:19 – Go therefore and make disciples of all the nations.... If we were to say *ethne* only meant non-Jewish nations here we would be excluding the Jews from the Great Commission. Yet in Acts 1:8 Jesus declares "you shall be witnesses to me in Jerusalem, and in all Judea and Samaria, and to the end of the earth." In other words, He was telling the disciples to share the Gospel with the Jews FIRST, then to the other peoples of the earth. Sharing the Gospel with all the earth's peoples is still the mandate of all Christians today! For our present purpose, it is enough to note that these words show that it is ALL PEOPLES, including the Jews and Gentiles, believers and unbelievers, and whether or not raptured, who will be gathered before Him for this judgment.

44 "Then they also will answer Him, saying, 'Lord, when did we see You hungry or thirsty or a stranger or naked or sick or in prison, and did not minister to You?' 45 Then He will answer them, saying, 'Assuredly, I say to you, inasmuch as you did not do it to one of the least of these, you did not do it to Me.' 46 And these will go away into everlasting punishment, but the righteous into eternal life."

In this part of the discourse, Jesus picks out one criterion to determine the condition of the soul: whether the person had empathy for and compassion on the suffering. There are many more issues which will also be examined at this final judgment, as we shall see. Matthew, in his inspired account, does not attempt to write a complete description. We will build up a picture by examining other scripture passages and comparing scripture with scripture. But surely of all issues to examine, this treatment of other fellow human beings must be the central issue. Jesus summarised the law as "love the Lord your God with all your heart, with all your soul, and with all your mind"; and "… love your neighbour as yourself". Some have said the point at issue is limited to how we have treated Jesus' disciples, based on verse 40, "inasmuch as you did it to one of the least of these My brethren". This is also one possible understanding. It is always vital for us to receive, aid and honour God's servants. But I think loving our neighbour as ourselves means extending love and care to everyone in need as far as possible. I am sure that this is what the Jesus who told the story of the good Samaritan had in mind.

How do we know that this is the final judgment? From verse 46: "And these will go away into everlasting punishment, but the righteous into eternal life." We have seen from the parables how everyone is judged individually. This is the outcome of life for every person for eternity. There will be no appeal, no early release for good behaviour, no family visits and no escape for those who go on the left side of Jesus the King into eternal punishment. On the other hand, those on the right side of the King inherit "a kingdom prepared for them since the foundation of the world" and eternal life. We may initially be gathered as nations, but we believers at some point will be gathered as the "Holy Nation" (1 Peter 2:9). And every person will each individually be judged for what they themselves have done.[5] There is no other outcome. Let's pray that we are in the group on His right side! In the Book of Revelation, John writes of the same event:

Rev 20:12 And the dead were judged according to their works, by the things which were written in the books.

It is notable that Matthew, like Mark and Luke, and the other writers of the Epistles, makes no mention at all of a seven-year tribulation or a thousand-year reign on earth. Matthew's timeline specifically rules out both events. Only John makes mention of the thousand years in the Book of Revelation, which is written in a symbolic genre, and therefore cannot be properly cited in support of pre-trib and Premillennial beliefs. We will discuss these issues in due course, but first let us survey in more depth the views of the church over the approximately 2000 years of history since Jesus' ministry on earth.

LIGHT ON THE LAST JUDGMENT FROM THE CATECHISM OF THE CATHOLIC CHURCH.

As mentioned earlier, I found while I was doing the research that my findings were very much in accord with official Catholic teaching. I will highlight this at intervals in the book by quoting relevant paragraphs of the Catechism. Paragraph 678 sheds considerable light on the sheep and goats judgment in Matthew 25, and makes it plain that it takes place at the end of the age, and that we will all be present:

"678 Following in the steps of the prophets and John the Baptist, Jesus announced the judgement of the Last Day in his preaching. Then will the conduct of each one and the secrets of hearts be brought to light. Then will the culpable unbelief that counted the offer of God's grace as nothing be condemned. Our attitude to our neighbour will disclose acceptance or refusal of grace and divine love. On the Last Day Jesus will say: "Truly I say to you, as you did it

---

[5] Some have said that this judgment is for nations, and judgment of individuals is a separate issue. But surely this teaching makes no sense. The judgments handed down here are final. It is not possible that individuals walk out of here and go to some other judgment. "A nation" being judged here means "all the individuals in that nation". And each individual will be judged for their own individual deeds. How else could they be consigned for eternity to either everlasting life or everlasting punishment (verse 32)?

to one of the least of these my brethren, you did it to me." (Catechism of the Catholic Church, 1997)

But what of the majority who have died prior to Jesus' coming? The Catholic Church holds that every person undergoes their "particular judgment" at the end of this life:

1021 Death puts an end to human life as the time open to either accepting or rejecting the divine grace manifested in Christ. The New Testament speaks of judgment primarily in its aspect of the final encounter with Christ in his second coming, but also repeatedly affirms that each will be rewarded immediately after death in accordance with his works and faith. the parable of the poor man Lazarus and the words of Christ on the cross to the good thief, as well as other New Testament texts speak of a final destiny of the soul -a destiny which can be different for some and for others.

1022 Each man receives his eternal retribution in his immortal soul at the very moment of his death, in a particular judgment that refers his life to Christ: either entrance into the blessedness of heaven-through a purification or immediately, or immediate and everlasting damnation.

At the evening of life, we shall be judged on our love.

So, according to Catholic teaching, each one of us will be judged immediately on death. But this judgment will be ratified at the final, universal judgment at the end of the age:

1038 The resurrection of all the dead, "of both the just and the unjust," will precede the Last Judgment. This will be "the hour when all who are in the tombs will hear [the Son of man's] voice and come forth, those who have done good, to the resurrection of life, and those who have done evil, to the resurrection of judgment. Then Christ will come "in his glory, and all the angels with him .... Before him will be gathered all the nations, and he will separate them one from another as a shepherd separates the sheep from the goats, and he will place the sheep at his right hand, but the goats at the left.... and they will go away into eternal punishment, but the righteous into eternal life."

1039 In the presence of Christ, who is Truth itself, the truth of each man's relationship with God will be laid bare. The Last Judgment will reveal even to its furthest consequences the good each person has done or failed to do during his earthly life:

All that the wicked do is recorded, and they do not know. When "our God comes, he does not keep silence."

Much Catholic Church teaching on the end times still follows Augustine, though his theology was never formally adopted by the church. He had a huge influence. (See chapter 10)

ORTHODOX AND EPISCOPAL CATECHISMS CONFIRM FINAL RESURRECTION AND JUDGMENT

The same has been true of Orthodox teaching, though the Orthodox Catechism and most other church catechisms are much less detailed than the Catholic catechism of 1997. The sections quoted below from the Orthodox and Episcopal / Anglican catechisms recognise that there will be a final resurrection and judgment:

With death, the soul is separated from the body. It receives a particular judgement and remains separated until the Second Coming of Christ and the final judgement. At the final judgement, man will be presented before Christ as a full person, with a body and soul. For man to be presented like this, his body must be resurrected and be united with the soul. This will happen immediately before the final judgement. Holy Scripture absolutely assures us of this. (Orthodox Catachism, 2017)

Q. What do we mean by the last judgment? A. We believe that Christ will come in glory and judge the living and the dead. Q. What do we mean by the resurrection of the body? A. We mean that God will raise us from death in the fullness of our being, that we may live with Christ in the communion of the saints. (Episcopal Church, 1979)

Chapter Ten

THE DEVELOPMENT OF DIFFERING VIEWS ON THE END TIMES – APOSTOLIC CHURCH TO AUGUSTINE

✝ ✝ ✝

Here are eight basic positions, or systems of interpretation taken by different groups of Christians over the centuries. When we count likely combinations of views there are at least 13 possibilities.

1. **Amillennialism**, ("Amil") which was, as I understand it, the original position of the New Testament, and was held by church fathers such as Dionysius of Alexandria and Augustine of Hippo, and reformers such as Luther and Calvin. The actual theological term, "Amillennialism" was only coined in the 20th century and would have been unknown to all these supporters, but the doctrine, I believe, fairly represents their known views. It takes its name from "a" meaning "no" in Greek – so it means "no millennium" – in other words, no literal reign over the world by Jesus from Jerusalem. Some writers prefer the term "realized

millennialism" for the doctrine. It teaches that the millennial reign of Revelation 20 is the spiritual reign of the risen Christ during the Gospel era. Throughout this book we will shorten the term to "Amil" for easier reading.

2. The **Classical Premillennialism** of church fathers such as Papias and Justin Martyr. "Premil" derives from "pre" in Greek, meaning "before". It teaches that Jesus Christ will come to earth before the millennium and will set up His reign over earth literally from Jerusalem for a literal thousand years. Many Premils claim that this was the majority position in the early church. Amil scholars do not at all accept that claim. We will refer to Premillennialism as "Premil".

3. **Historicism –** This relates to the interpretation of the prophetic symbols of the Books of Revelation, Daniel, and certain other prophetic books. The historicist viewpoint is that the symbols represent historical events of the Gospel era, from Jesus' earthly ministry to His return to earth. Historicism was born at the time of the Reformation, and, controversially depicts the beasts of Revelation 13 and 17 as the papacy, and the Catholic Church. It is possible to be a Premil historicist, a Postmil historicist, or an Amil historicist.

4. **Futurism –** holds that the symbols of Revelation and other prophetic books have nothing to do with history but portray a time of future tribulation on the earth. Futurism was born from classical Premillennialism. For many centuries from Augustine onwards, it was very little heard of. It was revived by a Jesuit priest, Francesco Ribera, during the Counter Reformation.

5. **Preterism –** holds that the prophecies of Revelation and certain other books were fulfilled back at the time of the destruction of Jerusalem in 70 AD by the Romans, or earlier, and therefore do not address the world of our time. A person may be "full preterist" or "partial preterist".

6. **Postmillennialism –** (from the Greek "post', - "after") is the notion that Jesus will return after the millennium. The millennium as interpreted by Postmil is a golden age ushered in by the church, which, according to this theory, will triumph

in its teaching and preaching to the extent that the world will be won and transformed even before the return of Jesus. When He arrives, the job will be pretty much done, according to this view. We will refer to it as Postmil. Support for it is growing today.

7. **Dispensationalism** (including **Futurism** and **'Pretribulationism'**). Invented in the 1830's by JN Darby, it was the first system to include the 'Pretribulation rapture'. The governing idea of the system is that God has different dealings with different peoples at different times so the Jews according to this theory have their own dealings with God separate from the church. Futurism is another tenet. Dispensationalism insists that the Book of Revelation portrays a future 7-year tribulation for non-believers after Jesus has come and removed all the Christians out of the earth. According to this view, people who miss the rapture will still have a chance to be saved during the tribulation. We will refer to Pretribulationism/t as "Pretrib".

8. **Anglo-Israelism and similar** – is focused on the northern ten tribes of Israel, which were forcibly exiled by the Assyrians in about 780AD. The southern tribes, Judah and Benjamin, ancestors of today's Jews, were exiled by the Babylonians 150 years later. Anglo-Israelism holds that the northern tribes lost their identity and migrated to Europe, where they became modern-day peoples such as British, Dutch, Scandinavian, US and British Commonwealth.

Table 1: Simplified sequence of the emergence of different viewpoints.

1 Amil
- The normal position of the Catholic Church. In my opinion, the original position of New Testament. No literal thousand year reign on earth. Book of Revelation symbolic.

2 premil
- Classical premillennialism. Held by some early church fathers. Belief in literal thousand year reign from Jerusalem.

3. Historicist
- Started during Reformation. Prophetic metaphors in Revelation portray church history since Jesus.

4. Futurism
- Origin in classsical premillennialism. Revived during Counter Reformation. Prophecies in Revelation portray a future tribulation.

5. Preterism
- Prophecies in Revelation were fulfilled by 70 AD.

6. Postmil
- Postmillennialism was very popular in 19th century USA. Thousand-year golden age before Jesus returns.

7. Dispen
- Dispensationalism includes Pretribulation rapture and premillennialism. Separate redemption plans for the Jews and the Church.

8. Anglo-Israel
- Anglo-Israelism and other similar ideas attempted to identify the "lost 10 tribes" i.e. the tribes conquered by Assyrians in 2 Kings 17

THE ORIGINAL AMIL.

As we shall see, many modern opponents of Amil would dispute the title I have given this section. But it seems to me beyond any possibility of denial that the New Testament writers were Amil in their whole concept of the coming end of the age, the final judgment, the immediate reward for the believers, and God's everlasting kingdom. I think I have demonstrated that in my comments on Matthew and will discuss the other New Testament writers as we study the scriptures together. The modern Amil movement is growing as more and more sincere adherents of other persuasions consider the logic of Amil. Some fine writers are making a compelling case for it, as I have detailed at the beginning of the list of references.

One fundamental concept of Amil is the progression from "inaugurated" truth to "realised" truth. This is seen particularly in the advance of God's kingdom. One application of the concept is that Jesus totally defeated Satan at the cross. Satan is now a defeated foe. Jesus is Lord and King. But Jesus is not yet fully and visibly reigning. Mankind is still in rebellion, yet because of Jesus' great victory, the issue is not in doubt. The victory has been won and Jesus' reign has been "inaugurated". But in time the reality of His rule will be fully "realised". He will be visibly King of all the universe, surrounded with glory. This is not a strange doctrine to many modern Christians. I remember hearing the much-loved and respected Derek Prince comparing this victory of Jesus with the victory of the allies over Germany in 1944-5. Once the allies had landed on D-day, final victory was inevitable. In a sense they had already won the war – but this had to be fought through on the ground. Brother Derek was a convinced Premil Christian, but this aspect of Amil teaching would not have been strange to him.

Another way to express this is to see the coming of Jesus' universal reign as a two-step progression. The first step was accomplished by Jesus' defeat of Satan during His earthly ministry – this "inaugurated" reality is what we now see, and glorious it is. But one day, and perhaps soon, His reign over all will be fully realised. He will be visibly on the throne, receiving homage from all the universe.

The same may be seen in every Christian's individual walk. As soon as we are saved, we are raised up into the heavenly places with Him. And we do truly reign and rule with him. Our prayers shake the universe, and our bodies are filled with His glory. He has given life to our bodies. Praise God! That is the inaugurated Christian experience that is so precious to us. However, there is more. Paul describes what is in store:

2 Cor 5 For we know that if our earthly house, *this* tent, is destroyed, we have a building from God, a house not made with hands, eternal in the heavens. ² For in this we groan, earnestly desiring to be clothed with our habitation which is from heaven, ³ if indeed, having been clothed, we shall not be found naked. ⁴ For we who are in *this* tent groan, being burdened, not because we want to be unclothed, but further clothed, that mortality may be swallowed up by life. ⁵ Now He who has prepared us for this very thing *is* God, who also has given us the Spirit as a guarantee.

This is the body we will inherit if we stand fast until the day of Christ. Notice this body is "eternal in the heavens" and is filled and submerged in the immortal life of God. This is the fully realised Christian life. Romans 8 gives more details which we will discuss in chapter 15. Note also how this life is guaranteed by God's gift of the Holy Spirit.

According to the Amil perspective, the millennium is a symbol John used in Revelation to signify the church age. The beginning of the Church marked its inauguration, and its full realisation will be seen after the millennium with all Old and New Testament saints worshipping God in glory for eternity. Interestingly, this perspective once again aligns closely with the Catholic Church position. The Catechism explains:

670 Since the Ascension God's plan has entered into its fulfilment. We are already at "the last hour"; "Already the final age of the world is with us, and the renewal of the world is irrevocably under way; it is even now anticipated in a certain real way, for the Church on earth is endowed already with a sanctity that is real but imperfect." Christ's kingdom already manifests its presence through the miraculous signs that attend its proclamation by the Church.

. . . until all things are subjected to him

671 Though already present in his Church, Christ's reign is nevertheless yet to be fulfilled "with power and great glory" by the King's return to earth. This reign is still under attack by the evil powers, even though they have been defeated definitively by Christ's Passover. Until everything is subject to him, "until there be realized new heavens and a new earth in which justice dwells," the pilgrim Church, in her sacraments and institutions, which belong to this present age, carries the mark of this world which will pass, and she herself takes her place among the creatures which groan and travail yet and await the revelation of the sons of God. That is why Christians pray, above all in the Eucharist, to hasten Christ's return by saying to him: Maranatha! "Our Lord, come!" (Catechism of the Catholic Church, 1997)

RISE OF PREMIL.

The first deviation from Matthew's simple sequence was the belief we have now called *Premil*, so familiar to evangelicals and charismatics today. In the days of the early church, it was called *chiliasm*, and in the 19th century *millenarianism*. It is the belief that the 1000-year reign of Christ and the saints (the *"millennium"*) referred to in Revelation 20:4 is going to be a literal reign on earth at some time in the future. According to this doctrine, Jesus is going to return in a visible way *before* the millennium, and that the millennium will be a time before the final judgement when Jesus will rule the earth for 1000 years from Jerusalem.

Modern Premils have alleged that pretty well all the early Christians were Premillennial in belief. This claim is far from proven. The topic has been one of hot debate. For example, the Premil Dr Charles Ryrie of Dallas Seminary cited several early church fathers including Papias, Justin Martyr, Irenaeus and Tertullian in support of his contention that "Premil is the historic faith of the Church". "In the face of such overwhelming evidence, who can deny that Premil was the faith of the early church?" he wrote (Ryrie, 1953). But he had a Master's student, Alan Boyd, who set out to research the prophetic views of the early Christians for his Master's thesis. On completing his research, Boyd's conclusion was:

"It is the conclusion of this thesis that Dr Ryrie's statement is historically invalid..." (Bahnsen_and_Gentry, 1989), p. 235.

Some examples of scholars supporting Boyd's conclusion are: D.H. Kromminga, Ned Stonehouse, W.G.T. Shedd, Philip Schaff and Louis Berkhof. For instance Dr Berkhof, the respected Reformed theologian, said, "The name (Amillennialism) is indeed new, but the view to which it is applied is as old as Christianity." Since the second century it has "been the view most widely accepted, is the only view that is either expressed or implied in the great historical Confessions of the Church and has always been the prevalent view in Reformed circles" (Berkhof, 1932) p. 708.

PAPIAS

One example of a believer in the literal 1000-year reign of Jesus was Bishop Papias (c70-155AD), who left some fragments of writing on the topic. The fourth century church historian, Eusebius, has this to say about him:

"The same person, moreover, has set down other things as coming to him from unwritten tradition, amongst these some strange parables and instructions of the Saviour, and some other things of a more fabulous nature. Amongst these he says that there will be a millennium after the resurrection from the dead, when the personal reign of Christ will be established on this earth." It is interesting that Eusebius should consider the ideas of Papias "strange" or "fabulous".

JUSTIN MARTYR

Another early Premil was Justin Martyr, writing about 120-150AD. He wrote "Dialogue with Trypho the Jew" in order to defend Christian ideas against Jewish detractors. In the dialogue, Trypho asks:

"But tell me, do you really admit that this place, Jerusalem, shall be rebuilt; and do you expect your people to be gathered together, and made joyful with Christ and the patriarchs, and the prophets, both the men of our nation, and other proselytes who joined them before your Christ came? or have you given way, and admitted this in order to have the appearance of worsting us in the controversies?"

Justin replied, 'Then I answered, "I am not so miserable a fellow,

Trypho, as to say one thing and think another. I admitted to you formerly, that I and many others are of this opinion, and [believe] that such will take place, as you assuredly are aware; but, on the other hand, I signified to you that many who belong to the pure and pious faith, and are true Christians, think otherwise.'"

So, from this dialogue, Trypho is obviously aware that some Christians believed that Jerusalem would literally be rebuilt (it was still in ruins after the Romans had destroyed it in 70AD), and that the resurrected Christ would literally rule from there. We notice how Justin states that he personally believes that is the case, but there were many good and sincere Christians who did not agree. In other words, there was disagreement and controversy among the Christians even in that era on the millennium, with "many" believing in no literal millennium, just as there is disagreement among Christians of our era! It is most certainly not justifiable to claim the case for Premil as proven, to say the least.

DIONYSIUS OF ALEXANDRIA

One example of an early church father who was strongly opposed to the doctrine of the millennial reign was Dionysius, Bishop of Alexandria, in the third century. Nepos, an Egyptian bishop, taught the Premil doctrine and some of his followers brought it to Dionysius' diocese after Nepos' death. Dionysius wrote:

"…..they produce a certain composition by Nepos, on which they insist very strongly, as if it demonstrated incontestably that there will be a (temporal) reign of Christ upon the earth……" (Premil)

It seems then and now to be a characteristic of some of the Premil expositors that they argue as if there were no other possible interpretation of scripture and the facts but their view only. Dionysius sees their concept as doing great dis-service to the true Gospel, because he thinks that a mere temporal reign of Jesus from Jerusalem would be something very much inferior to the real future as he saw it, namely the immediate universal judgement and creation of the new heavens and new earth as the Gospel of Matthew outlined.

Dionysius continues:

"………there are unquestionably some teachers, who hold that the law and the prophets are of no importance, and who decline to follow the Gospels, and who depreciate the epistles of the apostles, and who have also made large promises regarding the doctrine of this composition, as though it were some great and hidden mystery, and who, at the same time, do not allow that our simpler brethren have any sublime and elevated conceptions either of our Lord's appearing in His glory and His true divinity, or of our own resurrection from the dead, and our being gathered together to Him, and assimilated to Him, but, on the contrary, endeavour to lead them to hope for things which are trivial and corruptible, and only such as what we find at present in the kingdom of God."

Dionysius shows in this passage that he has adopted the view of Matthew (quoting Jesus Himself) about the appearance of Jesus in glory, and our resurrection and gathering to Him. He shows a deep concern that Premil means that the believers' glorious hope is being substituted by a much lesser hope – a life in this world in Jerusalem, which Dionysius saw as vastly inferior to the revelation of Jesus' glory for eternity as described in Matthew 24 and 25. He is concerned that those who are weaker in the faith will be drawn away by this doctrine of and be intent on earthly rewards such as pleasant food, comfortable surroundings and worldly pleasures.

He goes on to describe how he tackled the issue. The passage shows just how intensely controversial Premil was even in that remote time. We also see the shepherd's heart of Dionysius, who wouldn't rest until the opposing party had seen the light, and renounced Premil:

"Being then in the Arsinoitic prefecture (in Egypt)—where, as you are aware, this doctrine was current long ago, and caused such division, that schisms and apostasies took place in whole churches—I called together the presbyters and the teachers among the brethren in the villages, and those of the brethren also who wished to attend were present. I exhorted them to make an investigation into that dogma in public. Accordingly, when they had brought this book before us, as though it were a kind of weapon or impregnable battlement, I sat with them for three days in succession from morning till evening and attempted to set them right on the subjects propounded in the composition. Then, too, I was greatly gratified by observing the constancy of the brethren, and their love of the truth, and their docility and intelligence, as we proceeded, in an orderly method, and in a spirit of moderation, to deal with questions, and difficulties, and concessions. For we took care not to press, in every way and with jealous urgency, opinions which had once been adopted, even although they might appear to be correct. Neither did we evade objections alleged by others; but we endeavoured as far as possible to keep by the subject in hand, and to establish the positions pertinent to it. Nor, again, were we ashamed to change our opinions, if reason convinced us, and to acknowledge the fact; but rather with a good conscience, and in all sincerity, and with open hearts before God, we accepted all that could be established by the demonstrations and teachings of the Holy Scriptures. And at last the author and introducer of this doctrine, whose name was Coracion, in the hearing of all the brethren present, made acknowledgment of his position, and engaged to us that he would no longer hold by his opinion (Premil), nor discuss it, nor mention it, nor teach it, as he had been completely convinced by the arguments of those opposed to it. The rest of the brethren, also, who were present, were delighted with the conference, and with the conciliatory spirit and the harmony exhibited by all."

What a wonderful end to the debate – an end characterised by humility and respect – entirely in the spirit of Paul's instructions to Timothy, namely "God has not given us a spirit of fear, but of power, of love, and of a sound mind. And finally, Dionysius got what he wanted – the agreement of all that Premil was a false doctrine. (Eusebius, c250AD). Can we discuss these issues today in a similar environment of sincere truth-seeking, love of the brethren (including sisters), and sweet reason and reasonableness?

BOOK OF REVELATION – INSPIRED OR NOT?

The clash of views inevitably brought up focus on the Book of Revelation. Then, as now, the source of Premil teaching was mainly an insistence on taking the Book of Revelation literally. In the days of the early church, this literal approach, felt by the early Christians to lead to conflicts with the Gospels and letters of the New Testament, caused a number of believers to reject Revelation as a Holy Spirit-inspired book. Revelation was thought by some to be sourced out of the Cerinthian heresy. Amongst other things, Cerinthus, the leader of a heretical cult which he founded in the first century, taught that the reward for believers would be part in an earthly kingdom of sensual pleasures. In addition to this, Cerinthus was a gnostic, who taught that Jesus was different from Christ, and was a sensual man, not born of a virgin. Dionysius, after mentioning these believers who rejected Revelation, and giving his opinion that it is impossible to interpret the book of Revelation literally, made his own attitude on Revelation clear. He did not reject the book but emphasised that it is symbolic:

"But I, for my part, could not venture to set this book aside, for there are many brethren who value it highly. Yet, having formed an idea of it as a composition exceeding my capacity of understanding, I regard it as containing a kind of hidden and wonderful intelligence on the several subjects which come under it. For though I cannot comprehend it, I still suspect that there is some deeper sense underlying the words. And I do not measure and judge its expressions by the standard of my own reason, but, making more allowance for faith, I have simply regarded them as too lofty for my comprehension; and I do not forthwith reject what I do not understand, but I am only the more filled with wonder at it, in that I have not been able to discern its import."

The Council of Nicea ruled Revelation to be part of the recognised cannon of scripture in 325AD. Today the inspiration of Revelation is not in doubt among orthodox Christians, who accept that God's providence over the centuries has led us to have a reliable and inspired Bible. But I think we must read Revelation in such a way as to do the book justice, yet at the same time not to contradict the equally inspired Gospel of Matthew.

THE NICENE CREED

The Council of Nicea also, however, provided powerful evidence that the Matthew's Gospel view of end time events was the majority view. The Christian leaders present agreed on what has come to be known as the Nicene Creed as a summary statement of what the church believed. Here is the wording:

"I believe in one God, the Father, the Almighty, maker of heaven and earth, and in one Lord Jesus Christ, the only-begotten Son of God, begotten of the Father before all worlds; God of God, Light of Light, very God of very God; begotten, not made, being of one substance with the Father, by whom all things were made.

"Who, for us men for our salvation, came down from heaven, and was incarnate by the Holy Spirit of the virgin Mary, and was made man; and was crucified also for us under Pontius Pilate; He suffered and was buried; and the third day He rose again, according to the Scriptures; and ascended into heaven, and sits on the right hand of the Father; and He shall come again, with glory, to judge the living and the dead; whose kingdom shall have no end.

"And I believe in the Holy Ghost, the Lord and Giver of Life; who proceeds from the Father [and the Son]; who with the Father and the Son together is worshipped and glorified; who spoke by the prophets.

"And I believe one holy catholic and apostolic Church. I acknowledge one baptism for the remission of sins; and I look for the resurrection of the dead, and the life of the world to come. Amen."

Millions of Christians over the centuries in the East and in the West, in Catholic, Orthodox and Protestant churches, have recited and reflected on these words, or a variant of them. Let's notice a few things about the creed:

COMMENTS ON THE NICENE CREED

1. It is a summary of important things Christians have believed since the time of the New Testament Apostles.

2. There is absolutely no suggestion that we will reign on the earth for a thousand years. If it were the case, surely this aspect would have been important enough to include in a summary of the faith!

3. When the leaders were writing paragraph 2, they could have had a copy of the Matthew 24-25 discourse we have studied out on the table. "He shall come again, with glory, to judge

the living and the dead; whose kingdom shall have no end" – exactly the elements of the Matthew account.

4. What will be His purpose in coming? To judge the living and the dead!

5. How long will the Kingdom He founds last? Forever! – No 1000-year temporary kingdom.

6. What do the believers look for? The resurrection from the dead, not temporal rule based from the earthly Jerusalem.

7. What kind of life do we expect? THE LIFE OF THE WORLD TO COME! Not the life of this world. The world to come is eternal, whilst this world is perishing.

I must admit that to me this all seems obvious. Perhaps I'm missing something?

THE VALUE OF CHURCH TRADITIONS

Many Christians today are sceptical of Church tradition. Perhaps this reflects the society-wide tendency to reject the "establishment" and "do our own thing". Many are influenced by the words of Jesus to the Pharisees in Matthew 15. They were avoiding giving proper support to their parents, falsely reasoning that because they were "serving God", their possessions were given to God anyway, and so didn't need to be given to their parents. Jesus rebuked them sharply:

Mat 15:6 "... you have made the commandment of God of no effect by your tradition," he said.

He was referring to putting man-made traditions ahead of the Bible injunctions. It was a tradition of the Rabbis that this reasoning was quite acceptable and allowed them to ignore the Biblical commandment.

But it is important to realise that there were good traditions in the New Testament times. Paul wrote:

2 The 2:15 Therefore, brethren, stand fast and hold the **tradition**s which you were taught, whether by word or our epistle."

All the early churches had their own "Rule of Faith" which was received direct from the original apostles and passed on from one generation to the next. They were all very similar. The churches did not consider it their duty to discover new knowledge. Their role was to preserve the original teachings of Jesus and the apostles. Here is one early example:

"The church, though dispersed throughout the whole world, even to the ends of the earth, has received from the apostles and their disciples this faith in one God the Father Almighty, Maker of heaven, earth, and the sea and everything in them; and in one Christ Jesus, the Son of God, who became incarnate for our salvation; and in the Holy Spirit, who proclaimed through the prophets the dispensations, the advents, the birth from a virgin, the suffering, the resurrection from the dead, and the ascension into heaven in the flesh of the beloved Christ Jesus, our Lord, and his appearance from heaven in the glory of the Father to gather all things into one and to raise up anew all flesh of the whole human race, in order that every knee should bow—of things in heaven, things in earth, and things under the earth—and that every tongue should confess to him, and that he should execute just judgment towards everyone......." Extract from Irenaeus' Rule of Faith, c. A.D. 185 (Pavao, 2014).

The Nicene Creed was developed from these "Rules of Faith" and, contrary to the opinions of some commentators, did not just appear in 325 AD to change the tenets of the churches. Most of its elements can be seen in the above much earlier example.

ACCORDING TO THE CREEDS, JESUS IS COMING TO JUDGE!

Similar comments could be made about the later Apostles' Creed and other creeds. The Apostles' Creed says of Christ:

"The third day He rose again from the dead; he ascended into heaven, and sits at the right hand of God the Father Almighty; from thence He shall come to judge the living and the dead....."

Once again we notice He is coming to judge. Even clearer is the Athanasian Creed (dating from the fourth century):

"He ascended into heaven, He sitteth on the right hand of the Father, God Almighty; from thence He shall come to judge the living and the dead; at Whose coming all men shall rise again with their bodies; and shall give account of their own works; and they that have done good shall go into life everlasting, and they that have done evil into everlasting fire. This is the catholic faith, which except a man believe faithfully, he cannot be saved."

Let's note here that the Athanasian Creed affirms not only that Jesus will come to the earth for the purpose of judging, but that at that time all people, the wicked and the just, will be raised with their bodies. The Athanasian Creed was written in the fourth century by Athanasius, the famous bishop who was willing to go into exile to defend the doctrine of the Trinity. This agrees 100% with Matthew's Gospel, and as we shall see, the other Bible writers who had anything to say on the resurrection and Return of Christ.

The three creeds, the Nicene Creed, Apostles' Creed and Athanasian Creed, are known as the Ecumenical Creeds, because they are foundational to the Catholic, Orthodox and Lutheran traditions.

THE SACK OF ROME 410 AD

Eighty-five years after the Council of Nicea, a catastrophic event occurred, which was to act as a catalyst in bringing another hugely influential Christian thinker and writer to the fore. The event was the sack of Rome by the Visigoths led by Alaric, in 410 AD. The pagans put it about that the cause of all this terrible misfortune was that the Romans had deserted the old pagan gods for Christ, and that the old gods were now punishing the city.

AUGUSTINE OF HIPPO – DOCTOR OF THE CHURCH, PHILOSOPHER - BACKGROUND

The sack of Rome and resulting criticisms of Christianity are important to our topic because it was against this backdrop that Augustine of Hippo was stirred up to write his greatest work, the *City of God*, which was then something like a manifesto of Christianity. He put together an exposition on many topics relating to Christian faith, including our present topic, end-time events and the Return of Christ. He had been converted and baptised in 386 AD, and was emerging as a hugely influential theologian who single-handedly impacted the whole Western mediaeval world view.

The City of God is a monumental work, the modern translation of which spans 1000 pages. Never before had anyone written a treatise with one continuous theme of this length. It is a wide-ranging attack on paganism and defence of Christianity.

In setting out his view of the events surrounding Jesus' coming and the judgment he cites the descriptions by Jesus of the judgment of the cities where He did great works compared with Tyre and Sidon and other ancient cities. He draws two conclusions: there will be a judgment; and this will be at the time of the resurrection of the dead. He goes on to distinguish between what he saw as the first and second resurrections, taking the first resurrection to be that of the soul when a person is converted and baptised, and the second to be that of all mankind at the last judgment. He draws from John chapter 5, then proceeds to Revelation chapter 20, where he describes as "ridiculous fancies" the idea that that the first resurrection of verse 5 is a future, bodily resurrection, as believed by Premil doctrine. He further links Revelation 20:1-3, the binding of Satan, with Jesus' binding of the strong man in Matthew 12, and views the 1000-year millennium as a symbolic picture of Jesus' present reign through the believers. We will consider in depth these interpretations in Chapters 15 and 16. For now we will note:

1. Augustine advocated a *symbolic* interpretation of the book of Revelation.
2. He supported what is now known to theologians as "Amil".
3. He regarded Premil doctrine as a ridiculous fancy.
4. He carried the day completely – after his treatise, no-one with any credibility advocated Premil again until the nineteenth century.
5. It is important to realise the influence this man's thoughts have had given over the centuries: Augustine is recognised as a saint in the Catholic, Anglican and Orthodox churches, and as a pre-eminent doctor of the church. Many Protestants consider him to be a forerunner of the Reformation because of his teachings

on salvation and grace. He had a huge influence on Luther and Calvin, who both accepted Amil.

6. Modern Premils have tried to suggest that Augustine, writing in the fifth century, was the first proponent of Amil. The reality is that on the contrary, there were many non-Premils from the earliest days of the church (including Jesus Himself if Matthew's account is to be believed! And certainly Matthew himself). These believers would not have counted themselves "Amils" as the term was unknown in their day, the term not being coined until the twentieth century. Nevertheless, that is in effect what they were. (b) Augustine was by no means the first advocate of the "Amillennial" position. As we have seen, he was not advocating new doctrine when reasoning from the scriptures that there was no literal millennial reign. He was merely discovering afresh what the scriptures have always taught. Jerome, also considered to be one of the more significant church fathers, said of him that he "established anew the ancient Faith."

Augustine's view prevailed in the church until the reformation and beyond. Even the reformers, though they wanted to reform the *practices of* the church and some doctrines such as salvation by faith, and the priesthood of all believers, they were not wanting to change many of the foundational doctrines which made the church what is was and is. Augustine more than any other writer left a body of theological writings which was foundational to the future development of the church, including the Catholic, Orthodox, Protestant and Reformed churches. Amil was part of this foundation.

Chapter Eleven

DEVELOPMENT OF DIFFERING VIEWS 2 – THE REFORMATION

✠ ✠ ✠

We now jump to the end of the 16th century as very little of note was written on eschatology after Augustine until then. The churches of the Reformation retained the Amillennial foundation of the early church, as can be seen in these extracts from their creeds:

1. LUTHERAN – AUGSBERG CONFESSION 1530

Quoted in Davis (Davis, 2014):

"(We) teach that at the Consummation of the World Christ will appear for judgment and will raise up all the dead; He will give to the godly and elect eternal life and everlasting joys, but ungodly men and the devils He will condemn to be tormented without end."

(We) condemn (those) who are now spreading certain Jewish opinions, that before the resurrection of the dead the godly shall take possession of the kingdom of the world, the ungodly being everywhere suppressed."

2. BELGIC CONFESSION – REFORMED 1561

"Finally, we believe, according to God's Word, that when the time appointed by the Lord has come (which is unknown to all creatures) and the number of the elect is complete, our Lord Jesus Christ will come from heaven, bodily and visibly, as He ascended, with great glory and majesty, to declare Himself the judge of the living and the dead. He will burn this old world in fire and flame in order to cleanse it. Then all human creatures will appear in person – men, women and children who have lived from the beginning until the end of the world. They will be summoned there by the voice of the archangel and by the sound of the divine trumpet…."

The Reformation popularised a way of interpreting Bible prophecy known as **historicism**. The historicist looks at history and finds in it examples of fulfilled prophecy. The Protestant reformers saw the Catholicism of their day as decadent and revealed in the symbols of the Books of Daniel and Revelation. Sometimes going through incredible persecution and trials, they derived great encouragement from the prophetic scriptures. Until the mid-19th century the historicist approach was by far the most common amongst Protestant Christians. Examples of commentators using this approach were Martin Luther, John Calvin, John Foxe, Sir Isaac Newton (who incidentally thought his Bible commentaries were more significant life achievements than his work on gravity!), Matthew Henry, H Grattan Guinness, Charles Spurgeon, AB Simpson and many others.

The central feature of the historicist approach is to see the Book of Revelation as a description in symbolic terms of Christian history from the earthly ministry of Jesus to His second coming. Details of individual commentators' interpretations of events over the centuries have differed, especially as the notable commentators have lived centuries apart, but the broad theme is the same.

THE REFORMATION PORTRAYED IN THE LITTLE BOOK OF REVELATION

The little book of Revelation 10 was widely regarded as symbolising the resurgence of knowledge of the Bible. At this time translations of it were becoming available in the languages of the day, and, because of the invention of printing, these were widely distributed:

I saw still another mighty angel coming down from heaven, clothed with a cloud. And a rainbow was on his head, his face was like the sun, and his feet like pillars of fire. [2] He had a little book open in his hand.…… Revelation 10:1-2

Note that the little book is open, indicating that it had at last become accessible to the masses.

THE TWO WITNESSES

The reformers saw themselves in the two witnesses of Revelation 11:

Rev 11:3-6 And I will give power to my two witnesses, and they will prophesy one thousand two hundred and sixty days, clothed in sackcloth. [4] These are the two olive trees and the two lampstands standing before the God of the earth. [5] And if anyone wants to harm them, fire proceeds from their mouth and devours their enemies. And if anyone wants to harm them, he must be killed in this manner. [6] These have power to shut heaven, so that no rain falls in the days of their prophecy; and they have power over waters to turn them to blood, and to strike the earth with all plagues, as often as they desire.

The witnesses were variously seen to be the new Protestant church and the Bible, or the Old and New Testaments. The power they had was interpreted as the power of Biblical preaching to destroy false religion and practices and ideas which held people in bondage.

HISTORICIST VIEW OF THE PAPACY

The classical historicist position has been to see the Papacy as an institutional "Antichrist" down the centuries[6]. It is important to realize,

---

[6] To us, living in the 21st century where tolerance is perhaps the cardinal virtue, the language of the reformers when referring to the Pope and Catholicism sounds very extreme and bigoted. However, the writings of the reformers become more understandable when we reflect on an incident like the Saint Bartholomew's Day Massacre. The massacre began in the night of 23-24 August 1572. France was probably the most staunchly Catholic monarchy in Europe, but many Frenchmen had been convinced by the arguments of the reformers and had become Calvinist Protestants, called Huguenots. Traditionally supposed

and surprising to modern protestant Christians, that the reformers didn't believe that all Catholic Christians were "lost", or that the Catholic Church was not part of the universal church. For example, Luther said:

"We on our part confess that there is much that is Christian and good under the papacy; indeed, everything that is Christian and good is to be found there and has come to us from this source. For instance, we confess that in the papal church there are the true holy Scriptures, true baptism, the true sacrament of the altar, the true keys to the forgiveness of sins, the true office of the ministry, the true catechism in the form of the Lord's Prayer, the Ten Commandments, and the articles of the creed . . . I speak of what the Pope and we have in common . . . I contend that in the papacy there is true Christianity, even the right kind of Christianity and many great and devoted saints. (Luther, 1528)

But the reformers were very much against the office of the papacy, and corrupt practices in the church. The two aspects, religious and political, were interpreted by the classical historicist commentators to be the two beasts of Revelation 13. In John's vision, the first beast emerges from the sea:

Rev 13:1-5 And I saw a beast rising up out of the sea, having seven heads and ten horns, and on his horns ten crowns, and on his heads a blasphemous name.

According to historicism, the ten horns and the mouth speaking great things and blasphemies link this beast with the beast of Daniel 7, which also had 10 horns and an additional little horn speaking "great things". Both beasts were seen as representing Rome, pagan and later

---

to have been at the instigation of Queen Catherine de Medici, the mother of the King, Charles IX, the massacre started on the wedding day of the King's sister, Margaret, to the Protestant Henry III of Navarre (the future Henry IV of France). Many Huguenots were in Paris for the event. They were lured off guard by generous gifts and hospitality. The King ordered the killing of a group of Huguenot leaders, and the killings spread across Paris, then to other urban centres and the French countryside. Huguenot shops and homes were pillaged and the occupants butchered. The number killed were claimed to be upwards of 100,000, though modern estimates are more in the range of 5,000 – 30,000. One question that has been raised about these massacres is "Did the Pope (Gregory XII) know about them, or encourage them?" We can't know for sure now whether or not he knew about the massacres in advance, but he did strike a commemorative medal to celebrate the event when he heard about it. In the future we will know for certain – on the Day of the Lord!

papal. In their denunciations of the church of Rome, the historicist commentators cited the Popes' inquisitions, tortures and executions.

It should be realised, though, that the Reformers themselves committed some terrible measures, including executions and torture, against the more radical reformers, the Anabaptists, or Mennonites as they are now called. Secondly, some modern historians have made a persuasive case that the number of those condemned to death and torture by the inquisitions has been substantially exaggerated by propagandists seeking to discredit Catholicism[7].

God alone knows the true extent and gravity of these violent episodes and corrupt practice in former centuries. But we do know the final outcome. Those who take violent, cruel or corrupt acts, unrepented of, to the grave, will face God's justice. But those who repent and ask forgiveness will find God's mercy and grace. In 2010 the Lutheran church officially apologised to the Mennonites. Many Mennonites said at the time they felt very liberated, and no longer felt as though they were a persecuted minority. As a community, they had carried the burden of that persecution for 500 years. (dw.com, 2010) (Wikipedia, Historical-revision-of-the-Inquisition) (Kirkus, The-Spanish-Inquisition)

---

[7] "The two most significant and extensively-cited sources of this revised analysis of the historiography of the inquisitorial proceedings are Inquisition (1988) by Edward Peters and The Spanish Inquisition: An Historical Revision (1997) by Henry Kamen. These works focus on identifying and correcting what they argue are popular modern misconceptions about the inquisitions and historical misinterpretations of their activities." – Wikipedia. Kamen notes for example that ``the Netherlands [in the mid-16th century] already possessed an Inquisition of its own" and that the courts in Antwerp (then part of Holland) ``between 1557 and 1562 executed 103 heretics, more than died in the whole of Spain in that period." Kamen also points out how Protestant and other writers mythified the Inquisition, exaggerating its cruelties in the service of anti-Catholic propaganda.

Chapter Twelve

MORE SYSTEMS OF INTERPRETATION EMERGE – FUTURISM, PRETERISM AND POST-MILLENNIALISM

✢ ✢ ✢

THE JESUITS RESPOND – (1) FUTURISM

To convinced Catholics, of course, the depiction of the Pope as Antichrist and the Roman church the beast of Revelation 13 and 17 was and is highly offensive. The Catholic Counter-Reformation was launched to counter the influence of the Reformation.

The Jesuit Francisco Ribera wrote a 500-page commentary on the Book of Revelation, published in 1590, to refute the Protestant view. He revived the doctrine of Futurism, which had been part of classical Premil. Ribera's version taught that the prophecies of Revelation had nothing to do with the Roman Catholic Church, and the Reformation, but rather concerned a seven-year period at the end of this age when a single evil individual would assume the role of Antichrist and rule the world.

Ironically, almost 250 years later, this doctrine was incorporated into *Dispensationalism,* the system for interpretation of Bible prophecy developed in the first instance by John Nelson Darby of the Plymouth Brethren. Through that route, it became the most widely believed doctrine amongst Protestant evangelicals. This will be covered in more depth in the section on Dispensationalism.

WHO IS THE ANTICHRIST? MORE THEORIES......

Over history there have been many guesses as to who this final Antichrist could be, and every age has had its candidates. Napoleon Bonaparte was one pick, but obviously was not the final Antichrist at the end of the age. Hitler was another candidate. There have been many options since Dispensationalist ideas became widespread, with even certain high-profile US politicians named as such.

Theologians influenced by Amil tend to see a multi-fulfilment to the prophetic beasts of Daniel 7 and Revelation 13 and 17. For example, Kim Riddlebarger (Riddlebarger, 2018) applies the metaphor to a series of world empires including Babylon; Persia; the original pagan Roman empire, especially under the Caesars; the Papal Roman[8] empire, especially under the mediaeval and renaissance Popes; extending to empires of today such as Russia and China. The common feature of the beast empires is that they have huge political power, exert control over people's lives, and demand worship. Even atheist empires could fit this description, with millions filing reverently past the mummified bodies of Lenin in Moscow, and Mao Tse Tung in Beijing. Beale sees the Antichrist as the spirit behind all these evil empires. It is a consistent theme through the ages that God's people have had an enemy. Daniel is generally held to be writing of the Babylonian, Median, Persian and Seleucid Greek empires, from the symbolism and explanations of chapters 2, 7, and implicitly of chapter 8, but it would be a mistake to limit the application to these empires only.

[8] It may be inflammatory to talk about the Papal States in this context, but I believe that very few Catholics would try to defend the activities of some of the Renaissance popes.

THE JESUITS RESPOND - (2) PRETERISM

Preterism is the third approach to the times depicted in Bible prophecy, which holds that much prophecy was fulfilled in the years immediately following Jesus' ministry, especially by the Roman-Jewish war of 70 AD. A systematic preterist exposition of prophecy was written by the Jesuit Luis de Alcasar, who wrote an extensive treatise on this, published in 1614. What is now termed as "Full Preterism" holds that all of Jesus' prophecies were fulfilled by 70 A D. Partial Preterism holds that some of Jesus' prophecy was fulfilled at this time. For the Antichrist, Preterism would identify either Caligula, Nero, Vespasian or Titus, all emperors in the time following Jesus' earthly ministry.

Preterism has been criticised on the grounds that Alcasar was only intent on deflecting what quickly became the standard Protestant view that the Pope was the "man of sin" and the beast of Revelation. But it seems there were other preterist commentators well before him (DeMar, 2013).

In our time, Preterism has some well-able and well-known champions, perhaps the best known of whom today is R.C. Sproule. Sproule is a "partial preterist" in that he believes many but not all prophecies were fulfilled by the Roman-Jewish war and is on record as saying "Full Preterism" is not an orthodox position (Sproule, 1998).

"Full Preterism", known as "Hyper-Preterism" to its detractors, holds that all prophecy, including the prophecies of Jesus' second coming, were fulfilled during the Roman-Jewish war. "How is this possible?" you may ask. We mentioned this view in the section on Matthew's Gospel, Chapter 7. The argument goes as follows:

Matthew 24:34 has puzzled commentators for centuries, and opponents of Christianity have cited it as an alleged failure of Christ to fulfil prophecy. Jesus said:

Mat 24:34 Assuredly, I say to you, this generation will by no means pass away till all these things take place.

"All these things" refers to all the disasters, including destruction of the temple, and, most importantly, the return of Jesus in glory. All the other things mentioned by Jesus have come to pass, as we have discussed. In some cases, Jesus prophesied with devastating accuracy.

However, Jesus has not returned. Does that mean He didn't keep His word? Or that He was a false prophet because He foretold something that didn't happen? Or could He have returned in a way people didn't expect?

VISITATIONS OF GOD IN THE PAST

Jesus and/or the Father visited the world several times during Old Testament times, for example the coming of the Lord to Hagar in the desert:

Gen 16:7 Now the Angel of the Lord found her by a spring of water in the wilderness, by the spring on the way to Shur.

Note the phrase "Angel of the Lord" usually means the Lord Himself. In another well-known example the Lord came to earth to be with Moses when he drew water from the rock:

Exo 17:6 God said, "Behold, I will stand before you there on the rock in Horeb; and you shall strike the rock, and water will come out of it, that the people may drink."

The following Psalm of David portrays the Lord coming down to earth in judgment. His presence is hidden in the darkness, the wind and the clouds.

Psa 18:9-12 He bowed the heavens also, and came down with darkness under His feet.

And He rode upon a cherub, and flew; he flew upon the wings of the wind.

He made darkness His secret place; His canopy around Him was dark waters

And thick clouds of the skies. From the brightness before Him, His thick clouds passed with hailstones and coals of fire.

This is how He comes in wrath. Another example was used by Isaiah:

Isa 66:15 For, behold, the LORD will come with fire, and with his chariots like a whirlwind, to render his anger with fury, and his rebuke with flames of fire.

Isaiah's prophecy is another one of the coming of the Lord to earth in judgment.

WAS THE SACK OF JERUSALEM IN 70 AD A VISITATION OF JESUS?

If God visited the earth before the ministry of Jesus, surely it must be possible that He visited again during or after completion of the New Testament events? Perhaps we can consider the sack of Jerusalem as a visitation of the Lord, or indeed as a "Day of the Lord" for the Jews at that time. Could it be a historical fulfilment of Mat 24:34?

The concept of God's wrath is an uncomfortable one for 21st century man and woman. In the Old Testament, however, God "judged" many nations, including His own two nations, Israel and Judah. He used Assyria to punish the northern kingdom of Israel for its on-going idolatry and injustices imposed on the poor by the nation's leaders. The Assyrians brutally destroyed the Israelites and their lands. The survivors were gathered, chained and underwent forced deportation to Media. He used Babylon to similarly destroy the land of Judah. Babylon was portrayed in Jeremiah as God's instrument of vengeance:

> Jer 50:10 You *are* My battle-axe *and* weapons of war:
> For with you I will break the nation in pieces;
> With you I will destroy kingdoms;

God brought punishment on the Judah of the 6th century BC because of the rank evil committed, both in idolatry and oppression of the poor. Could He have similarly brought judgment on the Jerusalem of the 1st century AD? Contemporary writers Josephus, Tacitus, and Dio Cassio reported the sighting of supernatural events in the sky. We have already quoted the report of Josephus, the Jewish historian, on the sighting of "many chariots and armed battalions".[9] Other examples in contemporary writings are:

Tacitus The Histories 5.13: "In the sky appeared a vision of armies in conflict, of glittering armour."

Sepher Yosippon, mediaeval Jewish historian on AD66 (the beginning of the Jewish war): "Moreover, in those days were seen chariots of fire and horsemen, a great force flying across the sky near to

---

[9] See page 47

the ground coming against Jerusalem and all the land of Judah, all of them horses of fire and riders of fire." (Yosippon)

If these visions are to be believed, they could, argues the preterist, have provided a fulfilment of scripture passages such as 2 Thessalonians 1:7 ".... the Lord Jesus is revealed from heaven in blazing fire with his powerful angels."

Revelation 19:11-14 also comes to mind: "Now I saw heaven opened, and behold, a white horse. And He who sat on him was called Faithful and True, and in righteousness He judges and makes war. His eyes were like a flame of fire, and on His head were many crowns. He had a name written that no one knew except Himself. He was clothed with a robe dipped in blood, and His name is called The Word of God. And the armies in heaven, clothed in fine linen, white and clean, followed Him on white horses.

When coupled with the great carnage in Jerusalem when Titus' army broke through and massacred the majority of the population, it seems that these events could be interpreted to be an early fulfilment of Matthew 24.

However, these events were recorded by non-Christian historians and there are no writings extant that suggest the early church fathers viewed these signs in the sky as an appearance of Jesus. This visitation, if such it was, fell well short of fulfilling the prophecies of the final coming of Jesus at the end of the age. It was certainly not the final Return of Christ. It is clear from Matthew's Gospel that the universal judgment that goes with the final Day of God will be upon all humanity, from all periods of history. So, as we are still on earth, the final Return of Christ and universal judgment must be still in the future. Moreover, we have not yet fully entered the age to come! More of this soon – but for now let's stay with our survey of positions. There are still two to go!

POSTMILLENNIALISM

A third view of the millennium emerged in the 17th century. The Protestant reformation was obviously here to stay and it seemed that great progress was being made. The early Protestants were generally historicists as regards interpretation of Revelation and related prophecy, and Amil as regards the millennium, following Augustine, Luther and Calvin.

The Postmillennial view was first articulated by Puritans such as John Owen in England in the 17th century, then in the 18th century by Jonathan Edwards (1703-1758) in the US. It holds that the millennium is a long period of time (not necessarily literally 1000 years), a golden age during which Christ will reign not literally in person from Jerusalem, but through the victorious church, by the progress of the Gospel. This will result, so the theory goes, in the majority of the world's population being saved. Good will eventually triumph over evil, and Christian morals and institutions will become the dominant forces in the world.

The view began to really capture the imagination of Protestant Christians during the New England-wide revival which started from Edwards' church in the 1740's. Edwards was a devoted student of Scripture, including the Book of Revelation. He also entertained fervent hopes that God might do something special among the people of New England. He was low key when revival broke out in his own congregation in the 1730' s, but when all of New England was experiencing spiritual awakening in the early 1740' s, he wrote: "Tis not unlikely that this is a work of God's Spirit, it is so extraordinary."

By the 19th century Postmillennialism was the most common understanding of Protestant Christians in the US. It gave rise to a tremendous optimism on the part of many Christians, who believed that they were on the verge of seeing the Kingdom of God on earth. Many Christian institutions were founded in this era. This optimism was expressed in hymns like the "Battle Hymn of the Republic":

"Mine eyes have seen the glory of the coming of the Lord, / He is trampling out the vintage where the grapes of wrath are stored / He hath loosed the fateful lightning of his terrible swift sword, / His truth is marching on."

It is a surprise to many today to learn that Postmillennialism eventually dominated the religious press, the leading seminaries, and most of the Protestant clergy, and it was ingrained in the popular mind, much as Pretrib and Premil have captured the popular evangelical mind today. Postmillennialism gradually gave way in popularity to these two doctrines, as we shall see in the next section. The First World War ended the optimism of Postmillennialism. The doctrine became the view of a very small minority.

It subsequently appeared again to some extent with the coming of Christian Reconstructionism and Dominion Theology from the 1970's. The extremist doctrine of Christian Reconstructionism, originated by R J Rushdoony, advocated that society should be governed by the laws of the Israelites in the Old Testament. It was one form of "Dominion theology", which in general advocates that Christians should rise in society's institutions and take control of society. Another variant of Dominion theology is the "New Apostolic Reformation" championed by Peter Wagner.

How does this look in practice? When asked whether he believed in "the rapture and all that" by journalist Julie Ingersoll, Wagner said he used to but not anymore. "….. the Gospel will be preached to all nations... I believe the world is going to get better... we believe God has sent us out to restore things... when that has happened enough, Jesus will return to a very strong world, reflecting the Kingdom of God." (Ingersol, 2011) It is difficult to see how that fits in with our core discourse[10], Matthew chapters 24 – 25! There are many scripture passages which show the church under extreme pressure when Jesus returns.[11]

ANGLO-ISRAELISM

The 19th century saw the growth in popularity of the Anglo-Israel movement in the British Empire and the USA, which believed that the Northern Israelite tribes, after their conquest by Assyria (as recorded in 2 Kings chapter 17 and 18), no longer practising the religion taught

---

[10] In discussion with a postmill friend, I challenged my friend on his application of Matthew 24 and 25, the signs of Jesus' coming, and the sheep and goats judgment. He maintained that Mat 24 was fulfilled by the AD70 rebellion, and that the Mat 25 judgment described the final judgment at the end of the age, effectively. Of course, this would mean two visitations of Jesus, His second and third coming, separated by 3000 or more years, whereas the entire New Testament teaches one, and one only, second coming of Christ. Under this scenario, some would presumably be judged at Jesus' second coming and some at His third coming.

[11] For example 2 Thess 1:6-9; Dan 12:1-3; Mat 24:21-25

by Moses, and with no access to the temple in Jerusalem, lost their identity and went on separately to migrate to other lands. From this point on, the northern tribes of Israel had a completely different destiny from the southern tribes of Judah and Benjamin (see for example Hosea 1:6-7). The southern tribes carried on another 150 years until they were conquered by the Babylonians. The northern tribes were the progenitors of peoples such as Celts, Anglo-Saxons, Vikings, Normans and other peoples. One after another they entered Britain, so the theory goes, so that the British people and their descendants are Israelites without knowing it. Descendants of course would include the people in the USA, South Africa, Canada, Australia and New Zealand.

Modern commentators holding to derivatives of this view, referred to as the "recognition view" (Hickey, 2013) emphasise other ancient peoples as the descendants of the Israelites such as the Parthians, Scythians, Sacae, Goths and various others. These peoples became the nucleus of modern nations such as Britain, but also Denmark, Finland, Holland, France and other European nations. According to this view, the Jews we see today are predominantly descended from the kingdom of Judah. The descendants of the northern tribes migrated in ignorance of God's purposes and to this day are for the most part entirely ignorant of their Israelite ethnicity. Scriptures cited include:

> Isa 42:16 I will bring the blind by a way they did not know;
> I will lead them in paths they have not known.
> I will make darkness light before them,
> And crooked places straight.
> These things I will do for them,
> And not forsake them.

Or again

> Isa 42:18-20 "Hear, you deaf;
> And look, you blind, that you may see.
> 19 Who *is* blind but My servant,
> Or deaf as My messenger *whom* I send?

Who *is* blind as *he who is* perfect,
And blind as the Lord's servant?
[20] Seeing many things, but you do not observe;
Opening the ears, but he does not hear."

Holders of this view look to the future time when God will regather all the tribes of Israel as foretold.[12] At this point, it is held, it will be revealed where and who the descendants of the Northern tribes are.

---

[12] Eg Amos 9:8-15; Hos 1:10-11; Isaiah 11:10-16; Jer 31:1-30; Ezek 37:15-23

Chapter Thirteen

DISPENSATIONALISM: A NEW DOCTRINE IS BORN

✠ ✠ ✠

DISPENSATIONALISM: THE PRETRIB RAPTURE – ANCIENT REVELATION OR RECENT INVENTION?

As mentioned already, by far the most common teaching in many evangelical churches today is the "Pretribulation rapture" doctrine (as mentioned previously, "Pretrib" for short). The most common version of this teaching is that before Jesus returns to rule, He will come secretly to gather all the believers together in the sky. He will take all the Christians to some place in Heaven where we will experience the marriage supper of the lamb. During this time, God will pour out incredible tribulation on the world for seven years.

ORIGINS OF DISPENSATIONALISM

There is some disagreement as to how this originated, with proponents anxious to establish credibility for their doctrine. A recent claim is that the rapture was described in "Pseudo Ephraim", a document written purporting to be a sermon of Ephraim of Nisbis 306–373AD, shown by scholars to be in fact of later date, perhaps 7th century (Ice, 2016). The document is about the afflictions of the early Christians at the hands of the Huns and later the Muslims, which the writer saw as fulfilment of Jesus' prophecy in Matthew 24. The claim that the writer believed in a Pretrib rapture is based on one sentence in the Latin version of the text: "For all the saints and elect of God are gathered, prior to the tribulation that is to come, and are taken to the Lord lest they see the confusion that is to overwhelm the world because of our sins."

But the Syriac manuscript, probably the original, says that the saints who escaped the tribulation did so by death, not by rapture: "People will flee to cemeteries and hide themselves among the dead, pronouncing the good fortune of the deceased who had avoided the calamity: 'Blessed are you for you were borne away (to the grave) and hence you escaped from the afflictions!" The document goes on to say, as in Matthew, that the Lord will shorten the days of the tribulation for the sake of the elect (who are obviously then on earth, not raptured). It goes on to say that both the just and the unjust will go through this tribulation (Pseudo-Ephraim, estimated 9th century). So, when everything is taken account, there seems to be no support for Pretrib from Ephraim of Nisbis.

MARGARET MACDONALD – INVENTOR OF PRETRIB?

It appears that nobody, including Pretrib supporters, has presented a strong case for any Pretrib rapture belief before the 1800's. Writer Dave McPherson (MacPherson, 1975) has made a persuasive argument for the original Pretrib inventor to have been one Margaret McDonald, a fifteen year-old girl, speaking in what was claimed to be a prophetic utterance in 1830. The event was during a revivalist meeting conducted by Edward Irving, a co-founder of the "Catholic Apostolic Church", also known as the "Irvingite" church. This is an extract from McDonald's "vision":

"…… it is not known what the sign of the Son of man is; the people of God think they are waiting, but they know not what it is. I felt this needed to be revealed, and that there was great darkness and error about it; but suddenly what it was burst upon me with a glorious light. I saw it was just the Lord himself

descending from Heaven with a shout, just the glorified man, even Jesus; but that all must, as Stephen was, be filled with the Holy Ghost, that they might look up, and see the brightness of the Father's glory. I saw the error to be, that men think that it will be something seen by the natural eye; but 'tis spiritual discernment that is needed, the eye of God in his people.

".......... Only those who have the light of God within them will see the sign of his appearance. No need to follow them who say, see here, or see there, for his day shall be as the lightning to those in whom the living Christ is. 'Tis Christ in us that will lift us up - he is the light - 'tis only those that are alive in him that will be caught up to meet him in the air..........................."

JUDGING MCDONALD'S PROPHECY

We can surely see McDonald's error here. She is interpreting Matthew 24 to say that only the spiritually-minded Christians will be able to see Jesus at His coming described in verses 30-31. It is not, she says, an event to be seen with the natural eye. Even quite a superficial reading of Matthew 24 will show that this was not at all what Matthew intended, as we have seen. Wars, rumours of war, famine, persecution, the preaching of the Gospel in all the world, cataclysmic events, then the coming of Jesus with the angels – all are concrete happenings described in a straightforward, narrative style which rules out an over-spiritual application. Verse 30: "Then the sign of the Son of Man will appear in heaven, and then all the tribes of the earth will mourn, and they will see the Son of Man coming on the clouds of heaven with power and great glory." The spiritually minded Christians will not be mourning at the appearance of Jesus, so ALL will see Him. This idea is repeated even more explicitly in Revelation 1:7 "Behold, He is coming with clouds, and every eye will see Him, even they who pierced Him. And all the tribes of the earth will mourn because of Him." "All the tribes of the earth", then, obviously refers to the whole of humanity, not just the sanctified Christians. We must judge McDonald's prophecy as false because it doesn't agree with the written word of scripture. Added to that is the fact that McDonald prophesied at the same time that a contemporary socialist, Robert Owen, a well-known opponent of Christianity, and praised by Engels, would be the "man of sin". While not wishing to be uncharitable to a 15-year-old no doubt exercising her faith as well as she could, history has shown that this was another false prophecy. It is a Bible principle that if a prophecy foretells an event that does not happen, it is not from the Lord.

THE PROPHECY GAINS CIRCULATION

What is utterly amazing is how much currency this prophecy gathered, to the extent that many evangelical Christians attend churches influenced by it even today! It became one of the most important tenets of what would be called Dispensationalism, a system of interpretation of Bible prophecy which holds that God deals differently with mankind during different "dispensations". During the first half of the nineteenth century, though, it was not initially widely accepted. The first to give it attention was her church leader, Edward Irving. By December 1830, Irving seems to have been preaching a two-stage return of Jesus, the first stage coming to gather the believers, and the second to rule the earth. Also, in 1830 the Irvingite magazine "The Morning Watch" had an article about part of the church being taken out of the world before the "tribulation". The ones to go were to be the spiritual, devoted, "holy" ones – early Pretrib views were that only part of the church would be raptured.

Some confusion can be experienced by modern readers when reading the works of the early Pretrib writers until it is realised that by "the church", they often meant the lukewarm segment of the church which is to be left behind to suffer the tribulation, while the true saints are enjoying the marriage supper of the Lamb.

So, what about the girl Margaret McDonald and her "prophecy"? Every believer is encouraged to prophesy in the New Testament: "Pursue love, and desire spiritual gifts, but especially that you may prophesy…" wrote Paul in 1 Cor 14:1. John 10:27 says "My sheep hear My voice". Everyone who is born of the Spirit of God can hear the voice of God. Many churches encourage their members to learn to prophesy and practice all the gifts of the Holy Spirit listed in 1 Cor 12. The environment should be such that people are allowed to make mistakes.

However, there are some guidelines in the Bible. One is that prophecy should be judged, especially if it has some element of direction for the future, or it is going to be circulated or published. If a person brings a prophecy which is judged not to be from the Lord, it does not mean that person should be rejected. If our prophecy is considered not accurate, it's an opportunity to go back to the Lord and ask His help in getting it right. In my experience everyone gets it wrong sometimes. Prophets tend to be people who have had a go, made a few mistakes, and become practised in hearing God's voice through experience. If a person is judged to be bringing false prophecies persistently and not being open to some corrective discussion, they should be discouraged from making prophetic contributions in meetings. But the more common problem is that people are not willing to have a try. The environment should be such that people can make mistakes. Margaret's prophecy should have been judged, and Margaret herself given some teaching or mentoring to help her bring her gifting to maturity. But alas it was not to be. A huge section of the universal church fell into significant deception. At least that is the way I see it. Of course, many good men and women of God see it differently! I only ask that you study the scripture and form your own conclusion.

DISPENSATIONALISM: JOHN NELSON DARBY

The next Pretrib proponent was John Nelson Darby, of the Plymouth Brethren. Several pro-Brethren writers, unwilling to think that Darby got his ideas from MacDonald and Irving, tried to make a case that Darby developed Pretrib theory before them. The "Catholic Apostolic Church" was a rather unusual mixture of high Anglicanism, Pretrib theory, and speaking in tongues, and Irving, who started out as a Scottish Presbyterian minister, was expelled from the Presbyterian ministry for "heresy", so this foundation was unattractive to Brethren commentators. But it seems certain that Darby did not adopt the Pretrib rapture teaching until at the earliest the end of 1831, and it is likely that he was very influenced by Irving (Bennett, 2014).

Darby from then on played a major role in promoting the new doctrine. He included the Pretrib rapture as a foundational doctrine of the Dispensationalist system of understanding the Bible, developed in the main by himself. Other foundations included the Futurist interpretation of the Book of Revelation, after he found the treatise on the Book of Revelation by Francisco Ribera, the Jesuit (see previous section on "futurism"). He became convinced that Revelation portrayed a traumatic series of events prior to Jesus' return.

Another Dispensationalist fundamental which has been massively influential is Christian Zionism, born out of the idea that God still has a separate plan for the Jews, which involves their return to the physical land of Israel, rebuilding of the temple, and re-institution of animal sacrifices.

Darby was a man of extraordinary energy, with a very dominating personality, and well-travelled. He was convinced the church had fallen away from the true faith and joined the Brethren Assemblies which were exclusive and had no relationship with other churches, believing themselves to be the sole representatives of the true Gospel. He personally started Brethren assemblies in Germany, Switzerland, France, and the USA, which in turn sent missionaries to Africa, the West Indies, Australia and New Zealand. He wrote over 40 books and many hymns (Sizer, 2000) But for all his energy, it would be others who were to introduce the new doctrine to the mainstream.

Chapter Fourteen

DISPENSATIONALISM GOES MAINSTREAM!

✠ ✠ ✠

DWIGHT MOODY – CHAMPION OF DISPENSATIONALISM

One influential champion of Dispensationalism was the US evangelist Dwight Moody. Moody was a prolific evangelist, leading multitudes to a relationship with Christ. Many people at his meetings made commitments to follow Jesus. He made a personal vow that every day he would share the Gospel with someone who did not know the Lord.

Part of his appeal was the "Bible reading" method of preaching and study common to Plymouth Brethren adherents at the time, and which he popularized. In this method, when he wanted to preach on a topic, he used a concordance to find all the scripture passages on that topic (eg "grace", "hope" etc.), and compiled his own anecdotes, illustrations and comments to link the verses together.

Critics have claimed that having done this exercise, he was left with a speech which was much more composed of his own thoughts than Biblical content. It has been said that many "converts" at Moody's meetings were more drawn by emotion and razzmatazz than by scriptural conviction. This was especially so as Moody increasingly made his appeals based on a generalized understanding of the love of God, which placed little emphasis on the timeless themes of man's disobedience to God, the mercy of God, the necessity of true repentance and saving faith. Thus, he has been regarded by some as one of the originators of "easy believism" or "hyper-grace" – the notion that if a person just "prays a prayer" to Jesus, he or she is forever saved just on the grounds of having prayed that prayer, very much like "once saved always saved" which we discussed earlier.

Moody's "Bible reading" study method departed from the time-honoured methods of study which go back to the Reformation and earlier. As mentioned in chapter 2, this time-honoured method is composed of two parts: *exegesis* which is the analysis of what the author of a passage intended to say to his audience *in his own time;* and *hermeneutics,* the interpretation of how that passage applies to us in our time. Study carefully done by this method acts as a great defence against all sorts of outlandish interpretations never intended by either the author or the Holy Spirit. Is it possible that many cults such as Jehovah's Witnesses have arisen wholly or in part because of failure to apply these principles? Indeed the 19th century became a kind of golden age for the founding of cults, with Jehovah's Witnesses, Mormons, Christian Science, and others attracting many followers. Could it be that a reason for the mushrooming of cults and the meteoric rise of Dispensationalism was the decline of the use of time-tested methods of Bible study? Moody himself preached little on Dispensationalism, keeping his preaching simple and appealing to the public. But the merging of his movement with Dispensationalism ensured massive acceptance of the latter.

SCOFIELD JOINS THE DISPENSATIONALISTS; HIS BIBLE WINS MANY ADHERENTS

Another adherent of Dispensationalism was Cyrus Scofield, author of the Scofield Reference Bible. This Bible became the Bible of choice for many evangelicals and Scofield's dogmatic Dispensationalist notes were uncritically accepted by multitudes, and even adopted by many Bible colleges as a de-facto test for orthodoxy. One strong Dispensationalist doctrine advocated by Scofield's Bible notes was drawn from Genesis 12:3 "I will bless those who bless you, and I will curse him who curses you; and in you all the families of the earth shall be blessed." Scofield took this verse and interpreted it to mean that God's blessing was unconditionally on the Jewish people ever since. This view is common but, in my opinion, untenable – see for instance 1 Thessalonians 2:14-16.

MORE SUPPORTERS – CLARENCE LARKIN'S CHARTS

In the early 1900's Clarence Larkin, an engineer by background, drew a series of charts which became popular around the world, detailing Larkin's view of the sequence of end-time events. The wide circulation of Larkin's posters, copyright free, is the reason why so many posters, books and Bibles around the world even now carry similar charts detailing a fixed and unchangeable timetable of events around the second coming.

Others who took this Dispensationalist view included Jesse Penn-Lewis, T. Austin Sparks, Watchman Nee, John Walvoord and Charles C Ryrie. Hal Lindsey's book *The Late Great Planet Earth* (Lindsey, 1970), as mentioned earlier, was a popular expositor of the view. Today it is widely held still in Pentecostal, Brethren, Baptist, independent Bible and other evangelical and charismatic churches, though increasingly believers seem to be questioning it.

So, it can be seen that the Pretrib rapture theory, a key doctrine of Dispensationalism, is of very recent origin. None of the early church fathers, no theologians of the Middle Ages, and none of the leaders of the reformation such as Calvin, Luther, or Knox, had ever heard of such a thing. It seems the theory first surfaced in 1830. Even if we allowed the claims of pro-Brethren writers that Pretrib was taught before Margaret McDonald's vision, there is no credible claim that anybody thought of a Pretrib rapture before the 1820's. And if they had, it would have conflicted with Jesus' own end of the age discourse in the Gospel of Matthew, as has been discussed in Chapters 6 and 7.

SIGNS OF HIS COMING

The sequence of events according to Pretrib theory is first, as in Jesus' own account in Matthew, there are signs of His coming, which are all about us in the world now. One sign is the foundation of the Jewish State of Israel in 1948. Next, the theory goes, the "rapture" will occur. This is because the terrible 7-year tribulation is going to come on earth. Jesus does not want the church to go through this, so He will come to earth and gather all the believers in the world together to meet Him in the sky, then take them to the "marriage supper of the Lamb", while God pours out tribulation on the earth because of the prevalent sin. According to Dispensationalism, this gathering in the sky will not be seen by any of the non-believers, who are left to puzzle out where the believers have gone, as we saw in chapter 1.

PRETRIB SEQUENCE

The sequence of events according to Dispensationalism is roughly as follows. There are by now many variations on the theme, but the on-going scenario will look something like the following. Individual Dispensationalist teachers differ with each other in various particulars, and certainly Dispensationalist teaching has changed a lot over the nearly 190 years it has been taught. More recently "Progressive Dispensationalism" has developed. Nonetheless, I understand the basics (Pretrib and Premil) are still believed by most Dispensationalists. I have not attempted an in-depth presentation of the full range of Dispensationalist views[13].

RAPTURE AND TRIBULATION

About the time of the rapture, so the narrative goes, the Jewish temple will be rebuilt in Jerusalem, in place of, or next to the current Muslim Dome of the \Rock. Animal sacrifices and other Old Testament rituals

---

[13] Readers wanting to examine Dispensationalism in detail should consult one or more of the following authors: Charles Ryrie; Dwight Pentecost; David Jeremiah; John McArthur; Tim LaHay; John Walvoord; Hal Lindsay; and many others.

will resume there. When the Christians are gone in the rapture, this temple will spark off massive war and worldwide tribulation lasting seven years (or 3 ½ years according to "Mid-Trib" believers), during which the Antichrist will emerge and achieve a one-world government all over the earth. He will forbid the worship of God and force people to worship him. He will force everyone to take "the mark of the beast" on the forehead or the arm in order to be able to buy anything. When God pours out all judgments of Revelation on sinful humanity there will be wars, catastrophes, famines, and diseases. Things will be worse than ever before. Despite the difficulties, 144,000 Jewish evangelists will be sent out all over the world and they will lead multitudes to Christ. Those who respond will have missed out on the rapture and the marriage supper of the Lamb, but at least they will be saved. Satan will bring his armies against Jerusalem. When things are absolutely beyond the capacity of people to endure, Jesus will return to earth with the believers who have been raptured earlier. He will deliver the Jews from their enemies. The tribulation will end and Jesus will establish His kingdom, with Jerusalem the capital.

THE MILLENNIAL KINGDOM

This kingdom will be centred around and governed by the Jews. The Biblical David will be resurrected and appointed prime minister under Jesus. Animal sacrifices and other Old Testament customs will continue. The raptured Christians will also assist in the government of the world but will be lower ranked than the Jews. During the millennial reign, in addition to these glorified Christians, there will be other Christians without glorified bodies who were converted during the tribulation or born during the millennium. Their bodies will not be glorified, but they will lose the curse, which was placed on Adam when he disobeyed God, and so be able to live to the same kind of age as the patriarchs before the flood. Non-glorified Christians will carry on raising children and will be able to "backslide".

Satan will remain bound for nearly all the thousand years. Towards the end of this period, he will be released and will stir up rebellion against Jesus. None of the glorified saints would rebel, but Satan will gather his rebel army from non-glorified, backslidden Christians, either survivors of the tribulation or born as children in the millennium. Satan and his forces will attack Jerusalem but be defeated and he will be consigned to the lake of fire. The last judgment will be held and all those without Christ will be cast into the lake of fire with him. The new heaven and the new earth will appear, with eternal rewards for those belonging to Christ. Presumably there will be no need for the raptured saints to appear at this judgment. (Bible Study Tools, 2019) (McArthur, 1969)

So a summary of the Pretrib, Premil version of events could be:

1. Signs of His coming are apparent to some extent now, but will increase.
2. Jesus will come to earth to rescue the church. He will be invisible to those who don't know Him.
3. "Rapture" of the church.
4. Antichrist seizes power and rules the world.
5. Rebuilding of the temple.
6. Seven-year tribulation.
7. Jesus will return with the raptured saints and will be seen by all (Mat 24 – elect are Jews only).
8. Satan will be bound.
9. Start of thousand-year reign on earth by Jesus, Jews and Christians.
10. Types of people on earth during millennium: Jewish rulers who survived the tribulation (mostly in ordinary bodies); raptured and returned Christians in glorified bodies; people who became Christians during the tribulation and survived (in ordinary bodies); people born during the millennium (in ordinary but healthier bodies).
11. At the end of the 1000 years, Satan will be released and will start a rebellion.
12. Satan's rebellion will be defeated.
13. Mat 25 / Final judgment / rewards will apply only to gentiles who lived in the millennium according to some writers.

Others get rewards at either the rapture or the return after the tribulation.

14. New heavens and new earth created; eternal life will begin for the saved and eternal punishment for the lost.

MATTHEW'S GOSPEL AND THE PRETRIB-PREMILLENNIAL VERSION OF EVENTS

It appears that Pretrib theory presents a very different picture than Matthew's Gospel. As we have seen, Jesus, as reported by Matthew, gave a simple scenario for His return. It was summarised as follows at the beginning of chapter 2:

1. Signs of His coming are apparent to some extent now, but will increase.
2. Jesus will come and be seen by all.
3. Final reward / judgment.
4. New heavens and new earth created; eternal life will begin for the saved and eternal punishment for the lost.
5. Issues regarding the Pretrib view
6. Jesus, in Matthew's account, repeatedly urges believers to watch for His coming, which will be like lightening flashing from East to West, with the sign of the Son of Man in the sky, and much other commotion, including sun, moon and stars dropping out of the sky! The event of Jesus' coming will a massively public affair, which will be known everywhere. The non-believers will see Jesus and "mourn" with regret for their decision during their lives not to follow Jesus. How does this fit in with the rapture as portrayed in the movie, "Left Behind", that we outlined in Chapter 2?
7. The angels will gather the believers from all over the world WITH A GREAT SOUND OF A TRUMPET – again nothing secret about this. Note: the unbelievers are gathered BEFORE the believers. It is the believers who are Left BEHIND! (Mat 13:43) If there were to be a rapture years before the events of

Matthew 24-25, why didn't Jesus refer to it when He gave the Olivet discourse?

8. And let us have a look at this "tribulation". When reading Dispensationalist teaching, one could be forgiven for thinking that the 7-year tribulation is an established fact on the same level as the crucifixion, the resurrection or the second coming of Jesus, as discussed earlier. In fact, it is not! There is no plain straightforward teaching anywhere in the Bible about a seven-year tribulation. The teaching is mainly built on one non-traditional teaching on Daniel's seventy-week prophecy in Daniel chapter nine. We will look at this in chapter 18 of this book.

9. In the Pretrib theory, the believers are caught up in the air to meet Jesus BEFORE the tribulation. However, in Matthew's Gospel, they are caught up AFTER the tribulation (24:29 "immediately after the tribulation of those days...")

10. In Matthew's account there is ONLY ONE coming of Jesus. There is no reference to His coming to earth, taking the believers away, then coming back with them 7 years (or 3 ½ years for mid-trib theorists) later. The sequence in Matthew's Gospel is: He comes (once); then the judgment. See Matthew 25:31-32. Matthew's description of the judgment starts at Matthew 25:31 – When the Son of Man comes in His glory, and all the Holy angels with Him, then He will sit on the throne of His glory. All the nations will be gathered before Him..." This verse links the judgement (v 25) with Matthew 24:30 – "…. they will see the Son of Man coming on the clouds of heaven with power and great glory, and He will send His angels......" The Matthew 25 verse establishes the time of the judgment as the time when Jesus appears. And what comes next? Matthew 25:46 – the wicked go to eternal punishment but the righteous to eternal life. Matthew 24 and 25 have always been seen as one continuous discourse (the "Olivet discourse"), so it seems there is no possibility that Matthew 25 could describe some different judgment at some other time, as held by some Dispensationalist teaching

11. This brings us to the next point: not only could there be no rapture if Matthew is accurate, but also there could not be one 1000-year reign of Jesus on earth! A literal thousand-year millennial reign could not fit into Matthew's narrative. It certainly could not fit in after the appearance of Jesus in Matthew 24. As already mentioned, this appearance is followed immediately by the judgment of Matthew 25, which in turn is followed by eternal punishment or reward! It could not fit in before Jesus' coming either, or surely He would have mentioned it in this dialogue and alerted His followers to prepare for it, rather than for the events of chapters 24-25.

12. To account for the discrepancies between the Matthew 24-25 and Pretrib theory as outlined here, Dispensationalist teachers have come up with a number of proposed solutions. We have seen how early Dispensationalist writers thought that the events of Mat 24 would only be seen by Christians with a high degree of sanctification.

13. Many modern Dispensationalists now teach that the elect in Mat 24 refers not to the believers but to the ethnic Jews and that this chapter describes events at the end of the tribulation, at (according to their theory) the third coming of Jesus (Ice, 1996). But in New Testament usage the elect are always seen as the believers. For example, "What then? Israel has not obtained what it seeks; but the elect have obtained it, and the rest were blinded (Rom 11:7)." In the context of Matthew 24, certainly the meaning of the "elect" is the believers, because it is the believers who have asked the questions to which Jesus is responding. They happened to be Jews as well, as all believers at that time were Jews, but Jesus is telling them, in effect, what their position was as believers, in contrast to the rest of the Jews who were not believers. He addresses the disciples as "you". When He refers to the opponents of Christ, including the main body of Jewry, He refers to "them". The whole tenor of the passage would change if we were to think that the Jews are the elect. Jesus was talking to His disciples, whom He knew were about to be furiously persecuted by fellow Jews. It

is inconceivable that in this context He could have been using the word "elect" to mean the main body of the Jews, who were just about to crucify Him!

14. The oneness of the people of God (see Ephesians chapter 2) provides another compelling reason to reject this idea. If Dispensationalism were true, Mat 24 would be only marginally relevant to Christians today. It is as if the chapter has been stolen from the believers! However, believers of all ages have derived great encouragement from this discourse and will continue to do so.

15. The teaching of John Calvin, Martin Luther and the other reformers was very different from modern Dispensationalist teaching. There was no doubt at all in the minds of the reformers that believing Christians are the Elect (Dressler, 2014). The word "elect" (Greek "eklektos" – "favourite", "chosen") throughout the New Testament refers to the believers. (Lee-Warner, 2000)

16. In the face of points 4 and 5 above, many writers relegate Matthew 25 to the end of the millennial reign and teach that only gentiles who were saved during the tribulation or during the millennium will appear before this judgment. This violates the fact that Mat 24 and Mat 25 are a continuous discourse.

CATHOLIC VIEW – ONE COMING ONLY

Our view, which is becoming apparent, is given support by Catholic teaching.. The following extract from the Catholic Catechism outlines the position that there will be only one coming of Jesus and that will be in glory. It could happen at any time. "All Israel" will recognise Him. When He comes, it will be time for the fulfilment of all the prophets have spoken.

673 Since the Ascension Christ's coming in glory has been imminent, even though "it is not for you to know times or seasons which the Father has fixed by his own authority." This eschatological coming could be accomplished at any moment, even if both it and the final trial that will precede it are "delayed".

674 The glorious Messiah's coming is suspended at every moment of history until his recognition by "all Israel", for "a hardening has come upon part of Israel" in their "unbelief" toward Jesus. St. Peter says to the Jews of Jerusalem after Pentecost: "Repent therefore, and turn again, that your sins may be blotted out, that times of refreshing may come from the presence of the Lord, and that he may send the Christ appointed for you, Jesus, whom heaven must receive until the time for establishing all that God spoke by the mouth of his holy prophets from of old. St. Paul echoes him: "For if their rejection means the reconciliation of the world, what will their acceptance mean but life from the dead?" The "full inclusion" of the Jews in the Messiah's salvation, in the wake of "the full number of the Gentiles", will enable the People of God to achieve "the measure of the stature of the fullness of Christ", in which "God may be all in all". (Catechism of the Catholic Church, 1997)

THE CONTEXT OF DISPENSATIONALISM

I am not an enemy of the many godly believers who embrace the Dispensationalist view. The important doctrines we share include the eternal life of the saved; the eternal punishment of the lost; the supreme authority of Jesus and His forgiveness; the Great Commission for believers to take the Gospel to every person on the planet; and many other precious truths of the faith. Dispensationalism arose in a particular context in the late 19th and early 20th centuries. It gave a fresh focus on the return of Jesus to planet earth, in an age where the believers laid little emphasis on it. We share belief in the fact of our infinitely precious Lord Jesus coming to earth again, though we have different ideas on what that is going to look like.

Secondly, Dispensationalism laid great emphasis on taking the Word of God literally. It thrived in an age where liberal Christianity was also on the rise in society at large. All the certainties of previous generations were being questioned. Darwinian evolution was becoming widely accepted, and the Biblical account of creation rejected by many. Liberal theologians challenged the scriptures, holding that human reasoning is the source of ultimate truth, and that man is fundamentally good, without the need of a saviour. They held that Christ is only our saviour in the sense that He was a great teacher, and that he was not unique in any sense, and certainly not divine. The supernatural events of Old and New Testaments, including the resurrection of Jesus, were held to be mere stories and products of imagination. Christianity, in the eyes of these liberals, and indeed of liberals today, may possibly be the best religion, but not essentially different in kind from other religions (Muehlenberg, 2017).

Dispensationalism presented a foil to this growth of liberalism, and many believers flocked to its banner. Dispensationalists even until today have defended the Word of God and staunchly insisted on the bodily resurrection of Jesus, who died for all our sins, and other fundamental doctrines. To me, however, much of the detailed theory cannot be right. It is my prayer that believers everywhere should engage in discussion on eschatology, and that the Holy Spirit should guide us into all truth. I am prayerfully in disagreement about the teachings of Dispensationalism on a number of issues.

SEPARATE DESTINIES?

This separation of the destinies of the church and Israel is surely contrary to scripture. God now sees no difference between ethnic Jews and gentiles. We are one: God only has one people today, which is called "the Israel of God" (Gal 6:16). He only has one way of salvation, which is the same for Jews and gentiles, that is the preaching of the cross, giving rise to repentance and faith.

THE JUDGMENT OF MAT 25 RELEGATED UNTIL AFTER THE MILLENNIUM

The idea the judgment of Mat 25 will not take place until a literal millennial rule is ended poses some additional major problems of its own.

1. If it is correct, by the time the Mat 25 judgment comes along, the original disciples and all believers until today will have been raptured and will have ruled the earth 1,000 years before the

judgment even occurs. If this is so, why did Jesus even bother to give the discourse? Surely the obvious topic for Jesus would have been the first eschatological event to occur relevant to His audience - that would be the rapture if the Dispensationalist timeline were true.

2.   The Dispensationalist version of events would mean that: all believers from the past until now would be in the rapture, Jesus' second coming; all people who become believers during the tribulation would meet Jesus in some other way at Jesus' third coming (to start the millennium); and that all who become believers during the millennium would meet Jesus at His fourth coming, which is the coming allegedly described in Matthew 24-25.

3.   These ideas ignore the clearly universal nature of the Matthew 24-25 day of judgment. The scene is perhaps the most majestic in the Bible, and throughout the passage, the language is the language of universality. "All nations" will be gathered to Him. Matthew 10:15 tells us that, for example, the men and women of Sodom and Gomorrah, and the people visited by the 70, will be there at the day of judgment. Jesus was speaking about people who would not receive the Gospel in his own day: Mat 10:15 "Assuredly, I say to you, it will be more tolerable for the land of Sodom and Gomorrah in the day of judgment than for that city!" In Matthew 11, we are told that the people of Chorazin, Bethsaida (11:21) and Capurnaum (11:23) living in Jesus' own day, and the ancient people of Tyre and Sidon (11:21), who were massacred by Alexander the Great in 332 BC, will all be judged on the day of judgment. Matthew 12 adds the following examples to the list of people to be judged: the people of Nineveh in Assyria, who were preached to by Jonah, who lived in the eighth century BC (12:41); and the Queen of Sheba, from what is today the Yemen, in the 10th century BC (12:42). Jesus and all the Bible writers only ever refer to one day of judgment, so we can say with certainty that the judgment is universal, and everybody who has ever lived will be judged on that day.

4. The earliest ideas were those of Jesus Himself, as reported by the New Testament writers. We have shown that, at least in Matthew's case, there was no expectation of a millennial reign, and even less of a "rapture of the church" before the visitation for the purpose of final judgment. It would seem that there is nothing in the New Testament to correspond to the Pretrib rapture as described by modern writers. In Chapter 15, we will consider the whole of the book of Matthew and the other New Testament writers to check that we are not just taking an isolated part of the Gospel to suit our own narrative. Chapter 16 will consider Revelation 20, the source of Premil and Postmil teaching on the supposed thousand-year reign of Jesus on earth. Does Revelation 20 really teach this? We will see.

Chapter Fifteen

NEW TESTAMENT VIEW OF THE TIME OF THE END

✠ ✠ ✠

THE END OF THE AGE

The end of the present age is a major theme, if not the major theme, of the Bible, which has a large body of passages on the topic. As we will see the elements of "Day of the Lord" include:

1. The return of Christ in glory (the *Parousia*)
2. The final battle won by Christ's resounding victory over Antichrist
3. The resurrection of the dead
4. The destruction of the present heavens and earth
5. The universal last judgment
6. The creation of a new heavens and earth
7. The consignment of the wicked to the lake of fire
8. The reward of God's faithful people – new bodies and more
9. The final establishment of the Kingdom of God

All these elements are present, either explicitly or implicitly, in Matthew's account. For those who are willing to lay pre-conceptions aside, an honest, straight-forward reading of the New Testament text will reveal that all these events all happen on or approaching "the Day".

In this chapter we will survey what the rest of the Gospel of Matthew and the other New Testament writers had to say on the topic. The main study method will be to go straight to the relevant passages, rather than to commentaries, and where there is doubt about the meaning, to give priority initially to clear, simple narrative or explanatory passages rather than symbolic or metaphoric passages. First then, we will look at the rest of Matthew:

DESCRIPTION OF JESUS' SECOND COMING

As we covered earlier, the clearest description of His second coming is in Jesus' Olivet discourse: Mat 24:3 – Matthew 25:46. To recap, the actual moment of His coming is described:

Mat 24:29-31 "Immediately after the tribulation of those days the sun will be darkened, and the moon will not give its light; the stars will fall from heaven, and the powers of the heavens will be shaken. [30] Then the sign of the Son of Man will appear in heaven, and then all the tribes of the earth will mourn, and they will see the Son of Man coming on the clouds of heaven with power and great glory. [31] And He will send His angels with a great sound of a trumpet, and they will gather together His elect from the four winds, from one end of heaven to the other."

Mat 25:31 "When the Son of Man comes in His glory, and all the holy angels with Him, then He will sit on the throne of His glory. All the nations will be gathered before Him, and He will separate them one from another, as a shepherd divides his sheep from the goats."

This vision of Jesus coming with the clouds, and in great glory is described several times in Matthew and in the rest of the New Testament[14]. Jesus confirms the manner of his coming again in Matthew 26:

Matthew 26:63 And the high priest answered and said to Him, "I put You under oath by the living God: Tell us if You are the Christ, the Son of God!" Jesus said to him, "It is as you said. Nevertheless, I say to

---

[14] Eg Mark 14:62

you, hereafter you will see the Son of Man sitting at the right hand of the Power and coming on the clouds of heaven."

On this occasion Jesus didn't specify that He will be coming for the judgment. But in Matthew's Gospel, we don't see even the slightest suggestion there is any other occasion in which He will come. The whole Gospel describes one coming – the Return of Christ. This is reinforced by the inclusion of the detail about Him coming "on the clouds of heaven" – agreeing with Mat 24:31 and 25:31-32. This passage adds the information that He will be "sitting at the right hand of the Power", that is God. This means that God the Father's full power and authority will be backing and upholding the Son.

We see from Matthew 24 that the appearance of Jesus coincides with cataclysmic events which are outlined in several places in the Bible. The sun and moon will be darkened, and the stars fall out of the sky. Is this vision literal or symbolic? We understand today with our modern scientific and astronomical knowledge that if the stars literally fall from the sky, the whole universe will be destroyed. It does seem that all the earth will know about this extraordinary event, which rules out the Pretrib rapture theory and its insistence that only the believers will see the first return of Jesus. Are there any other clues in the Gospel of Matthew to pinpoint Matthew's opinion on this point? I believe that the parable of the wheat and tares in Matthew 13, which we studied in chapter 3, is conclusive on the point. And as Matthew was directly quoting Jesus I for one am ready to accept the truth of what he wrote.

In fact, Matthew's Gospel is full of references to the coming end of the age and Kingdom of Heaven, to the extent that it could be said that the main theme of the Gospel is the coming of the Kingdom, which means the rulership of God. It comes in two stages:

1. The birth and earthly ministry of Jesus (from our perspective, in the past) leading to a period commonly called the era of proclamation, which we are still in.
2. His second coming (from our perspective, still in the future) followed by the "time of fulfilment" – which is the eternal Kingdom of God.

The coming age was proclaimed by John the Baptist, "Repent, for the kingdom of heaven has come near." (Mat 3:2) He asked the pharisees, "Who warned you to flee from the wrath to come?" Of course, John's knowledge came from the Old Testament, as we shall see, and he could not know of the worldwide bringing of the Gospel which was to come after Jesus was crucified. But, unlike many people today, he understood that the wrath of God will come at the end of the age, which we will discuss presently. Jesus picked up the same theme in Matthew 4:17, repeating John's words: "Repent, for the kingdom of heaven has come near."

THE END OF THE AGE ACCORDING TO SCRIPTURE.

Let's consider "the end of the age". What does Matthew mean when he refers to the "end of the age" (E.g. Mat 13:39)? And how do other New Testament writers see "the end of the age", either explicitly or by implication? Here are some quotes:

Mat 12:32: but whoever speaks against the Holy Spirit, it will not be forgiven him, either **in this age or in the age to come**.

Mark 10 Assuredly, I say to you, there is no one who has left house or brothers or sisters or father or mother or wife or children or lands, for My sake and the Gospel's, who shall not receive a hundredfold now in this time—houses and brothers and sisters and mothers and children and lands, with persecutions—and in **the age to come**, eternal life.

Galatians 1:3: Grace to you and peace from God the Father and our Lord Jesus Christ, who gave Himself for our sins, that **He might deliver us from this present evil age....**

2 Corinthians 4:3-4 But even if our Gospel is veiled, it is veiled to those who are perishing, whose minds **the god of this age** has blinded, who do not believe, lest the light of the Gospel of the glory of Christ should shine on them.

Hebrews 6:4-6 For it is impossible for those who were once enlightened, and have tasted the heavenly gift, and have become partakers of the Holy Spirit, and have tasted the good word of God and the powers of **the age to come**, if they fall away, to renew them again to repentance, since they crucify again for themselves the Son of God and put Him to an open shame.

Rom 12:2 And do not be conformed **to this age** (world), but be transformed by the renewing of your mind, that you may prove what is that good and acceptable and perfect will of God.

Note the word "world" in Romans 12:2 could be translated "age" as the Greek word in the original is *"aion"* (age).

DIFFERENCE BETWEEN THE AGES – SUMMARY

The paradigm of the New Testament is that there are two ages: this present (evil) age and the age to come. Some characteristics of this present age as shown in scripture are:

1. It is clearly distinct from the age to come.
2. People of this age are subject to sickness, suffering and death.
3. It requires faith to relate to Christ and God.
4. We can receive material gifts, and blessings for obeying God, but we also receive persecution.
5. Satan has been "the god" of this age, and rules in the lives of those who have not received Christ. He can blind those whose hearts are not seeking God.
6. We have a taste of the age to come but we do not experience the full reality of it until we get there.
7. Actions of God are "inaugurated" in this age, e.g., a person is saved in this age, but salvation is not complete until they receive a new body in the age to come (1 Cor 15:20-28).
8. We can be taken by sin, temptation, and the devil's attacks if we do not stay watchful.
9. We need to take care we do not model our behaviour on the norms of this age.
10. This present age is soon coming to an end and will be finalised with the universal judgment.

CHARACTERISTICS OF THE AGE TO COME:

1. The Age to Come will be ushered in when this present age ends – as marked by the "Day of the Lord".

2. Suffering, sickness and death will be finished.

3. No faith will be required to relate to Christ. We will be able to see Him as He is.

4. People receive eternal rewards or punishment.

5. Satan, all his power, and all his subordinates, will be completely destroyed.

6. The age to come is the home of the Word of God and supernatural gifts and powers, in which we will walk all the time.

7. We will see the completion of things inaugurated in the present age. For example, salvation will be completed by the giving of a new body, shining like the sun.

8. We are no longer vulnerable to sin, temptation and the devil's attacks.

9. The norm will be holy behaviour so we will be aligned with the norm.

10. The age to come starts after the universal judgment and will never end. It is full of light, joy and the glory of Christ.

SEPARATION OF THE WICKED AND THE JUST AT THE END OF THE AGE

Jesus, in the parable of the wheat and tares and His explanation of it, clearly shows that this gathering of the wicked and the just takes place at the END of this present age. It is not explicitly mentioned in the wheat and tares parable (see chapter 3) but of course the means of their separation for reward or punishment can only be the judgment. FROM THAT POINT the new age begins. Premil is therefore inconsistent with the account of the Judgement given in Matthew 25. It is the end of the age so nothing can happen after this other than the age to come. And it would seem there is no possibility of either a Pretrib rapture or a thousand-year reign on earth before this because the Master orders that both righteous and unrighteous, wheat and tares, should be left to grow together until the angels are sent out to gather them at the end of this age; i.e. on the Return of Christ. Whether they know it or not, both are headed for the Judgment! But the believers go in confidence, rejoicing in the Saviour, whereas the non-believers will go in the dread of certain punishment.

The Parable of the Dragnet also confirms that the wicked will be separated from the righteous at the end of the age:

Mat 13:47 "Again, the kingdom of heaven is like a dragnet that was cast into the sea and gathered some of every kind, which, when it was full, they drew to shore; and they sat down and gathered the good into vessels but threw the bad away. So it will be at the end of the age. The angels will come forth, separate the wicked from among the just, and cast them into the furnace of fire. There will be wailing and gnashing of teeth."

THE SEQUENCE OF EVENTS: GLORY AND JUDGMENT GO TOGETHER

Luke and Mark confirm that the Judgment coincides with Jesus' coming in glory:

Luke 9:26, Mark 8:38 For whoever is ashamed of Me and My words, of him the Son of Man will be ashamed when He comes in His own glory, and in His Father's, and of the holy angels.

Matthew confirms that the time of Jesus' coming in glory is the time when the righteous are rewarded:

Mat 16:27 For the Son of Man will come in the glory of His Father with His angels, and then He will reward each according to his works."

Because we know the unbelievers receive their sentences at the same time (Mat 13:30; Mat 13:47-50; Mat 25:31-32; 46) there is only one scenario that can fit the facts as described. That is the one universal judgment, and immediate consignment of believers to everlasting life and unrepentant sinners to everlasting punishment.

In fact, the judgment is the very reason for His coming, not only to judge the work done in faith by the believers, but to award punishment to unrepentant sinners. Peter tells Cornelius the nature of his commission from Jesus:

Act 10:40-43 Him God raised up on the third day, and showed Him openly, [41] not to all the people, but to witnesses chosen before by God, *even* to us who ate and drank with Him after He arose from the dead. [42] And He commanded us to preach to the people, and to testify that it is He who was ordained by God *to be* Judge of the living and the dead. [43] To Him all the prophets witness that, through His name, whoever believes in Him will receive remission of sins."

Receiving remission of sins was a vital issue to the Jews of New Testament times, and to those such as Cornelius who had been influenced by the Jewish worldview. Unhappily, in our time, very few in the "West" now hold to that Biblical worldview, Those of us who believe in the authenticity and divine authorship of the Bible have a deep responsibility to warn people about this coming judgment.

THE SEQUENCE OF EVENTS: THE LAST DAY

John, in chapter 6 of his Gospel, fixes the time of the resurrection of the believers as *the last day*. Remarkably, He states four times in the chapter that He will raise believers on the *last day*:

John 6:38-40 For I have come down from heaven, not to do My own will, but the will of Him who sent Me. This is the will of the Father who sent Me, that of all He has given Me I should lose nothing, **but should raise it up at the last day**. And this is the will of Him who sent Me, that everyone who sees the Son and believes in Him may have everlasting life; and I will **raise him up at the last day**."

......43-44 Jesus therefore answered and said to them, "Do not murmur among yourselves. No one can come to Me unless the Father who sent Me draws him; and I **will raise him up at the last day**..... ....

......54 Whoever eats My flesh and drinks My blood has eternal life, and I will **raise him up at the last day**."

If words have meaning, *the last day* must mean the same as *the end of the age*. Jesus could not possibly have meant the end of the age to come – because that will never end. So, John is in agreement with Matthew as to when believers are raised up – the end of (this present) age. The John 6 discourse pinpoints *the last day* as the time believers are raised.

THE SEQUENCE OF EVENTS: THE REAL "RAPTURE"

Now let's go to Paul's account of the dead in Christ being raised, for more details:

1 Thessalonians 4:13-18 But I do not want you to be ignorant, brethren, concerning those who have fallen asleep, lest you sorrow as others who have no hope. For if we believe that Jesus died and rose again, even so God will bring with Him those who sleep in Jesus. For this we say to you by the word of the Lord, that we who are alive and remain until the coming of the Lord will by no means precede those who are asleep. For the Lord Himself will descend from heaven with a shout, with the voice of an archangel, and with the trumpet of God. And the dead in Christ will rise first. Then we who are alive and remain shall be caught up together with them in the clouds to meet the Lord in the air. And thus, we shall always be with the Lord. Therefore comfort one another with these words.[15]

This is the passage cited by Pretrib as the main "rapture" passage. Yes, Jesus does meet the believers in the air. All true believers can be assured we will be part of this incredible event. The dead will precede the living. So, I know my friend's wife who died recently will be one of this crowd. And if I do not die before Jesus comes, she will be with Him before me! But let us just think of the scenario in the *Left Behind* movie. After the rapture, according to the movie, all the people are at a loss to know where these hundreds of thousands or millions of people who have disappeared, have gone. As we have seen, the film script is based on the Pretrib idea of the "secret rapture" of the church before the tribulation. In other words, the rapture is supposed to be secret so that the rest of the people don't know where the Christians have gone.

But on reading the original passage, I cannot imagine any scenario less secret, with the Lord himself shouting, the voice of the archangel, and the Lord's trumpet. This scene is where the "dead in Christ rise" according to Paul. The "dead in Christ" can only be a subset of the ones talked about in John chapter 6:

1. "all the Father has given Me (Jesus);" v 39
2. "everyone who sees the Son and believes in Him"; v 40
3. everyone whom "the Father draws"; v 44
4. "whoever eats My flesh and drinks My blood"; v54

---

[15] 1 Thes 4:13-18

These are all in Christ, either dead (first subset) or still living (second subset). The only possible third subset are children, including the pre-born, too young to be morally accountable. Many believe that Jesus will raise all these up at the "last day", or, as we have explained, at the "end of the age". So we have the timing for the 1 Thessalonians 4:16 dead who rise first: *at the last day*! If words have any meaning, and simple rules of grammar apply, surely this CANNOT mean 7 years earlier in secret or after 1000 years.

USING SCRIPTURE TO INTERPRET SCRIPTURE

Further confirmation comes when we compare 1 Thessalonians 4:16-18 with our core passage Matthew chapters 24 and 25. Here, once again, is a summary of events and signs from Mat 24:

1. Wars, disasters, tribulation, deception
2. Gospel preached in all the world
3. Sun and moon darkened
4. Stars fall from heaven
5. Powers of the heavens shaken
6. Sign of the Son of Man appears
7. All tribes on earth mourn
8. Jesus comes with clouds, power and great glory.
9. Angels sent out with the great sound of a trumpet
10. The elect gathered from all the earth by the angels
11. Judgment of all nations
12. Righteous inherit "kingdom prepared from the foundation of the world", eternal life.
13. Unrighteous depart from Jesus and are consigned to the "everlasting fire prepared for the devil and his angels", everlasting punishment.

Jesus' discourse in Matthew chapters 24 and 25 is the most detailed description of the Return of Christ in the Bible, but still does not give nearly the whole picture. Other scriptures can fill out our total understanding of this all-important day. Similarly, the Matthew discourse can complete our understanding of other scriptures. For instance, when we compare 1Thes 4:13 with the Mat 24-25 account, 1 Thes 4:13 adds to our understanding of point 10. We see that not only those of the believers who are alive at the time will rise to meet Jesus in the air, but also those believers who have died will precede them. The process of comparing scripture with scripture and using scripture to interpret scripture gives us a comprehensive picture.

Matthew 24:30-31 describes the same event as 1Thessalonians 4:13-18

Features that are common to the Matthew account and the passage being compared, suggest that the same overall event is being discussed. The Lord's shout is suggestive of His coming with power and great glory. The trumpet of God, point 9 in the Mat 24-5 summary, matches 1 Thes 4:16 and is a pointer, if we needed any more convincing, that it is the same event being described from a different perspective. The righteous are rewarded with eternal life in both scripture passages and the context means that both the passages are talking about ALL the righteous. Comparison with the parable of the wheat and the tares in Mat 13 clarifies that the angels gather both wicked and righteous at this time.

At first glance, someone may object that important pieces of information are missed in some of the passages, so how can we be certain of our timetable of events? Can we trust these passages? For example, in 1 The 4:13-18 there is no mention of the judgment, or the resurrection of the unrighteous. A little reflection will show that the selection of information for each passage depends on context. In this passage Paul's purpose is not to give a comprehensive description of the last day. He is just wanting to encourage Christians experiencing persecution, so he just picks out some of the facts relevant to his purpose.

Someone may ask how is Jesus' raising of the Christians (with the dead preceding) as in 1Thes 4:13-18, compatible with Him sending out the angels to first gather the tares, then gather the wheat into his barn as in Mat 13:30? There is a historical explanation which might help us see the course of events. It was the custom of that time that when an important personage visited a city, that a deputation of citizens would go and meet the personage outside the city, and then escort the personage to the city. It could be that the believers will meet Jesus in the sky as described, then return to earth with Him. Then He will send out the angels to gather the unrighteous. The main point is that we can be satisfied in the interpretation of the events if the main outlines of the relevant passages agree.

BELIEVERS RECEIVE SPIRITUAL BODIES; DEATH IS SWALLOWED UP IN VICTORY!

Another vital scripture that cannot be reconciled with the time sequence of the pre-tribulation rapture theory is this one. We are given a step-by-step account of how the believers will receive new bodies:

1 Cor 14:50-58 I declare to you, brothers and sisters, that flesh and blood cannot inherit the kingdom of God, nor does the perishable inherit the imperishable. [51] Listen, I tell you a mystery: We will not all sleep, but we will all be changed— [52] in a flash, in the twinkling of an eye, at the last trumpet. For the trumpet will sound, the dead will be raised imperishable, and we will be changed. [53] For the perishable must clothe itself with the imperishable, and the mortal with immortality. [54] When the perishable has been clothed with the imperishable, and the mortal with immortality, then the saying that is written will come true: "Death has been swallowed up in victory." [55] "Where, O death, is your victory? Where, O death, is your sting?" [56] The sting of death is sin, and the power of sin is the law. [57] But thanks be to God! He gives us the victory through our Lord Jesus Christ. [58] Therefore, my dear brothers and sisters, stand firm. Let nothing move you. Always give yourselves fully to the work of the Lord because you know that your labour in the Lord is not in vain.

Dispensationalism interprets 1 Cor 15:50-58 as describing the rapture seven years before Jesus' coming to reign and rule. However, there is no reason to doubt that this is yet another description of what the most dramatic and exciting event in human history will be – the general resurrection on the Return of Christ. Of course, only the righteous will be changed in the way described to receive a spiritual body. Pointers to the general resurrection include the "last trumpet" of verse 52, presumably the same trumpet that sounds in Mat 24:31 and in 1Thess 4:16. Perhaps of more significance is that the point in time this scripture passage describes is pinpointed in verse 52b as being the time "the dead will be raised". This is the "day of the Lord", "the last day", the time of the "last trumpet", the day of judgment and, as we shall see, the "day of wrath"! Nowhere in the New Testament is there any suggestion that there will be two or more resurrections. There is only ever one general resurrection, inextricably associated with Jesus' return and the judgment.

JESUS' COMFORTING WORDS

Next are Jesus' famous comforting words prior to crucifixion. He tells the disciples He is going to prepare a place for them (and us) which is obviously from the context not on earth but in heaven / the heavenly realm. He then says He will come again to receive us so we will go to this place and be with Him there. Once again, no mention of a thousand-year reign. No suggestion He will give us a governmental role on this earth in between His coming to receive us and taking us to His place He has prepared – in Heaven!

John 14:1-6 "Let not your heart be troubled; you believe in God, believe also in Me. In My Father's house are many mansions; if it were not so, I would have told you. I go to prepare a place for you. And if I go and prepare a place for you, I will come again and receive you to Myself; that where I am, there you may be also. And where I go you know, and the way you know." Thomas said to Him, "Lord, we do not know where You are going, and how can we know the way?" Jesus said to him, "I am the way, the truth, and the life. No one comes to the Father except through Me.

THE JUST AND THE UNRIGHTEOUS ALL STAND TOGETHER BEFORE THE JUDGMENT (1)

If it is established beyond all doubt that the righteous and wicked are all judged together at one time, it is difficult to see how this could be reconciled with the doctrines of Pretrib and Premil. In the case of Pretrib, if all will appear at the Judgment and obtain rewards or punishment there, who would have been part of a rapture seven years earlier? In the case of a millennial reign, when would it occur? Before or after the judgment? If before, who would be ruling with Jesus? Everyone would still be awaiting their case to be heard. After is impossible because the judgment will take place at the end of the age. The last trumpet will have sounded, the last day will have arrived. There would quite simply be no time left for a millennium, nor any purpose to be served by it.

It has already been shown in comments on Matthew 25 that the sheep and the goats will all be gathered together for judgment. For confirmation that both the wicked and the just shall appear and be judged together, let's read the following passage from Paul:

Rom 2:5-16 But in accordance with your hardness and your impenitent heart you are treasuring up for yourself wrath in the day of wrath and revelation of the righteous judgment of God, ⁶ who "will render to each one according to his deeds": ⁷ eternal life to those who by patient continuance in doing good seek for glory, honour, and immortality; ⁸ but to those who are self-seeking and do not obey the truth, but obey unrighteousness—indignation and wrath, ⁹ tribulation and anguish, on every soul of man who does evil, of the Jew first and also of the Greek; ¹⁰ but glory, honour, and peace to everyone who works what is good, to the Jew first and also to the Greek. ¹¹ For there is no partiality with God.

¹² For as many as have sinned without law will also perish without law, and as many as have sinned in the law will be judged by the law ¹³ (for not the hearers of the law *are* just in the sight of God, but the doers of the law will be justified; ¹⁴ for when Gentiles, who do not have the law, by nature do the things in the law, these, although not having the law, are a law to themselves, ¹⁵ who show the work of the law written in their hearts, their conscience also bearing witness, and between themselves *their* thoughts accusing or else excusing *them*) ¹⁶ in the day when God will judge the secrets of men by Jesus Christ, according to my Gospel.

Paul's main thrust is that Jews and gentiles will receive the same judgment. His first concern is to rebuke hypocritical judgment especially by Jews, who consider themselves immune from the wrath of God. But they will themselves be punished as well as those they are criticising if they do the same things. When will this punishment come? The day of wrath and revelation of the righteous judgment of God (verse 5). This is another expression for the "Day of the Lord", as the end of the age is often referred to in scripture, especially in the Old Testament. "Wrath" is God's anger. His "righteous judgment" will be seen by all to be impartial, as everyone is rewarded according to his or her deeds. Great rewards will be given to those who exercise "patient continuance in doing good"; whereas those who are self-seeking and do not obey the truth will be subjected to God's wrath. Again, these punishments or rewards will be given out on the day when God will judge the secrets of men by Jesus Christ (Rom 2:16). This can only be on the Return of Christ. This is confirmed again by Matthew: (Mat 16:27) For the Son of Man will come in the glory of His Father with His angels, and then He will reward each according to his works. For each person to be rewarded according to his or her works, their secrets must be brought to the light and judged (Luke 12:3). Verse 16 declares that there is a day when God will judge the secrets of men. It will not necessarily be literally 24 hours. The "day" may be a metaphor for a comparatively short, discrete, period of time. But it will be right at the end of this universe as we know it.

THE JUSTICE OF GOD

How terrible God's wrath is, as Paul makes clear in these verses. We live in an age where some people believe the preaching we hear in church must be sugar-coated. Many churches will not hear solid truth about sin, the devil, and God's wrath. We notice:

1. Whether people like it or not, God will reward or punish everyone ACCORDING TO THEIR DEEDS. This is a strong theme in scriptures pertaining to God's judgment. People are always judged according to their DEEDS, not their doctrine. This is a rebuke to Western Christianity which over the centuries has put so much emphasis on having the right doctrine. By contrast our actions really show whether we are genuinely in the faith, as in Matthew 25 (verses 6-8).
2. Note there is no conflict here between Rom 2:5-16 and Ephesians 2:8-10: For by grace you have been saved through

faith, and that not of yourselves; *it is* the gift of God, [9] not of works, lest anyone should boast. [10] For we are His workmanship, created in Christ Jesus for good works, which God prepared beforehand that we should walk in them. The works of Eph 2:10 are the works God has prepared for us to do in the power of His Spirit, rather than those done in our own strength.

3. EVERYONE who has done evil will be punished; EVERYONE who has done good will be rewarded. This is one more confirmation that it is a universal judgment (Rom 2:9-12).
4. There is no reward for just hearing or knowing the law – we must OBEY it! (verse 13). Note he is talking about the moral law, the thrust of which is to love God with all our hearts, souls and minds and our neighbours as ourselves, not the ceremonial and sacrificial law of Moses.
5. Those who have done good are those who have put faith in Christ and as a result He has changed their life. There is no other way to please God.
6. As we read above, the Day of the Lord is also referred to as "the day when God will judge the secrets of men by Jesus Christ" (Rom 2:16). Nothing will be hidden unless it is a sin which has been thoroughly repented of and renounced.

Many think that in the case of the true believers God knows their hearts and so there is no need for them to appear at the judgment. Well God does know the hearts – but WE do not! We will see again when we look at the Sermon on the Mount that everything that is hidden now will be revealed. The day will declare our works, and every thought will be revealed. Justice must not only be done but it must be seen to be done. All the universe will see the greatness and the justice of God, His incredible mercy and tender love to the righteous, and His terrible wrath against the unrepentant. We will discuss this further in chapter 19.

As we have already noted, the Parousia coming of Christ, the Day of the Lord, the judgment, the rewards for the righteous, and the punishment of the wicked under God's wrath are all inextricably linked. If we take plain scripture as our authority, it is inconceivable that there should be another coming of the Lord, or another judgment. "The day when

God will judge the secrets of men" can only possibly happen once, and it's firmly understood all people will be there. It cannot be a different judgment for different peoples. If we take Dispensationalist commentaries as our authority, we will end up on intellectually shaky ground.

THE JUST AND THE UNRIGHTEOUS ALL STAND TOGETHER BEFORE THE JUDGMENT (2)

Earlier we noticed that the resurrection of Daniel 12:1-3 must be the same event as Matthew 24-25, because both passages place the general resurrection of the dead after the time of the worst tribulation ever experienced on earth. In the Daniel passage we learned that some of those raised will be raised to everlasting life, and some to everlasting contempt. The following passage in John also confirms that both righteous and unrighteous will be raised together, to appear at the universal judgment.

John 5:24-30 "Do not marvel at this; for the hour is coming in which all who are in the graves will hear His voice and come forth—those who have done good, to the resurrection of life, and those who have done evil, to the resurrection of condemnation."

The scenario described here matches the Romans 2 passage exactly. Once again it is a judgment of WORKS. There are two categories of people:

1. Those that have DONE good and
2. Those who have DONE evil.

More confirmation again comes from Acts 25:14-15 ...I worship the God of my fathers, believing all things which are written in the Law and in the Prophets. [15] I have hope in God, which they themselves also accept, that there will be a resurrection of *the* dead, both of *the* just and *the* unjust. This passage also indicates that the New Testament description of reality agrees with what was known in Old Testament times. We will return to this.

ONE DAY OF THE LORD / ONE JUDGMENT / ONE RETURN OF JESUS ONLY

Jesus' "appearing" is mentioned in almost every book of the New Testament. There are three different Greek words used:

1. "parousia" – means the personal arrival or appearance of someone.
2. "apokalupsis" – uncovering, unveiling, manifestation. When used of a person the word always denotes physically appearing.
3. "epiphania" – appearance, manifestation, shining upon.

Dispensationalists have tried to argue that the different words denote different types of appearing and have defended the Dispensational concept of several returns of Jesus on that basis. However, scholars have refuted this idea convincingly and demonstrated that the three words are interchangeable, and while depicting slightly different aspects of the return of Jesus, they all undoubtedly describe the same event, the (one) appearance of our blessed Lord. See for example the thorough article on the topic by Robert Brown, who documents every occurrence of each of the three words in the New Testament (Brown, 2015)

Most importantly, whether it's called "the Day of the Lord", "the day of Jesus Christ", "that Day", "the day of God" or "the last Day", there is only one! No Bible writer ever refers to "when Jesus comes the second time" or "when Jesus comes the third time"! Read this statement from Paul:

Truly, these times of ignorance God overlooked, but now commands all men everywhere to repent, because He has appointed a day on which He will judge the world in righteousness by the Man whom He has ordained. He has given assurance of this to all by raising Him from the dead (Acts 17:30-31)

Paul is addressing the people of Athens, telling them there is a (ie one particular) day when the world will be judged. The raising of Jesus from the dead is God's guarantee this day of judgment is coming. A single resurrection and judgment will apply to all including Satan and the demons. Even the demons know this as the time they will be cast into the lake of fire as exemplified when Jesus casts out the legion of demons into the swine. They cried,

"Mat 8:29 What have we to do with You, Jesus, You Son of God? Have You come here to torment us before the time?"

Notice how they talk about "THE" time. They know there is one particular time when everything that has been prophesied will come to pass.

TIME FOR THE WORK TO END!

The parable of the workers in the vineyard (Matthew 20:1-16) gives a picture of the work of God until the end of the age. The heavenly rewards for people who follow the call to bring the Gospel to all the world and make disciples are symbolised by the wages. Different groups of labourers are recruited at intervals throughout the day. Then suddenly the time for the work is over, and all the workers are paid. There is no staggered end – the time comes when the work is finished. No mention of a Pretrib banquet before the next step for the workers.

"So when evening had come, the owner of the vineyard said to his steward, 'Call the laborers and give them their wages, beginning with the last to the first" (Matt 20:8).

There will come a day when believers will be all gathered together to receive their reward. Imagine being gathered before the Lord with all the labourers of all ages– the Biblical apostles, Mary the blessed mother of Jesus, the other New Testament women, the early church fathers, Martin Luther, John Wesley, David Livingstone, Watchman Nee, Augustine and other men and women of God. Who do you look forward to meeting? You don't need to worry about the mechanics of how it happens. You only need to keep yourself "sincere and without offense" until that day.

THE DAY OF THE LORD – THE WICKED DESTROYED BY FIRE, THE BELIEVERS JOYFULLY UNITED WITH JESUS

The following passage by Paul shows the dramatic difference between what the righteous receive and what the wicked receive on the Day of the Lord. Here, as elsewhere, Paul merely refers to the day as "that day" – all his readers and hearers know the day he is referring to.

2 Thessalonians 1:6-10 it is a righteous thing with God to repay with tribulation those who trouble you, and to give you who are troubled rest with us when the Lord Jesus is revealed from heaven with His mighty angels, in flaming fire taking vengeance on those who do not know God, and on those who do not obey the Gospel of our Lord Jesus Christ. These shall be punished with everlasting destruction from the presence of the Lord and from the glory of His power, when He comes, in that Day, to be glorified in His saints and to be admired among all those who believe, because our testimony among you was believed.

Once again, it is the same day, the Day of the Lord, when those who do not obey the Gospel will be punished with fire and everlasting removal from God's presence and Jesus will be glorified in His saints and admired by all who believe. When the prophecies around Jesus' birth, life and ministry were fulfilled in minute detail at His first coming, there was only wonder on the part of the believers. They might have said "Oh, so *that's* what He meant!" When the Holy Spirit fell on the believers they exclaimed "Ah – *that's* what Joel was writing about!" Surely that is what it will be like on the Day of the Lord. Let us not build sophisticated systems for interpreting prophecy and develop cut and dried theories on how everything will fit together. Let us come to God's Word in humility and simplicity of heart and meditate on it, seeking such revelation as He pleases to give, above all being determined to OBEY His word, and be pleasing to Him. If words have any meaning, the above passage from 2 Thessalonians gives confidence that Jesus will come ON ONE DAY (at one discrete time) to judge the wicked and reward the righteous.

2 DO PETER'S WORDS SUPPORT THE MILLENNIAL REIGN DOCTRINE?

The following passage from 2 Peter is perhaps the most difficult statement in the Bible for the Dispensationalist position:

2 Peter 3:7-10 But the heavens and the earth which are now preserved by the same word, are reserved for fire until the day of judgment and

perdition of ungodly men. But, beloved, do not forget this one thing, that with the Lord one day is as a thousand years, and a thousand years as one day. The Lord is not slack concerning His promise, as some count slackness, but is longsuffering toward us, not willing that any should perish but that all should come to repentance. But the day of the Lord will come as a thief in the night, in which the heavens will pass away with a great noise, and the elements will melt with fervent heat; both the earth and the works that are in it will be burned up.

EARTH DESTROYED BY FIRE

Dispensationalists claim that they alone interpret the scriptures literally. They take the verses about the thousand-year millennial reign literally, whereas Amils interpret them symbolically. But what about 2 Peter 3? The passage clearly talks about the Day of the Lord, which is clearly the same Day of the Lord as described in Mat 24:31, Mat 25:32, and the many other instances where the day of Christ/the Lord is mentioned in the New Testament. It is THAT DAY when Christ returns to raise up the believers and to judge the world. Consider the 2 Peter passage, especially verse 10: THE DAY will come unexpectedly, and IN THAT DAY the heavens will pass away with a great noise, and the elements will melt with fervent heat; both the earth and the works that are in it will be burned up. This is the *parousia* return of Christ to earth. My simple question to our Premillennial brothers and sisters is, if the heavens pass away, the elements melt and the earth and all its works burn up, where will the millennial reign take place?

WHICH SCRIPTURE IS LITERAL?

If we take 2 Peter 3:10 literally, it is beyond dispute that we go straight into the age to come on the day Jesus manifests Himself on the earth. So it is surely the case that either 2 Peter 3 is literal and Revelation 20 is symbolic, or Revelation 20 is literal and 2 Peter 3 symbolic. It is surely not possible for them both to be taken literally because if so they would be contradictory! If we look at the genre of the two passages, 2 Peter is a straight explanatory letter, whereas Revelation belongs to the

THE RETURN OF CHRIST

genre of apocalyptic literature and is highly symbolic. To establish a base understanding therefore, it is advisable to give precedence to the former.

One simple passage expressing Paul's thinking is this one, written to his beloved Timothy

2 Tim 4:1 I charge *you* therefore before God and the Lord Jesus Christ, who will judge the living and the dead at His appearing and His kingdom...

It is clear that Jesus' role will be to judge. When? At His appearing. That is His one appearing referred to by all the New Testament writers.

Another emphasis of Paul is the glory to be received by the believers. Jesus' very own glory will shine in us:

Philippians 3:4 When Christ *who is* our life appears, then you also will appear with Him in glory.

Once again, a simple verse brings out a profound truth. Question: when will we appear with Him in glory? Answer: when He appears. Not complicated. Only one return of Jesus was expected by the New Testament Christians – and THAT will be when we appear in glory.

Rom 9:23-4 .... He might make known the riches of His glory on the vessels of mercy, which He had prepared beforehand for glory, [24] even us whom He called, not of the Jews only, but also of the Gentiles.

He is preparing us for glory. This agrees with Matthew:

Mat 13:43 Then the righteous will shine forth as the sun in the kingdom of their Father. He who has ears to hear, let him hear!

ALL CREATION LONGS FOR THE REVEALING OF THE CHILDREN OF GOD

Not only we ourselves, but all of the creation will shine with the glory of God:

Rom 8:18-22 For I consider that the sufferings of this present time are not worthy *to be compared* with the glory which shall be revealed in us. 19 For the earnest expectation of the creation eagerly waits for the revealing of the sons of God. 20 For the creation was subjected to futility, not willingly, but because of Him who subjected *it* in hope; 21 because the creation itself also will be delivered from the bondage of corruption into the glorious liberty of the children of God. 22 For we know that the whole creation groans and labours with birth pangs together until now.

The whole of creation longs for the "revealing of the sons of God". This is a very humbling truth when we meditate on it. This state of glory will be the fully realised Christian life mentioned earlier. Paul in 2 Corinthians 5 illustrates this full life of Christ, and Romans 8:19 tells us that all creation longs for the moment when the sons and daughters of God enter this glory phase. The deliverance from bondage for the creation itself can only refer to the new heavens and earth promised by Jesus. Romans chapter 8 is very relevant to eschatology, though very little seems to be written on this topic.

Please note: A study guide for this book, The New Testament End Time Study Guide, is available through the 222 Foundation website, https://222foundation.net. The New Testament passages on the end times may be studied in more detail using the guide.

Chapter Sixteen

WHAT ABOUT REVELATION 20?

✛ ✛ ✛

GENERAL PRINCIPLES

Revelation 20 has perhaps generated more controversy than any other chapter in the Bible. If it were not for this one passage, nobody would have thought of a thousand-year reign of Jesus on this planet. It is true that many books have been written on the topic and many writers have tried to synthesize the doctrine of the literal 1000-year reign with the rest of the Bible. I have a deep respect for the many men and women of God who have examined the scriptures and sought God for the true interpretation. Sincere Christians from all sides have studied and arrived at different positions on the whole Book of Revelation. As we have seen, right from the earliest writings of the post-New Testament church, it has been a strongly contended topic. We will start by identifying five general principles for the study of scripture.

INTERPRETING REVELATION (1): INTERPRETING SCRIPTURE BY REFERRING TO OTHER SCRIPTURE

It is a well-known truism that we cannot "hang a doctrine" on one single passage of scripture alone. To use one passage, especially in a symbolic book, to assert a theological doctrine breaks the rules of scriptural interpretation. We read that some of the early Christians rejected Revelation as canonical scripture because they did not believe in a literal 1000-year reign. "Orthodox" Christians today don't have that option because the Council of Nicaea made the decision to regard the book as part of the scriptural canon[16]. I have the faith that the Bible the universal church has accepted for so many centuries is the true revelation of God. But we must look to see how scripture passages inter-relate to get the full meaning of the Bible. There must be a way of understanding Revelation which does not contradict the other scriptures mentioned so far.

INTERPRETING REVELATION (2): INTERPRET THE SIMPLE NEW TESTAMENT BOOKS FIRST

Where the whole counsel of scripture is not obvious, we should give precedence to the simple, clear passages ahead of the complex ones; then interpret the complex in a way that is compatible with the simple. Many writers, especially on eschatology, start by interpreting the complex, metaphorical passages, and then manipulate the straightforward, clear passages to fit their interpretation of the complex ones. This is why, in this book, I took the comparatively straightforward Matthew 24-25 first, because it is the clearest, most detailed explanation of His return, from Jesus Himself.

INTERPRETING REVELATION (3): GIVE PRECEDENCE TO NEW TESTAMENT DIDACTIC TEACHING

The didactic passages of the New Testament are the peak of Biblical revelation. God has progressively revealed His truth to mankind. His

---

[16] The "canon" is the body of writings which are considered to be scripture by the church.

supreme goal is to impart to us the knowledge of Jesus Christ, His beloved Son. We can build our knowledge of Him by reading the Old Testament, which in fact, though the writers did not know it, is about Him! (John 1:1-5, John 5:39-40, 45-46, Luke 4:18-21, Luke 24:27, 44-45). The Gospels quote Jesus in many places and are accounts of His life, so we need to give His words precedence over the Old Testament, in the knowledge that the Old Testament, if understood correctly, will not contradict Him.

We should give especial regard to the Acts and Epistles, because they represent New Testament knowledge given in accordance with Jesus' promise here:

Joh 16:12-13 "I still have many things to say to you, but you cannot bear *them* now. [13] However, when He, the Spirit of truth, has come, He will guide you into all truth".

The epistles are Jesus' "many things to say" which were revealed by the Holy Spirit after Jesus' return to heaven, and when the apostles were mature enough to receive them. Therefore, they represent the very highest truth, being Jesus' own explanatory words on the whole Bible.

INTERPRETING REVELATION (4): THE METAPHORICAL NATURE OF APOCALYPTIC LITERATURE

When we read Revelation, it is obvious that it is different from any other Bible book. The closest books to it in the Bible are the Old Testament books Daniel and Zechariah with their extended visions with the meanings explained by angels. The genre the Book of Revelation was written in is called "apocalyptic". In the literature of the time there were several other apocalypses including 1,2 and 3 Enoch; 4 Ezra; 2 and 3 Baruch; and the Apocalypse of Zephaniah.

In these books literary devices are used for effect. For example, the narrator is taken to be some well-known man of God from the past such as Enoch or Abraham, who gains revelation through a dream, or by supernaturally traveling to a spiritual region guided by angels. It is unlikely that people thought that the narrator had literally been taken to those regions by real angels. Many of these apocalyptic books have images, symbols and symbolic numbers to clarify or expand on this message. Most likely no contemporaries thought that they should take these images and symbols literally, but rather that they were an understood and accepted literary technique.

The Book of Revelation is similarly constructed. It is the revelation of Jesus Christ which the angel **signified** to John (Rev 1:1). The word "signified" in Greek is *semaino* which means *to signify, indicate, make a sign.* (Kercheville, Undated) That is obvious anyway from the language and images used. There will never be a woman clothed in scarlet and purple, wearing gold and precious stones, with a golden cup in her hand, sitting on a scarlet beast, as described in Revelation 17. You can visit every place in the world, and you will never see her. Why not? The answer is given in Rev 17:18. She is not a woman, but a symbol for a city, often interpreted as Rome from the description. So, this principle is that Revelation uses signs and symbols to convey its meaning and is largely metaphorical. Jesus used metaphor extensively in the parables, and in His analysis of Old Testament prophecy. For example, He regarded the coming of John the Baptist as the fulfilment of Malachi's prophecy about the coming of Elijah in Malachi 4. So, we can safely say that some features of Rev 20, such as the 1000 years, the chain, the dragon and other images, may be symbols.

INTERPRETING THE BOOK OF REVELATION (5): EVENTS ARE NOT SEQUENTIAL

A fifth principle in interpreting Revelation is that we do not have to view the events portrayed by the symbols as sequential[17]. In my earlier days as a Christian, I always enjoyed reading commentaries with a historicist understanding of Revelation. Commentators of this school try to interpret the symbols in such a way as to represent a continuous narrative of events from Jesus' ministry to the present day. I was

---

[17] The idea that the events of Rev 19:11-21 are preceded by those of Rev 20:1-6 is a key to understanding these events. It is apparent Rev 20:7-10 is parallel to Rev 19:11-21, and also to Ezek 39:17-29.

puzzled at the portrayal of obviously end-time events in Revelation 6, which seemed to be right out of sequence as Jesus' birth and early ministry do not figure until Revelation 12. The problem disappears if we see Revelation as a sequence of visions, each portraying largely the same events and time period, but giving new information and perspective.

"PROGRESSIVE PARALLEL" INTERPRETATION

The idea that the episodes of Revelation are non-sequential is known as the "progressive parallel" interpretation. It is in response to the observation there are at least seven times in the book of Revelation where one would expect the book to end - because the end of the age has come. So, what do we do? Start the next section assuming the story is beginning again - and it makes sense! Table 5 shows one such interpretation, based on division into sections suggested by Hendriksen (Hendriksen, 1940). Each portrays an aspect of kingdom history from Jesus' early ministry to His return in glory. This is an important concept, because if we believed the whole of Revelation represented a continual chronological sequence, we would have to conclude that the binding of Satan followed the return of Jesus to earth depicted so graphically in Revelation 19. But looking at the table, we can see that the end of the age has been portrayed at the end of each of the seven sections. So it is perfectly in accord with the structure of Revelation to see section 6 as another parallel account ending in Christ's dramatic appearance and total defeat of the enemy in Rev 19. Each section has covered the time from Jesus' earthly ministry until His return but has brought additional insight or a different perspective. In this view section 7 (chapters 20-22) starts the time sequence again, with the binding of Satan occurring during Christ's earthly ministry. From all the scriptural evidence we are examining, this seems to me to be the only possible conclusion.

Table 2: Scenes in Revelation

Parallel sections in Revelation (Hoekema, 1977), (Beale, 1999), (Hendriksen, 1940)

There is minor disagreement on where each section starts and ends. This table uses Hendriksen's section divisions.

Verse ref	Description	End of section shown by:
Section 1: 1:1 – 3:22 Letters to seven churches.	Introduction and vision of the risen Christ. Letters to seven of the churches of John's day, addressing issues which were relevant to them, but also relevant to churches of all ages.	3:22 "He who has an ear, let him hear what the Spirit says to the churches." The seven churches are symbolic of all churches of all periods of history and all locations. As such it covers the whole period of operation of the Church until the return of Jesus. (Day of the Lord)
2: From cross to new heavens and earth. 4:1 – 6:17	This second section also covers the whole church age. It begins with the vision of God's glory. Then we see Christ pictured as killed and ruling from Heaven: ...5:6 in the midst of the throne and of the four living creatures, and in the midst of the elders, stood a Lamb as though it had been slain...	Rev 6:17 Then the sky receded as a scroll when it is rolled up ...For the great day of His wrath has come, and who is able to stand? ...6:17 or the Lamb who is in the midst of the throne will shepherd them and lead them to living fountains of waters. And God will wipe away every tear from their eyes. Like section 1, this section also ends with the day of the Lord – the time of the "great day of His wrath" on the wicked, and eternal rewards (living fountains of waters) for the believers.
3: 7:1 – 11:19 Overcomers.	First, we see the saints sealed, then rejoicing. The judgments of God are poured out; the overcoming church is portrayed in the little book and the two witnesses. This third section ends very clearly in the last judgment, and reward of the saints.	You have taken Your great power and reigned. [18] The nations were angry, and Your wrath has come, and the time of the dead, that they should be judged, and that You should reward Your servants the prophets and the saints. Again, we come to the day of the Lord, time to judge the wicked and reward the Lord's servants.
4: Journey to the harvest. 12:1 – 14:20	A metaphorical journey through kingdom history, beginning with the birth of Christ then the rise of the beast, and ending with the harvest at the end of the age. 14:19-20 So the angel thrust his sickle into the earth.	...and gathered the vine of the earth, and threw it into the great winepress of the wrath of God. [20] And the winepress was trampled outside the city, and blood came out of the winepress, up to the horses' bridles, for one thousand six hundred furlongs. Again, the end of the age, and time for God's wrath on His enemies, those who refuse to believe.
5: God's wrath outpoured. 15:1-16:21	God's wrath poured out on the enemies of the Church. The end of this section is clear. We are told God's wrath is complete, then the section ends with the last battle 15:1...seven last plagues, for in them the wrath of God is complete.	16:14,16 For they are spirits of demons, performing signs, which go out to the kings of the earth and of the whole world, to gather them to the battle of that great day of God Almighty....to the place called in Hebrew, Armageddon. Again, the scene ends with the end of the age, the famous battle of Armageddon.

6: Babylon falls. 17:1-19:21	The fall of Babylon (idolatry) and the beast, culminating again in the last battle and return of Christ.	19:21 And the rest were killed with the sword which proceeded from the mouth of Him who sat on the horse. And all the birds were filled with their flesh. Ends with the end of the age – the last battle again.
7 : Consummation 20:1 – 22:21	Satan's defeat; the metaphorical 1000-year reign; the final judgment; the new heavens and the new earth.	Starts with Jesus' victory at the cross. Ends with Satan being released for a little while, totally defeated in the last battle. The consummation. Visions of the new heaven and earth 22:20-21 "Surely I am coming quickly." Amen. Even so, come, Lord Jesus! [21] The grace of our Lord Jesus Christ *be* with you all. Amen.

REVELATION 20 VERSE BY VERSE

With these principles in mind, then, let's look at Revelation 20:1-10, and analyse the symbols to see whether there is a ring of truth in interpreting Revelation this way:

REV 20:1 THE ANGEL

Then I saw an angel coming down from heaven, having the key to the bottomless pit and a great chain in his hand.

Let us start with the angel who binds Satan. The image of a key is used to denote Jesus' authority throughout Revelation. For instance:

> Rev 1:18 *I am* He who lives, and was dead, and behold,
> I am alive forevermore. Amen. And I have the keys of
> Hades and of Death.

Here it is shown that it was through His death and resurrection that He obtained the keys of Hades and of death. It is probable that "the key to the bottomless pit" held by the angel is the same key. This means the angel either represents Jesus or is an angel under Jesus' authority. It also strengthens our conviction that the place on the timeline of the angel binding Satan is at the crucifixion and resurrection of Jesus.

> Rev 20:1 (cont.) ....a great chain in his hand.

The fact of the chain adds weight to the case for a metaphorical interpretation. If it is a literal chain, what sort of chain would be best to use when binding Satan? What would it be made of? Steel? Copper? An alloy? How long would it be? How heavy? What tensile strength? Surely, we can dismiss any case for a literal chain fairly easily.

REV 20:2 THE DRAGON BOUND

He laid hold of the dragon, that serpent of old, who is *the* Devil and Satan, and bound him for a thousand years;

The dragon is the symbol for Satan – as explained by John. It is certain that if we interpret the chain and the dragon as metaphorical, we must likewise accept the "binding" as metaphorical. The binding is a symbol of defeat and loss of power and authority. The question is, how and when was Satan defeated and stripped of power and authority? We will turn to New Testament didactic teaching to get the answer. Jesus referred to binding Satan in Matthew 12:

> Mat 12: 28-29 But if I cast out demons by the Spirit of God, surely the kingdom of God has come upon you. [29] Or how can one enter a strong man's house and plunder his goods, unless he first binds the strong man? And then he will plunder his house.

In that situation, until Jesus came, Satan was in charge, with the demon as his agent. The demon was causing the man to be blind and mute. Jesus bound the "strong man" and cast the demon out. The result was physical healing of the man. We are not told whether this means that He bound Satan directly, or just Satan's representative on the scene, the demon. But it does not make any real difference for our present purpose. Satan's power was broken over this man.

Did it mean that Satan lost all power when he was bound? No – there were many other people at that time who were under the bondage of Satan, and many if not all nations were deceived by Satan. Let us consider for a moment the ministry of Jesus. His authority came from the Holy Spirit, whom He received when He was baptized in the river

Jordan by John the Baptist. It was tested when Satan tempted Him in the wilderness. This was a confrontation that had to happen – notice that it was the Holy Spirit who led Him into the wilderness for this encounter. And Jesus won the contest hands down – Satan could only have made any progress had Jesus been disobedient to the Father. He resisted the temptation and won a massive victory. Because of this, and because He had the Holy Spirit, His ministry was launched:

> Mat 4:23-25 And Jesus went about all Galilee, teaching in their synagogues, preaching the Gospel of the kingdom, and healing all kinds of sickness and all kinds of disease among the people. Then His fame went throughout all Syria; and they brought to Him all sick people who were afflicted with various diseases and torments, and those who were demon-possessed, epileptics, and paralytics; and He healed them. Great multitudes followed Him—from Galilee, and from Decapolis, Jerusalem, Judea, and beyond the Jordan.

Jesus came to inaugurate the Kingdom of God, which means He ushered in the spread of God's spiritual authority in all the world. He did not intend to complete this mission all Himself. He commissioned His followers, even down to today, to complete the task. Look at His words to the disciples as recorded in Luke's Gospel:

> Luke 10:19-20 "Behold, I give you the authority to trample on serpents and scorpions, and over all the power of the enemy, and nothing shall by any means hurt you. Nevertheless, do not rejoice in this, that the spirits are subject to you, but rather rejoice because your names are written in heaven."

He was able to give them that authority because He had bound the power of Satan. They had previously told Him: "Lord, even the demons are subject to us in Your name." And He said to them, "I saw Satan fall like lightning from heaven" (Luke 10:17-18). He can give us this authority too, to proclaim the coming of the Kingdom of God. This reality is what is expressed so eloquently in the symbol of the angel binding the dragon in Revelation 20:2. The question remains, when did this take place? Again, we go to other didactic New Testament teaching to interpret the meaning.

THE VICTORY OVER SATAN WAS WON AT THE CROSS AND RESURRECTION OF CHRIST.

As He contemplated His crucifixion, Jesus told His disciples (and us),

> "Now is the judgment of this world; now the ruler of this world will be cast out" (John 12:31)

The writer of Hebrews explains that it was through His death that He defeated Satan:

> Heb 2:14-15 Inasmuch then as the children have partaken of flesh and blood, He Himself likewise shared in the same, that through death He might destroy him who had the power of death, that is, the devil, and release those who through fear of death were all their lifetime subject to bondage.

Paul, in his letter to the Colossians used the image of a Roman triumph to illustrate the nature of Jesus' victory. A Roman triumph was a public spectacle, where the defeated enemy were led through the streets of Rome, bound by chains, and totally humiliated:

> Col 2:15 Having disarmed principalities and powers, He made a public spectacle of them, triumphing over them in it.

In Colossians, Paul places this triumph in time at the cross. In a further development, after He was taken up into heaven, Christ empowered His followers to complete the outworking of the victory by giving us the infilling of the Holy Spirit. In the words of the great evangelist, Charles Spurgeon, "Satan is now a defeated foe". There is an outworking of that reality, which will be finally accomplished at the "Parousia" return of Jesus, and general resurrection. But the outcome is not in doubt. Jesus has triumphed at the cross and through His resurrection!

THE 1000 YEARS

We are told in Rev 20:2-3 that the period of Satan's incarceration would be 1000 years. In interpreting this, we can learn from the mistakes of believers in the past. In the lead up to 1000 AD many people believed that 1 January 1000 would be the long-awaited day when Jesus would return. This expectation was based solely on the mesmerizing number 1000. As the day approached, people tried to behave properly. In December 999, many sold goods and gave the money to the poor; crowds of pilgrims set of for Jerusalem to meet the Lord there; crops were not planted; and there was huge expectation. However, nothing happened except widespread famine in Europe because the crops were not planted! (The Interactive Bible, 2012)

NUMBERS IN REVELATION

The mistake these believers made was to take the 1000 years literally, whereas Revelation being a book of symbols which uses many symbolic numbers, we should understand it symbolically. Numbers are often used symbolically in the Bible. For instance, Psalm 50:10 reads, "For every beast of the forest is Mine, and the cattle on a thousand hills." No-one would take this to mean that there are precisely 1000 hills; "1000 hills" stands for an indefinitely large number.

The number 1000 is the cube of 10, and 10 is the number of completeness, as for example in the 10 commandments, the 10 plagues which afflicted Egypt or the 10 virgins in the parable. The 1000 years is a symbol for an indefinitely long time[18]. Our study so far has pinpointed

---

[18] By contrast, "one hour" in Revelation 17:3 is a symbol for a short time: ".... ten kings who have not yet received a kingdom, but who for one hour will receive authority as

the beginning of the "1000 years" as the crucifixion. The end will be the Day of the Lord. The thousand years is a metaphor for the church age.

So we have seen that Jesus received the Holy Spirit and resisted temptation, and so was able to "bind the strong man (the devil) and "plunder his house". So far, as we shall see, Jesus had fulfilled His purpose: For this purpose, the Son of God was manifested, that He might destroy the works of the devil. (1 John 3:8). The Matthew 12 example we looked at was drawn from Jesus personal ministry to individuals. But the scope of His actions in destroying Satan's power was a lot broader, as we shall see.

REV 20:3 SATAN BOUND 1000 YEARS, THEN RELEASED.

.... and he cast him into the bottomless pit, and shut him up, and set a seal on him, so that he should deceive the nations no more till the thousand years were finished. But after these things he must be released for a little while.

Some object that verse 3 says he should "deceive the nations no more till the 1000 years were finished", whereas we see the nations under deception today. It is true that many if not all nations are under major deception in our times. But the devil is unable to hold them in deception. Before Jesus, there was no way out for the nations, but now there is a way out through the preaching of the Word of God and taking the Gospel to the nations. The intention of Christ was certainly to prevent the devil continuing to deceive the nations. The on-going work of removing deception from the nations depends on us, working with Him (Mat 28:20). As we discussed earlier, this

---

kings...." No-one would think that 10 literal kings would reign literally one hour. There are many symbolic numbers in Revelation. Another example is the 144,000 in Revelation 7:4 and 14:1. Nobody suggests that only 144,000 will be saved. It is the number of election (12 tribes of Israel, 12 Apostles) squared and multiplied by 1000, again standing for an indefinitely large number. So it stands for the multitude of saved people under both the old covenant and the new covenant (Kroll, 2016) (The International Bible Encyclopaedia, 2001).

work is going on today at an incredible pace. It may not seem so in the West, but in the developing world, the Gospel is advancing at a massive rate never imagined. Satan is completely under the authority of Jesus. So what about the millions who are now obviously under the deception of Satan. Does this mean Jesus has let His authority slip? No, not even in the slightest. We will get to this but first let us discuss verses 4 and 5.

REV 20:4 REIGNING WITH CHRIST

And I saw thrones, and they sat on them, and judgment was committed to them. Then I saw the souls of those who had been beheaded for their witness to Jesus and for the word of God, who had not worshiped the beast or his image, and had not received his mark on their foreheads or on their hands. And they lived and reigned with Christ for a thousand years.

The first part of this vision John saw was the thrones, which speak of authority. Secondly, he saw the martyrs for the Lord Jesus Christ. The verse references Revelation 13: 16-18, the famous "mark of the beast" passage:

> Also it causes all, both small and great, both rich and poor, both free and slave, to be marked on the right hand or the forehead, [17] so that no one can buy or sell unless he has the mark, that is, the name of the beast or the number of its name. [18] This calls for wisdom: let the one who has understanding calculate the number of the beast, for it is the number of a man, and his number is 666.

THE INTERMEDIATE STATE

The most common interpretation today amongst Amil commentators is that these beheaded saints are saved people who have died, and who are experiencing what theologians call the "intermediate state" This interpretation is very fully evidenced by Beale, and others. (Beale, 1999)

(Hoekema, 1977). Comparing this verse with others in Revelation and elsewhere[19], it is clear that the meaning is not limited to believers who have been martyred, but it applies to all God's people who have been faithful. The Bible makes it clear that, if we are not still alive on the return of Jesus, we will arise from our graves on the Day of the Lord and meet Him in the air if we have died in Him. But what about the time between our death and being raised up on the last day? Jesus said to "the good thief" who was crucified with Him, "Assuredly, I say to you, today you will be with Me in Paradise." (Luke 23:43) So there is a blessed state where our spirit goes to be with the Lord, but where we have not yet received the full promised spiritual body, and supernatural life in the new heavens and earth.

PAUL'S CONFIDENCE IN THE FINAL OUTCOME

Paul tells us about this blessed state in both the following passages. It is obvious that he is confident about the promise of God that this will be his experience after death. We know from what we have studied so far that final bodily resurrection will not occur until the "last day". But these passages reassure us that while we wait for that final glorious body, our souls will be resurrected to be with Jesus in the interim. This was so real to Paul he desired more to be with Jesus than to live the present life, though his on-going life here was of major benefit to his disciples. There is no doubt from the wording that he expected to be with Jesus immediately after death.

> 2 Cor 5:4-8 For we who are in *this* tent groan, being burdened, not because we want to be unclothed, but further clothed, that mortality may be swallowed up by life. [5] Now He who has prepared us for this very thing *is* God, who also has given us the Spirit as a guarantee. [6] So *we are* always confident, knowing that while we are at home in the body we are absent from the Lord. [7] For we walk by faith, not by sight. [8] We are confident, yes,

---

[19] For example, Rev 1:6

well pleased rather to be absent from the body and to be present with the Lord.

Phil 1:20-24 But if *I* live on in the flesh, this *will mean* fruit from *my* labour; yet what I shall choose I cannot tell. **²³** For I am hard-pressed between the two, having a desire to depart and be with Christ, *which is* far better. **²⁴** Nevertheless to remain in the flesh *is* more needful for you.

Perhaps the most moving declaration of this expectancy was by Stephen as he was being stoned by the Jews:

Acts 7:59-60 And they stoned Stephen as he was calling on *God* and saying, "Lord Jesus, receive my spirit." **⁶⁰** Then he knelt down and cried out with a loud voice, "Lord, do not charge them with this sin." And when he had said this, he fell asleep.

Adherents of the "soul sleep" doctrine of the Jehovah's Witnesses and Seventh Day Adventists[20] might object that the text says he then fell asleep, but it seems obvious he was entering into the real presence of the Lord. "Falling asleep" was an idiomatic way of expressing death in New Testament times.

Catholic teaching recognises this intermediate period between a person's physical death and resurrection on the last day:

1051 Every man receives his eternal recompense in his immortal soul from the moment of his death in a particular judgment by Christ, the judge of the living and the dead.

1052 "We believe that the souls of all who die in Christ's grace . . . are the People of God beyond death. On the day of resurrection, death will be definitively conquered, when these souls will be reunited with their bodies" (Paul VI, CPG # 28)

---

[20] This doctrine holds that on death the believer experiences a deep sleep of unconsciousness until resurrection on the last day. If it were true, Paul would hardly have been so expectant about seeing the Lord and departing to "be with Him"!

It is from this understanding that the idea of purgatory and prayer for the dead come:

1030 All who die in God's grace and friendship, but still imperfectly purified, are indeed assured of their eternal salvation; but after death they undergo purification, so as to achieve the holiness necessary to enter the joy of heaven.

1031 The Church gives the name Purgatory to this final purification of the elect, which is entirely different from the punishment of the damned. The Church formulated her doctrine of faith on Purgatory especially at the Councils of Florence and Trent. the tradition of the Church, by reference to certain texts of Scripture, speaks of a cleansing fire.

1032 This teaching is also based on the practice of prayer for the dead, already mentioned in Sacred Scripture: "Therefore Judas Maccabeus made atonement for the dead, that they might be delivered from their sin." From the beginning the Church has honoured the memory of the dead and offered prayers in suffrage for them, above all the Eucharistic sacrifice, so that, thus purified, they may attain the beatific vision of God. The Church also commends almsgiving, indulgences, and works of penance undertaken on behalf of the dead.

The teaching comes from 2 Maccabees, which along with other books, was excluded from the canon of scripture by the Protestants at the Reformation. The reasons for this exclusion are somewhat questionable as the books had been part of the Catholic and Eastern Orthodox Bibles for more than 1500 years at the time, and still are accepted by those churches today.

2 Maccabees 12:40-45 Then under the tunic of every one of the dead they found sacred tokens of the idols of Jamnia, which the law forbids the Jews to wear. And it became clear to all that this was why these men had fallen. [41] So they all blessed the ways of the Lord, the righteous Judge, who reveals the things that are hidden; [42] and they turned to prayer, beseeching that the sin which had been committed might be wholly blotted out. And the noble Judas exhorted the people to keep themselves free from sin, for they had seen with their own eyes what had happened because of the sin of those who had fallen. [43] He also took up a collection, man by man, to the amount of two thousand drachmas of silver, and sent it to Jerusalem to provide for a sin offering. In doing this he acted very well and honourably, taking account of the resurrection.

[44] For if he were not expecting that those who had fallen would rise again, it would have been superfluous and foolish to pray for the dead. [45] But if he was looking to the splendid reward that is laid up for those who fall asleep in godliness, it was a holy and pious thought. Therefore, he made atonement for the dead, that they might be delivered from their sin.

REVELATION GREATLY ENCOURAGED CONTEMPORARY CHRISTIANS WHO WERE UNDER PERSECUTION

John's visions would have encouraged the disciples of that time, who were struggling under heavy persecution. We do not know when Revelation was written, but the two most widely supported dates would be 95 AD or 65AD, with 95 being the clear favourite. If 65 was the date, it was at the high point of persecution under the infamous Nero, who soaked Christians in oil, hung them upside-down and set fire to them, using them as flaming torches in his garden. Or if 95, the Christians were under persecution by Roman Emperor Domitian, whose persecution was not quite as intense as that of Nero, but geographically it was much more widespread throughout the Empire, whereas Nero's persecution was more or less confined to Rome. Many surviving Christians of either date would have been mourning relatives and/or fellow Christians who had perished or been traumatised themselves by rejection or deprivation and this assurance of their raising to life would have greatly boosted their faith. Another idea in the text is the vindication of the Christians. The binding of Satan and their elevation showed the world that they had made the right decision to follow God. Comforting and encouraging them was probably one of John's foremost purposes in writing.

REFUSAL TO TAKE THE MARK OF THE BEAST.

There is an interesting allusion to the Old Testament in the mark on the forehead. The priests under the law of Moses had to take small copies of the scriptures in tiny containers called phylacteries and tie them on their foreheads and hands. This symbolized the law of God being obeyed with all their heart and soul (represented by the head) and strength (represented by the right hand). In Revelation 14:1 ...a Lamb stood on the mount Sion, and with him an hundred forty and four thousand, having his Father's name written in their foreheads. So the site of the seal or name of God on the forehead is significant. Satan's attempted goal is to substitute the seal of God with his mark, to claim the person for his own. To me this appears to be a much more satisfying and likely explanation than a literal planting of a chip or some other technological way which will bring people under the control of some worldwide government. Of course there could be some kind of literal fulfillment of the prophecy as well.

REV 20:5 THE FIRST RESURRECTION

But the rest of the dead did not live again until the thousand years were finished. This *is* the first resurrection.

Classical Premillennialism, insisting on a literal interpretation of Revelation, appeals to Revelation 20:4-6 to uphold its doctrine that there are two resurrections, one before the millennium for the righteous, and one after the millennium for the wicked. Dispensationalism compounds this, and postulates three resurrections: the above two plus the Pretrib rapture! Both these doctrines hold that the "first resurrection" must be a bodily resurrection for the believers (Scott, undated) (Larkin, Undated). Most evangelical / charismatic Christians I know take this passage, coupled with Revelation 13, to mean that at some point soon, the Antichrist will gain power over the whole world, and will enforce a literal mark / microchip / barcode or similar on everyone in the world who missed the rapture. They think that after 3 ½ or 7 years' appalling tribulation in the world, Christ will come a second time and the millennium, in the form of an actual rule from Jerusalem, will start. I guess if you have read this far into my book you are at least open to a different interpretation!

UNLIKELINESS OF THE LITERAL INTERPRETATION

We have discussed the idea that there is no Pretrib rapture and no literal 1000-year reign. It seems probable that that the "mark of the beast" from Revelation 13:15-18 has a symbolic interpretation. A little thought will show the literal explanation is not satisfactory anyway. Why should only those believers who have been beheaded get to reign with Christ? Turning our attention to our own day, that means the Egyptian Christians who were beheaded by IS militants recently qualify, but Indian Christians who were killed with machetes but not actually beheaded do not qualify? Or James and Paul who were beheaded qualify, but Peter who was crucified upside-down does not qualify? Additionally, can we believe that a global regime literally compelling every person to take a physical mark is what these passages of scripture imply? We know God could bring about such a thing if He wanted to, but surely a symbolic interpretation is more convincing and fits in better with chapter 20, and the whole Book of Revelation? A portion of scripture can be either symbolic or literal, but is unlikely to suddenly change mid-passage, then revert back again.

In my view, two clear facts refute the common literal view: (1) there is no clear scripture passage pointing to a 7-year period of great tribulation where the saints have been removed from the earth, as we shall see in chapter 18, and (2) as discussed earlier, everyone will be resurrected at the same time, the time of Christ's coming and the Judgment (Romans 2; John 5; John 6; Daniel 12:1-3; Mat 13; Mat 24; Mat 25 et al). We will continue to explore the metaphorical view and see how it enhances our understanding of the entire Bible.

REV 20:6 THE REWARD OF GOD'S FAITHFUL PEOPLE

Blessed and holy *is* he who has part in the first resurrection. Over such the second death has no power, but they shall be priests of God and of Christ and shall reign with Him a thousand years.

So far we have established that the first resurrection is indeed for the believers, though what is meant is not a bodily resurrection but a prior spiritual resurrection, where the believers' souls are resurrected to be with the Lord, and to join him in reigning and ruling. The thousand years, as we have discussed, stands for the church age, ending on the Day of the Lord, when we are bodily resurrected and given our glorious bodies.

But is the elevation to rule and reign with Jesus limited to saints who have died? Surely all believers experience reigning in life with Christ, are priests, and will not be under the power of the second death (incarceration in hell). All the way through the centuries some commentators, for example Augustine as we have seen, have held that the first resurrection does not only apply to saints who have died and been elevated to the intermediate state, but it applies to every born again Christian. The question is when does the believer start to reign with Christ? The scriptural answer to this question is surely at the moment of being born again, in other words, at the moment of conversion. God made us kings and priests and promised us deliverance from the second death from the beginning of our walk.

> Eph 2:6 (God) raised *us* up together, and made *us* sit together in the heavenly *places* in Christ Jesus...

> Rev 1:5-6 To Him who loved us and washed us from our sins in His own blood and has made us kings and priests to His God and Father, to Him be glory and dominion forever and ever. Amen.

So how can the living believer be included within the vision of the beheaded souls? True Christian faith involves death to ourselves. When we are baptized, we partake of Christ's death:

> Rom 6:3-4 ....as many of us as were baptized into Christ Jesus were baptized into His death? Therefore we were buried with Him through baptism into death, that just as Christ was raised from the dead by the glory of the Father, even so we also should walk in newness of life.

The passage goes on to explain that the same power which went into Jesus Christ to raise Him from the death, God the Father sends that same power into our bodies to live a new life. Paul characterized his Christian experience as follows:

Galatians 2:20 I have been crucified with Christ; it is no longer I who live, but Christ lives in me; and the life which I now live in the flesh I live by faith in the Son of God, who loved me and gave Himself for me.

Having given our lives to Christ, our lives now wholly belong to Him. This so radically changed Paul that he could write "it is no longer I that live, but Christ lives in me". Can we say "it's no longer I that live – but Christ lives in me"? This is the meaning of the Lordship of Jesus. He might be our saviour, but is He our Lord? The death here is death to ourselves, death to our selfishness, and death to our own plans. It is death to our old habits, addictions, and sins. It is discipline. It is sharing the Gospel when we do not feel like it. It is serving that person in need. It is giving our resources, time, money. It is standing when under persecution and, if need be, giving even our life if it is called for rather than betray our Lord. It may be a radical death. We follow the Master who, faced with the cross, said, "Father, if it is Your will, take this cup away from Me; nevertheless, not My will, but Yours, be done." Someone said, "He's either Lord of all, or He's not Lord at all." When I became a Christian, I understood that He gave everything to me; it was only right and proper that I should give everything to Him. We who have given ourselves to Him do not belong to ourselves anymore:

1 Cor 6:19-20 Or do you not know that your body is the temple of the Holy Spirit who is in you, whom you have from God, and you are not your own? For you were bought at a price; therefore glorify God in your body and in your spirit, which are God's.

So the beheaded soul can be seen as a radical image of the fully surrendered Christian as well as a Christian who has physically died.

Is there any conflict between the two interpretations? I cannot see any reason why there should be. There is one kind of authority promised to the believers now[21] and one kind of authority promise after death[22]. I cannot see any reason why both interpretations cannot be valid.

WHAT KIND OF AUTHORITY?

Would we expect to rise to political or economic power on the strength of these promises? No, Jesus said that the kingdom does not come with observation, and that His kingdom is not of this world. He had and has complete authority, but He was not made a king on this earth. He did not have political authority to overrule His crucifixion, even though He did not want to go to the cross and asked His Father if He could avoid it. His willingness eventually to go was a huge victory. His authority was authority over His own fears and temptations. Likewise, with Stephen in Acts 8. He had no influence, no troop of soldiers, that could save him from stoning. But he spoke with massive spiritual authority as he was surrendering his soul to the Father.

Jesus demonstrated spiritual authority when He cast out a demon or performed a miracle or won a victory over temptation. He also said:

> John 14:12-14 "Most assuredly, I say to you, he who believes in Me, the works that I do he will do also; and greater works than these he will do, because I go to My Father. And whatever you ask in My name, that I will do, that the Father may be glorified in the Son. If you ask anything in My name, I will do it.

As He enables and leads us, we should be casting out demons, healing the sick, performing miracles and seeing many come to Christ. In this way, we can reign with Him. We must both be under His authority and bringing His authority of the kingdom into every corner of the earth. Revelation 20 is God's word for us now – not for a future 1000-year reign. Now we are supposed to be demonstrating

---

[21] See for instance Luke 10:19

[22] See for instance Luke 22:30

that authority in the same way He did – by proclaiming the Gospel of the Kingdom, healing the sick and casting out demons (Luke 10:19; Mark 16:15-18). We should be walking by the Spirit and not the flesh, as Paul enjoined us in Romans 8. For someone who has started to walk in spiritual authority, life should look something like this:

> 2 Cor 10:3-5 For though we walk in the flesh, we do not war according to the flesh. ⁴ For the weapons of our warfare *are* not carnal but mighty in God for pulling down strongholds, ⁵ casting down arguments and every high thing that exalts itself against the knowledge of God, bringing every thought into captivity to the obedience of Christ...

This is what the Revelation 20 reign with Christ implies. After the Day of the Lord, in the new heavens and earth, we will have political authority under God; but not before.

REV 20:7 SATAN RELEASED FOR THE LAST BATTLE

Now when the thousand years have expired, Satan will be released from his prison

We are warned that before the end, Satan will be released. Paul has more didactic teaching. He warns us that just prior to Jesus' coming, we are to expect the "falling away", and Satan's agent will be revealed:

> 2 Thessalonians 2:1-4 Now, brethren, concerning the coming of our Lord Jesus Christ and our gathering together to Him, we ask you, ² not to be soon shaken in mind or troubled, either by spirit or by word or by letter, as if from us, as though the day of Christ had come. ³ Let no one deceive you by any means; for *that Day will not come* unless the falling away comes first, and the man of sin is revealed, the son of perdition, ⁴ who opposes and exalts himself above all that is called God

or that is worshiped, so that he sits as God in the temple of God, showing himself that he is God.

Is it possible we are now entering this time? We already have events, trends, and value-changes that nobody from a previous generation would have dreamed of. Globalism is now so advanced that no nation today can be examined in isolation. Global financial crises have taught us that a severe downturn can affect the whole world. Social experimentation and disregard or intentional overturning of Biblical principles has proceeded at a bewildering rate. We are all only too familiar with examples: same sex marriage; legalized prostitution; abortion practiced on a mega-factory scale; massive changes in values; militant promotion of transgenderism; nihilism; and a worldwide flood of pornography and violence via the internet. Twentieth century history has shown as never before how ideological conflict turns to military conflict, and today we have weapons with previously unimagined powers of destruction. At the same time, we see massive "falling away" by individuals, churches and denominations which once taught the truth but no longer do. Surely the signs of the final conflict with Satan and his agents are visible today. The "exalting of himself above all that is called God" and "showing himself that he is God" would appear to be the final "abomination of desolation standing in the holy place" of Daniel 9:27, Matthew 24:15, and Mark 13:14. There is no clear consensus among true Christians on the identity of the "man of sin". That he should be revealed suggests that consensus may be reached. Paul goes on to write about the restrainer. Ever since the letter was written, the debate has raged over his identity:

> 2 Thes 2:6-8 And now you know what is restraining, that he may be revealed in his own time. 7 For the mystery of lawlessness is already at work; only He who now restrains *will do so* until He is taken out of the way. 8 And then the lawless one will be revealed, whom the Lord will consume with the breath of His mouth and destroy with the brightness of His coming.

Could it be Jesus Himself who is the restrainer? We learned earlier from 2 Thessalonians 2:9-12 that it will be God's will for recalcitrant humanity to be deceived into coming under the rule of "the lawless one". We read here in Revelation 20:7 that Satan is "released from prison". Who apart from the Lord Himself could release Satan from prison?

POSITION OF THE CATHOLIC CHURCH

Interestingly, the position of the modern-day Catholic Church agrees with the scriptures we have studying much more closely than that of most other churches. The following is quoted from the Catechism of the Catholic Church. I have included at the end of this extract the scriptures it is based on.

The Church's ultimate trial

675 Before Christ's second coming the Church must pass through a final trial that will shake the faith of many believers (1). The persecution that accompanies her pilgrimage on earth (2) will unveil the "mystery of iniquity" in the form of a religious deception offering men an apparent solution to their problems at the price of apostasy from the truth. The supreme religious deception is that of the Antichrist, a pseudo-messianism by which man glorifies himself in place of God and of his Messiah come in the flesh. (3)

676 The Antichrist's deception already begins to take shape in the world every time the claim is made to realize within history that messianic hope which can only be realized beyond history through the eschatological judgement. The Church has rejected even modified forms of this falsification of the kingdom to come under the name of millenarianism, especially the "intrinsically perverse" political form of a secular messianism.

677 The Church will enter the glory of the kingdom only through this final Passover, when she will follow her Lord in his death and Resurrection. (4) The kingdom will be fulfilled, then, not by a historic triumph of the Church through a progressive ascendancy, but only by God's victory over the final unleashing of evil, which will cause his Bride to come down from heaven. (5) God's triumph over the revolt of evil will take the form of the Last Judgement after the final cosmic upheaval of this passing world.

1.   *Cf. Lk 18:8; Mt 24:12.*
2.   *Cf. Lk 21:12; Jn 15:19-20.*
3.   *Cf. 2 Th 2:4-12; I Th 5:2-3; 2 Jn 7; I Jn 2:1 8, 22*
4.   *Cf. Rev 19:1-9.*
5.   *Cf Rev 13:8; 20:7-10; 21:2-4.* (Catechism of the Catholic Church, 1997)

REV 20:8 DECEIVING THE NATIONS

......and will go out to deceive the nations which are in the four corners of the earth, Gog and Magog, to gather them together to battle, whose number *is* as the sand of the sea.

Now we can understand the import of Revelation 20:3 better. Satan was bound to prevent him deceiving the nations. At the end of time God will release him once more to again deceive the nations and lure the forces of evil to where God can destroy them. Our infinitely loving Father is giving humanity the wonderful opportunity to come to Him and be saved. Many have taken in the past this incredible offer of mercy, and all over the world today, millions are taking it and will continue to take it. But God cannot keep the gates of mercy open forever. There must come a time, like in the days of Noah, when the door must be shut and the flood of God's judgement comes on the Earth.

REV 20:9 SATAN'S ARMY DESTROYED BY GOD

They went up on the breadth of the earth and surrounded the camp of the saints and the beloved city. And fire came down from God out of heaven and devoured them.

Revelation 20:9 continues with the description of what theologians call the Last Battle, which, is the same as the battle described in Matthew 24, Mark 13, Luke 21, 2 Thessalonians 2, 2 Peter 3, and which has been alluded to earlier in Revelation, in Revelation 6:12-17, 11:18, 14:8-20, 16:1-16, and 19:11-21 (see table earlier in this chapter). It is on this point of the last battle that much of the Bible converges. Not only are the New Testament passages mentioned above focussed upon this battle. Also, the prophetic books of the Old Testament converge similarly. John's account of the battle in Revelation 20:7-10 is parallel especially to Ezekiel 38 and 39, which describe the same events.

> Ezek 38:16-17 It will be in the latter days that I will bring you against My land, so that the nations may know Me, when I am hallowed in you, O Gog, before their eyes." [17] Thus says the Lord God: "Are *you* he of whom I have spoken in former days by My servants the prophets of Israel, who prophesied for years in those days that I would bring you against them?

There is a difference. Whereas in Revelation we see it is Satan who deceives Gog and Magog into gathering all the nations together to fight Israel, in Ezekiel 38, it is God Himself who deceives them. This is not the contradiction it may first seem. We discussed when reading 2 Thessalonians 2:10-12 that, frighteningly for the unsaved, it will be God himself who deceives those who did not receive the love of the truth. We must conclude that God does this by releasing Satan once again to deceive the nations of the world as stated in revelation 20:7-8

Incidentally, the fact of the parallel accounts of the last battle is more persuasive evidence for Amil, as Amil writer Sam Storms notes: " The Amillennial reading of Revelation alone makes sense of the obvious parallel between the war of Revelation 16, 19, and 20. This parallel is reinforced when we note that the imagery in Ezekiel 39 related to Gog and Magog is used to describe both the battle in Revelation 19:17-21 and the battle in Revelation 20:7-10. Clearly, these are one and the same battle, known as Armageddon." (Storms, 2014)

Like everything else in the Book of Revelation, the account of the last battle, with all Gog's armies camped around Jerusalem, is probably a metaphor, though I believe there will be some literal fulfilment of prophecy at the same time. After all, surely all the armies of the world, along with their modern weapons, navies, and air forces, would not have room to fight together in the small state of Israel. It seems much more likely that the real last battle will be waged everywhere on earth, and once again, metaphor is being used to draw a picture which is far beyond the wildest imagination of the Bible writers.

It is not limited to military fighting. All the significant wars in the world's history have started not by fighting with weapons but fighting with words. If we think of the Second World war, the worst conflict to date in the world history, it all started with ideas and words. In today's world there are so many different ideologies, people seeking for power and philosophies. Surely these will ultimately collide, and the last battle will really start.

This picture from Revelation, gives a glimpse of things to come after the war, and, it would seem, after the universal judgment. We have already considered part of this passage, but now we will look at a longer extract:

> Rev 7:9-12 After these things I looked, and behold, a great multitude which no one could number, of all nations, tribes, peoples, and tongues, standing before the throne and before the Lamb, clothed with white robes, with palm branches in their hands, [10] and crying out with a loud voice, saying, "Salvation *belongs* to our God who sits on the throne, and to the Lamb!" [11] All the angels stood around the throne and the elders and the four living creatures, and fell on their faces before the throne and worshiped God, [12] saying:

> "Amen! Blessing and glory and wisdom,
> Thanksgiving and honour and power and might,
> *Be* to our God forever and ever. Amen."

We all need to examine ourselves and check that we are indeed walking in the faith that was once delivered to the saints of old. Then, if we are still alive on earth at the time of this terrible conflict, we will know that we are on God's side, and that by the Holy Spirit, He will make a way for us.

REV 20:10 ETERNAL PUNISHMENT FOR THE DEVIL, THE BEAST, AND THE FALSE PROPHET

The devil, who deceived them, was cast into the lake of fire and brimstone where the beast and the false prophet *are*. And they will be tormented day and night forever and ever.

We will arrive at last at God's final victory, which will be, in the event, so easy. The beast and the false prophet are metaphors for Satan's agents in the world from Revelation chapters 13 and 17. All commentators of whatever millennial persuasion are agreed that their portraits are metaphorical. This being so, it is difficult to see why some are so adamant that the thousand-year reign is literal.

WHY DOES REVELATION USE THESE SYMBOLS?

The question arises why John used all these mysterious symbols. There is a long tradition in the Bible of non-literal communication of important events or truths in mysterious visions, metaphorical actions and, particularly in Jesus' case, parables. Examples include Hosea, who was told by God to marry a prostitute as a prophetic action to convey to Israel the depth of its sin. Isaiah was another prophet who was given many riddles and mysterious oracles. When he was first called by God, God had these words for him:

> Isa 6:9-10 "Go, and tell this people:
>
> 'Keep on hearing, but do not understand;
> Keep on seeing, but do not perceive.'
> [10] "Make the heart of this people dull,
> And their ears heavy,
> And shut their eyes;
> Lest they see with their eyes,
> And hear with their ears,
> And understand with their heart,
> And return and be healed."

It seems that the Israelites had carried their depravity too far to be able to simply respond to didactic teaching. They would not have listened anyway.

JESUS' USE OF MYSTERIOUS AND METAPHORIC TEACHING

It was the same in Jesus' own day. In fact, He quoted these exact words from Isaiah when his disciples asked why He taught in mysterious parables, and not in plain speech. Jesus answered them:

Mat 13:11-14 He answered and said to them, "Because it has been given to you to know the mysteries of the kingdom of heaven, but to them it has not been given. [12] For whoever has, to him more will be given, and he will have abundance; but whoever does not have, even what he has will be taken away from him. [13] Therefore I speak to them in parables, because seeing they do not see, and hearing they do not hear, nor do they understand. [14] And in them the prophecy of Isaiah is fulfilled....

The response to such teaching was always that: the majority would reject; some who had been following God but had fallen away would be renewed to repentance and return to the ways of the Lord; and some who were non-believers but with a sincere hunger for truth would be converted.

JOHN'S USE OF MYSTERY AND METAPHOR IN REVELATION

John similarly used metaphor, mystery, and symbolism in his teaching in Revelation. The first point to note is that contrary to our literalist friends' expectations, as pointed out above, this is very normal in the Bible. It is true that much of the Bible is meant to be taken literally and historically. For instance, without the historical fact of Jesus being raised from the dead, we would have nothing of value. As declared by Paul:

Now if Christ is preached that He has been raised from the dead, how do some among you say that there is no resurrection of the dead?

[13] But if there is no resurrection of the dead, then Christ is not risen. [14] And if Christ is not risen, then our preaching *is* empty, and your faith *is* also empty.

Our Christian faith is based, at its most fundamental, on the historical fact of the resurrection of Jesus Christ. If the resurrection were not historically and literally true, we would have nothing of value at all. But that does not change the fact that elsewhere in the Book of Books, there is much beautiful and breath-taking poetry and metaphor.

THE LAST BATTLE IS PROPHESIED MANY TIMES IN THE OLD TESTAMENT.

The last battle is prophesied also in the Old Testament many times. But we do not read about the details pertaining to Christ's return until the New Testament. The Book of Revelation itself goes on to describe the last judgment. But we will leave Revelation for a while and take a detour to discover the Old Testament foundations of the New Testament.

Please note: A study guide for this book, The New Testament End Time Study Guide, is available through the 222 Foundation website, https://222foundation.net. The interpretation of the Book of Revelation may be studied in more detail using the guide.

Chapter Seventeen

THE OLD TESTAMENT – FOUNDATION OF THE NEW

✛ ✛ ✛

Many people are not aware of the extent to which the Old Testament provides a foundation for the New. For example, the events portrayed by John in Revelation 20:7-10, which we have just discussed, were prophesied in more detail by Ezekiel more than five hundred years previously:

Eze 38: 18-23 "And it will come to pass at the same time, when Gog comes against the land of Israel," says the Lord God, "that My fury will show in My face. For in My jealousy and in the fire of My wrath I have spoken: 'Surely in that day there shall be a great earthquake in the land of Israel, so that the fish of the sea, the birds of the heavens, the beasts of the field, all creeping things that creep on the earth, and all men who are on the face of the earth shall shake at My presence. The mountains shall be thrown down, the steep places shall fall, and every wall shall fall to the ground.' I will call for a sword against Gog throughout all My mountains," says the Lord God. "Every man's sword will be against his brother. And I will bring him to judgment with pestilence and bloodshed; I will rain down on him, on his troops, and on the many peoples who are with him, flooding rain, great hailstones, fire, and brimstone. Thus, I will magnify Myself and sanctify Myself, and I will be known in the eyes of many nations. Then they shall know that I am the Lord.'"

John, and those he was writing for, of course, would have been well familiar with the Book of Ezekiel. It would be inconceivable that the Gog of Revelation should be a different Gog from Ezekiel's Gog. Both books portray the time of the end, which is the time for the last battle and the restoration of Israel.

Eze 39:22 So the house of Israel shall know that I am the Lord their God from that day forward.

"From that day forward" means that after the battle, the survivors of Israel will come into a permanent new state of knowing the Lord.

Before we study this, we should look at some more of the Old Testament references to the end times, starting from the earliest writings in the Bible, where we can see the progressive growth of revelation among the Bible writers. More and more information about the Day of the Lord and attendant events is given as we read through the Old Testament. There will not be enough space in this book to give a comprehensive coverage of the Old Testament references, but for now a selection of themes will suffice.

JOB – THE EVERLASTING GOSPEL

The first writer is Job, whose book is considered to be the oldest book in the Bible. The passage below is breath-taking. He lived long before any preaching of the Gospel of Christ, even before any of the teachings of Moses, given for Israel. Scholars think he may have been a contemporary of Abraham. As you read the passage, consider what Job knew of the Gospel.

> Job 19:23-29 Oh, that my words were written!
> Oh, that they were inscribed in a book!
> [24] That they were engraved on a rock
> With an iron pen and lead, forever!
> [25] For I know *that* my Redeemer lives,

And He shall stand at last on the earth;

[26] And after my skin is destroyed, this *I know,*
That in my flesh I shall see God,
[27] Whom I shall see for myself,
And my eyes shall behold, and not another.
How my heart yearns within me!
[28] If you should say, 'How shall we persecute him?'—
Since the root of the matter is found in me,
[29] Be afraid of the sword for yourselves;
For wrath *brings* the punishment of the sword,
That you may know *there is* a judgment."

God poured His favour on this man. A little reflection will show that he had knowledge of all the following:

1. He was aware that what he knew of eternal life was incredibly significant and important, and wanted to write it in lead on rock with an iron pen.
2. He had more than a knowledge of God; he understood the concept of a redeemer, so he was close to knowing Jesus, or had some intuitive knowledge about Him.
3. He knew the Redeemer would come to earth at the end of the age.
4. He knew his body would rot in the ground, but he was also confident that he would be resurrected bodily and see God, as he was yearning.
5. He knew the wrath of God is directed towards those who persecute His people, and specifically that it would be directed to his own tormentors.
6. There is a suggestion that he knew about the last judgment.
7. He was conscious and intentional about being a servant of God.

This is in essence the everlasting Gospel (see Revelation 14:6). Most people believe that the first Gospel was preached by John the Baptist and Jesus – but they were not the first. It was preached by Job. The

Gospel has been in the Bible from the beginning, not fully explained in clarity as today, but in an earlier, less developed form, as it was at an earlier stage in God's revelation of truth to mankind. The essence is nevertheless the same. "I know that my Redeemer lives."

MOSES: CONFLICT BETWEEN JESUS AND SATAN

Moses, in Genesis, alludes to the conflict between Jesus and Satan, and so sets the scene for the greatest conflict of the age:

Gen 3:15 And I will put enmity between you and the woman, and between your seed and her Seed; he shall bruise your head, and you shall bruise His heel."

Exodus 32 records some of Moses' prayer to the Lord. Moses knew about the judgment:

Exo 32:31 If I whet My glittering sword,
And My hand takes hold on judgment,
I will render vengeance to My enemies.

God is speaking of His role of "rendering vengeance" on His enemies. In the Old Testament His enemies were the peoples who attacked His people, Israel. Also, those from His own people who broke His laws became enemies. These two types symbolise people who have never known the Lord, and people who are backslidden, having believed in the Lord but changed their minds and opposed Him. He also knew about the Book of Life, which is referred to on various occasions in the Bible, as demonstrated by this verse:

Exo 32:32-33 .... if You will forgive their sin—but if not, I pray, blot me out of Your book which You have written. And the Lord said to Moses, "Whoever has sinned against Me, I will blot him out of My book."

Moses laid the foundation of knowledge of the Book of Life, which eventually will be used in the final judgment.

Moses foresaw that Israel would backslide from obedience to the Lord. He could see the terrible future in front of them, coming under the judgment of the Lord, being overrun by merciless enemies, and being scattered among the nations of the world into bitter exile. But he also foresaw the great regathering of the tribes of Israel that was to become the most abiding theme of the prophets:

Exo 30:1-6; 9-10; "Now it shall come to pass, when all these things come upon you, the blessing and the curse which I have set before you, and you call *them* to mind among all the nations where the Lord your God drives you, [2] and you return to the Lord your God and obey His voice, according to all that I command you today, you and your children, with all your heart and with all your soul, [3] that the Lord your God will bring you back from captivity, and have compassion on you, and gather you again from all the nations where the Lord your God has scattered you. [4] If *any* of you are driven out to the farthest *parts* under heaven, from there the Lord your God will gather you, and from there He will bring you. [5] Then the Lord your God will bring you to the land which your fathers possessed, and you shall possess it. He will prosper you and multiply you more than your fathers. [6] And the Lord your God will circumcise your heart and the heart of your descendants, to love the Lord your God with all your heart and with all your soul, that you may live."

The incredible promise here is that the Lord would "circumcise their heart" and change their disposition to serve Him if they would start by turning to Him. The passage goes on to emphasise the magnificence of the promises of God, and the dire nature of the punishment to be meted out in the case of disobedience. To our ears today this at first seems unjustified until we consider the awe of God's promise and the appalling ingratitude of rejecting such promises. It cannot be that rejection of God's promises by His created beings should be seen as an inconsequential thing. God Himself must exalt His own honour for the benefit of the whole universe. The condition for blessing? Turning to Him with our whole heart and soul

For the Lord will again rejoice over you for good as He rejoiced over your fathers, [10] if you obey the voice of the Lord your God, to keep His commandments and His statutes which are written in this Book of the Law, *and* if you turn to the Lord your God with all your heart and with all your soul."

The circumcision of the heart was later picked up as a theme by Paul in Romans 2:

Rom 2:28-29 ....or he is not a Jew who *is one* outwardly, nor *is* circumcision that which *is* outward in the flesh; [29] but *he is* a Jew who *is one* inwardly; and circumcision *is that* of the heart, in the Spirit, not in the letter; whose praise *is* not from men but from God.

God has always desired a people who would not just obey Him legalistically according to a set of rules, but who would enter into a loving, intimate relationship with Him.

DAVID – REVELATION FROM THE PSALMS

Psa110:5-6 The Lord shall execute kings **in the day of His wrath.** He shall judge among the nations...

Psalm 110 is one of a number of references where David shows that he had revelation of the judgment at the end of the age. Paul's writing in Romans 2 refers to the day of the Lord as the day of wrath, a concept which would have been well familiar to the early Christians and the Jews. The Gospel writers referred to both Jesus and John warning of the "wrath to come".

THE "WRITING PROPHETS"

Almost all the writing prophets had something to say about the end times. Usually, they started by prophesying about an issue in their own time, but the Holy Spirit took them into glimpses of the universal and eternal. For example, Amos chastises Israel for their sins, and prophesies they will go into captivity (e.g. Amos 5:3, 5:27, 6:8, 7:11). This was fulfilled in 722 BC when Assyria conquered Israel and deported the population to Assyria, as described in 2 Kings 17. But at times in his prophetic discourse Amos switches to prophetic revelations which apply to the end of the age:

Amos 8:9 And it shall come to pass in that day," says the Lord God, "That I will make the sun go down at noon and I will darken the earth in broad daylight;

Amos here is introducing a prophetic theme which will be picked up by later prophets and in due course by Matthew and John in the New Testament:

Isa 13:10 For the stars of heaven and their constellations
Will not give their light;
The sun will be darkened in its going forth,
And the moon will not cause its light to shine.

Isa 24:23 Then the moon will be disgraced
And the sun ashamed;
For the Lord of hosts will reign
On Mount Zion and in Jerusalem
And before His elders, gloriously.

We know that Isaiah is speaking of the end time because it is from this time that the Lord will reign in Jerusalem. The Jerusalem spoken of here is not the earthly Jerusalem but the heavenly Jerusalem. This must be the case because the old earth, including the present Jerusalem, will be destroyed on the coming of Jesus when He returns on the Day of the Lord (see 2 Peter 3:10).

Eze 32:7-8 When I put out your light,
I will cover the heavens, and make its stars dark;
I will cover the sun with a cloud,
And the moon shall not give her light.
8 All the bright lights of the heavens I will make dark
over you,
And bring darkness upon your land,"
Says the Lord God.

Zep 1:14-16 The great day of the Lord *is* near;
It is near and hastens quickly.
The noise of the day of the Lord is bitter;
There the mighty men shall cry out.
15 That day *is* a day of wrath,
A day of trouble and distress,
A day of devastation and desolation,
A day of darkness and gloominess,
A day of clouds and thick darkness,

¹⁶ A day of trumpet and alarm
Against the fortified cities
And against the high towers.

The trumpet in Zephaniah recalls the trumpet of Matthew 24 and other verses.

Mat 24:29 "Immediately after the tribulation of those days the sun will be darkened, and the moon will not give its light; the stars will fall from heaven, and the powers of the heavens will be shaken.

Rev 6:12-13 I looked when He opened the sixth seal, and behold, there was a great earthquake; and the sun became black as sackcloth of hair, and the moon became like blood. ¹³ And the stars of heaven fell to the earth, as a fig tree drops its late figs when it is shaken by a mighty wind.

Modern man knows that when the stars drop out of the sky, we are looking at the destruction of the present universe. Is this a warning that this is going to happen in our time? Many Biblical prophecies have found literal fulfilment over the centuries, especially when Jesus was living out His earthly ministry. Many found metaphorical or symbolic fulfilment as we saw when we studied the Book of Revelation. Some found both literal and symbolic fulfilment, and many are still waiting for fulfilment today. Many prophecies began or picked up a theme that was later taken up and expanded by later prophets or the New Testament writers, as in the theme of the sun becoming dark above.

THE DAYS SPOKEN OF BY PROPHETS AND NEW TESTAMENT WRITERS

How can we be sure that the "Day of the Lord" spoken of by the prophets is the same as the "Day of the Lord" spoken of by the New Testament writers? It is apparent that the days were the same. It is clear in many passages that the events of Jesus' time were in fulfilment of the Old Testament prophets' words. Here are some verses:

Mat 26:56 But all this was done that the Scriptures of the prophets might be fulfilled."

Luk 24:25-27 Then He said to them, "O foolish ones, and slow of heart to believe in all that the prophets have spoken! 26 Ought not the Christ to have suffered these things and to enter into His glory?" 27 And beginning at Moses and all the Prophets, He expounded to them in all the Scriptures the things concerning Himself.

Not only did the prophets reveal many things about Jesus' earthly ministry, but they also revealed much about the end of the age, which complements the teaching of the New Testament on this topic. The following passage from Acts specifically endorses the teaching of the prophets on the "restoration of all things", one important feature of the end of the age.

Acts 3:21 ...whom heaven must receive until the times of restoration of all things, which God has spoken by the mouth of all His holy prophets since the world began.

That the two testaments are in harmony is affirmed by Peter, who places the holy prophets and the apostles of Jesus on the same level of authority:

2 Pet 3:2 ...that you may be mindful of the words which were spoken before by the holy prophets, and of the commandment of us, the apostles of the Lord and Saviour...

If any doubt remains on this point, the following passage from Revelation confirms that the judgment of the dead, and rewards given to the righteous of both Testaments, happen at the same time – because it all happens at ONE time!

Rev 11:18 The nations were angry, and Your wrath has come, And the time of the dead, that they should be judged, and that You should reward Your servants the prophets and the saints, and those who fear Your name, small and great, and should destroy those who destroy the earth."

ETHNIC OR SPIRITUAL ISRAEL?

Our interpretation of the prophecies of the kingdom of God will be quite different according to whether we are considering ethnic Israel of today, or "spiritual" Israel – which is the believers in Christ (see Galatians 6:16), whether ethnic Jews or gentiles. In the case of ethnic Israel, there have been some remarkable prophetic fulfilments in a literal sense. An important theme in prophecy is the re-gathering of scattered ethnic Israel[23]. Against all expectation, the Jewish State of Israel literally became a nation in one day in 1948. Many have considered this a fulfilment of the prophecy of Isaiah 66:8:

> Shall the earth be made to give birth in one day? Or shall a nation be born at once? For as soon as Zion was in labour, she gave birth to her children.

The gathering and settling in the State of Israel of Jews from all over the world is no doubt at least a step on the way to physical fulfilment of the prophecies of the regathering of the tribes of Israel and suggests the closeness of the Day of the Lord (Rom 11:13-32). We must, however, be aware that most Jews in our time firmly reject the Gospel, so while they are being physically regathered in the territory of Israel, they are not fulfilling the spiritual part of the prophecy.

It is noteworthy that the Old Testament prophesies were always applied to the Church by the New Testament writers, and they were applied spiritually, or metaphorically. For example, the following passage shows James quoting from Amos 9:11-12 during the Jerusalem Council recorded in Acts 15. First Barnabas and Paul give a report of their successful mission among the Gentiles. Observe how James then uses the Amos passage to draw a conclusion on how the church should respond.

Act 15:12-17 All the multitude kept silent and listened to Barnabas and Paul declaring how many miracles and wonders God had worked through them among the Gentiles. [13] And after they had become silent, James answered, saying, "Men *and* brethren, listen to me: [14] Simon has declared how God at the first visited the Gentiles to take out of them a people for His name. [15] And with this the words of the prophets agree, just as it is written:

[16] 'After this I will return

---

[23] See for example Isa 11:11-12; Jer 31:38-40; Eze 37:11-12, 14, 21-22, 25; Hos 2:2-7; 3:5; Zec 10:8-10

And will rebuild the tabernacle of David, which has
fallen down;
I will rebuild its ruins,
And I will set it up;
[17] So that the rest of mankind may seek the Lord,
Even all the Gentiles who are called by My name,
Says the Lord who does all these things.'

When Amos originally penned this prophecy, he probably
thought Israel would one day become once again militarily powerful
and would literally build David's tabernacle, an ornate tent-like
structure, for worship. But as interpreted by James under the guidance
of the Holy Spirit, such a physical structure was not envisioned by
the prophecy at all. The fulfilment spoke of all mankind coming to
the knowledge of God, in great jubilation. The tabernacle itself can
be thought of as Jesus Himself, or as the Gospel whereby all people
are led by God to know Him. The act of building the tabernacle
is the work of preaching the Gospel, as Barnabas and Paul did at
that time, and as so many inspired men and women do in our day,
resulting in the salvation of millions. The fulfilment of the prophecy
is therefore entirely metaphorical – in the same way as I have urged
the thousand year millennial reign in Revelation 20 be interpreted.
To insist on a literal fulfilment would do no service to the Word
of God. Biblical literalism brings many problems to interpretation
which are easily solved when we accept the metaphorical nature of
many prophecies.

THE DEFEAT OF DEATH

One reassuring theme of the prophets and apostles, a thread which runs
through the Old and New Testaments, is the defeat of death. Death will
be annihilated at the end of the Last Battle: the last enemy of mankind
will be destroyed. Death, along with Satan, will be committed to the
lake of fire.

1Cor 15:20-Then comes the end, when He delivers the kingdom to
God the Father, when He puts an end to all rule and all authority and

power. For He must reign till He has put all enemies under His feet. The last enemy that will be destroyed is death.

Paul exulted in the defeat of death:

1 Cor 15:54-55 "Death has been swallowed up in victory." [55] "Where, O death, is your victory? Where, O death, is your sting?"

He was quoting directly from Isaiah, who wrote about 700 years earlier:

Isaiah 25:8 He will swallow up death forever,

It seems Isaiah himself drew on the probably earlier revelation of Hosea:

Hos 13:14 O Grave, I will be your destruction!

Chapter Eighteen

DANIEL'S 70 "SEVENS" PROPHECY

✛ ✛ ✛

I will devote a chapter to this prophecy because, when understood, it presents an inspiring picture, as well as a warning of the events of the end time. It is also very controversial. Many interpretations have been proposed over the centuries.

It was around 540 B.C. The period of Judah's enforced exile was almost completed. Daniel noticed Jeremiah's prophecy that God would keep Jerusalem desolate for 70 years (2 Chron 36:21; Jer 25:11-12; Jer 29:10-11; Dan 9:2), after which He would allow the restoration of the city. He was confessing to God the sins of the nation and praying fervently for the promised restoration of Judah when the angel Gabriel came to him with this prophecy, which amounts to a mysterious promise that God would grant full restoration of His people within "70 sevens". We will summarise the distinctives of three different approaches to understand this prophecy: the Traditional View (TV); the Dispensationalist view (DV); and what I have called the Davis / Leupold/ Amil view (AV). Note that many commentators have written about this prophecy. There are many differences of detail within these broad categories.

THE PROPHECY

Dan 9:24 (NIV) "70 'sevens' are decreed for your people and your holy city to finish transgression, to put an end to sin, to atone for wickedness, to bring in everlasting righteousness, to seal up vision and prophecy, and to anoint the Most Holy Place.

9:25 "Know and understand this: From the time the word goes out to restore and rebuild Jerusalem until the Anointed One, the ruler, comes, there will be 7 'sevens,' and 62 'sevens.' It will be rebuilt with streets and a trench, but in times of trouble.

9:26 After the sixty-two 'sevens,' the Anointed One will be put to death and will have nothing. The people of the ruler who will come will destroy the city and the sanctuary. The end will come like a flood: War will continue until the end, and desolations have been decreed.

9:27 He will confirm a covenant with many for one 'seven.' In the middle of the 'seven' he will put an end to sacrifice and offering. And at the temple he will set up an abomination that causes desolation, until the end that is decreed is poured out on him."

OVERVIEW (DAN 9:24)

All commentators agree that the six outcomes of 9:24 would be the accomplishments of Christ in His earthly ministry to bring God's blessing and restoration on His people. The Traditional view (TV) and the Amillennial view (AV) would have in mind that God's people for whom these blessings were reserved would be the people of faith, the church. The Dispensationalist view (DV) is that this prophecy relates to the Jews only, who are held by DV to have their own special and independent destiny, as we saw in Chapter 14.

Let's have a look at the six outcomes of 9:24. Leupold writes, "The six statements...cover the sum total of the purposes of God with man."

To finish transgression – this outcome has the sense that sin is going to come under control and will no longer flourish.

To put an end to sin – here the sin of the wicked is securely locked away.

To atone for wickedness – even godly people sin unintentionally, and these sins are atoned for under this outcome, and the sinner reconciled to God.

To bring in everlasting righteousness – this is the imputed righteousness of Jesus, won at the cross.

To seal up vision and prophecy – realised prophecy will be assigned to the category of "no longer needed" and sealed up.

To anoint the Most Holy Place – a statement that implies God's holy presence will be manifested in all eternity.

Dan 9:24, then, is describing the blessing of God, and promising it to Daniel and "his people". The 70 "sevens" of the NIV translation represent the period during which the prophesied actions will take place. Most translations render the Hebrew word *sabu im* as "weeks", so the prophecy is often referred to as Daniel's 70 week prophecy. Many of the Traditional view (TV) and of the Dispensational view (DV) writers apply what is known as the "day/year" principle to determine the length of this period of time. Under this principle, a day in prophetic writing is held to represent a year of time. A week consists of 7 days, and so represents 7 years. According to this school of thought, in Dan 9:24, the 70 weeks of prophetic time represents 490 years.

TRADITIONAL VIEW (TV)

Supporters include Julius Africanus (3rd century, cited by Schaff, 1893); many interpreters from the Reformation era; I Duguid; E Hengstenberg; K Riddlebarger.

TV identifies the six outcomes of 9:24 as the benefits won by Christ for all who believe. It adds the 7 weeks (sevens) of Dan 9:25 (when Nehemiah was leading the rebuilding of Jerusalem), and the 62 weeks mentioned in Dan 9:25 and Dan 9:26, to make a period of 483 years. In 9:25 we learn that the period ends at the coming of Christ (the "Anointed One"). In 9:26 the Anointed One is put to death, which is taken to be Jesus' death on the cross. "The people of the ruler that will come" are taken to be the Roman legions under Titus in 70 A.D. who destroyed the city.

The most obvious distinctive of the TV is the way that it interprets the 70th week. The "He" of the beginning of the verse who "confirms the covenant with many" is held to be the Messiah, and the covenant is the New Covenant. He is cut off in the middle of the week (i.e. after 3 ½ years); "He will put an end to sacrifice and offering" refers to Jesus' ending of the Jewish Levitical sacrifices, according to TV. From now on He is our perfect sacrifice. The last half of the 70th week is sometimes taken to be the ministry of the Holy Spirit.

The last sentence of 9:27 in the NIV does not fit the TV. TV would challenge the translation. Here is the NKJV, which could be used instead: "And on the wing of abominations shall be one who makes desolate, even until the consummation, which is determined, is poured out on the desolate."

DISPENSATIONAL VIEW (DV)

Supporters include e.g. C Scofield; H Lindsay, C Misler; (McArthur, 1969); D Jeremiah; T Ice.

DV largely follows TV for Dan 9:24-26 with some significant exceptions, the most important of which is that TV looks to see the prophecy fulfilled in people of faith (i.e., "the Israel of God", Gal 6:16) whereas DV looks for fulfilment in ethnic Israel. Secondly, DV lays more emphasis on the day/year principle than TV.

In Dan 9:27, DV diverges completely. DV holds that the 70th week did not take place at the time of Christ's earthly ministry, but rather it was projected forward in time, and has still not occurred after 2000 years. It is held to be a 7-year period in the future, when the alleged end time events that we examined in Chapters 13 and 14 are due to take place, i.e. the rapture; the temple rebuilt; and the rise of Antichrist. According to DV the Antichrist is "he who will confirm a covenant with many". According to the theory, this covenant will be made by the Antichrist with the Jews during the 70th week, allowing them to worship in the temple. The 70th week is the much talked about "7-year tribulation". The Antichrist will break the covenant and forbid the worship halfway through the 7-year period, defiling the temple with gross blasphemy, and leading to major worldwide war. Tribulation will be intensified for 3 ½ years. The Jews will suffer terribly, but at the end of the 3 ½ years Jesus will return and annihilate Antichrist and his armies. The remaining Jews will convert and will receive Jesus as Lord. They will, with Jesus, reign in a glorious millennial kingdom.

PROBLEMS WITH THE DISPENSATIONALIST SYSTEM.

1. It seems to me that the day/year principle is problematic. The question for the interpreter is to find a starting point for the prophetic time, and a way of rendering the 70 "sevens", which takes the reader to some appropriate time in the ministry of Jesus. One common approach is to take Artaxerxes' letter to Nehemiah giving him permission to uplift supplies for Jerusalem (Neh 2:7-9; 445 B.C.). If the interpreter uses lunar years in the calculation it does "work". The reader will come to Jesus in 30 A.D. But is Neh 2 the right place to start? The decree of Cyrus (Ezra 1:2-4, 538 B.C.) is the real command to rebuild the city and fits the prophecy much better. This was the turning point for Jerusalem. The Neh 2 letter was only an order for provisions.

2. It is difficult to agree with the rationale for the day / year correspondence. It is usually based on Ezekiel 4:5-6 and/or Num 14:34. These scriptures are in a totally different context and have little or nothing to say about a day / year principle in Daniel.

3. There is nothing pointing to it in Daniel 9 anyway. The Hebrew *sabu im* does not mean weeks. It means "sevens".

4. There is no evidence in the text for the rapture, the gap of 2,000 or more years in between the 69th and the 70th "seven", or the covenant between Antichrist and the Jews.

5. The time covered by the prophecy only stretches to the beginning of a millennium, not to the fullness of God's kingdom, which will last until eternity.

6. It invents a separate eternal destiny for Jewish people, in contradiction to Ephesians 2.

LEUPOLD/DAVIS AMIL VIEW

Supporters include C F Keil; (Leupold, 1969); (Davis, 2014); T Klifoth; G Beale.

Kyle, in the 19th century, grew dissatisfied with both the Traditional and Dispensationalist views, and wrote a commentary which was a forerunner of this interpretation. Since his time others, notably Leupold, have worked on their own commentaries within this genre. In studying this interpretation, we will bear in mind some of what we learned while studying Revelation in Chapter 16 about metaphor, which is commonly used in scripture, and enables us to derive the full meaning of the text. We also need to compare scripture with scripture to get a comprehensive picture.

The numbers do not represent calendar days, weeks or years. They are idealistic numbers and further amplify the meaning of the text. The 70 "sevens" are equivalent to 7x7x10, which represents perfect completeness (see Mat 18:22). The message is that the six promised outcomes of 9:24 will have been perfectly accomplished by God at the consummation, i.e. after the final resurrection/judgment, and the time covered by the prophecy reaches that point at the end of the age.

This means that the period set aside for the prophecy is not merely the time between Daniel's day and Jesus' earthly ministry, but rather it extends all the way in time to His return in glory. This is much more in tune with the whole Book of Daniel. The first 7 "sevens" are not weeks of years, but rather an era of salvation history, at the close of which Jesus starts His earthly ministry. The 62 sevens span the era during which He builds His church. The rebuilding with a wall and moat is a metaphor for restoring the kingdom of God, with defences provided by God for its citizens. Dates are not relevant to AV. We do not know the date of His return anyway.

Dan 9:26 pictures a period where the divine mission appears to have failed. This is not about the death of Jesus on the cross. This "Anointed One" "will have nothing" after his execution. He cannot be representative of Jesus because Jesus was given everything after His mighty victory on the cross. He was raised up to be seated on the eternal throne at the right hand of God. Rather, this second mentioned messiah has been interpreted to be the community of anointed servants of God, akin to the two witnesses of Rev 11:3-12, who will be killed by the beast while speaking out God's word. We are told of this reverse in 2 Thes 2:1-12.

"The people of the ruler who will come" are not the legions of Titus. They are the people of the Antichrist. They are the people who are portrayed in Revelation, who worship the beast and take his mark. The Antichrist will "confirm a covenant with many" – this is interpreted as a bond between him and his supporters. Antichrist-type historical figures have exercised a hero-worship type relationship with their followers. Portrayed in the prophecy is the final Antichrist but there have been Antichrist figures throughout history motivated by the same spirit. Hitler, Napoleon, Genghis Khan and Alexander the Great are all examples, modern day and ancient, of dictatorial leaders who built a strong bond even to the extent of worship, with their followers, and especially with their armies. The Roman emperors at the time of Christ and the early church did the same, establishing emperor cults which the masses had to bow down to or die.

Ultimately he will ban all worship. We foresee a time when public worship is impossible, and Christians will be forced to worship "underground". Who knows what the "abomination that causes desolation" will be? There are many possibilities, but I'm sure it will not only take place at a Jewish temple in Jerusalem but will be something which will affect people all over the world. He will turn against God's people, but Christ will finally rescue his people and annihilate him and his armies. "The end that is decreed will indeed be poured out on him.

So, as we can see, this prophecy brings us right to the end of the age, where the universal judgment and God's eternal rewards await us all.

Please note: A study guide for this book, The New Testament End Time Study Guide, is available from the 222 Foundation website, https://222foundation.net. Daniel's 70 "sevens" prophecy may be studied in more detail using the guide.

Chapter Nineteen

THE FINAL JUDGMENT

✝ ✝ ✝

THE GREAT WHITE THRONE JUDGMENT

So, having journeyed through many prophecies, having thought many thoughts, we have arrived at the finale of the age, the Judgment. Let's look at it again, this time in more depth, and discuss some aspects of it. The extended descriptions of the judgment specifically in the New Testament are those by Matthew (Mathew 25), Paul (Romans 2) and John (Rev 20:11-15). The first two we have examined already. Here we return to the Book of Revelation and John's description. We pick up again where we left off before – at Revelation 20:11.

Rev 20:11-15 Then I saw a great white throne and Him who sat on it, from whose face the earth and the heaven fled away. And there was found no place for them. [12] And I saw the dead, small and great, standing before God, and books were opened. And another book was opened, which is *the Book* of Life. And the dead were judged according to their works, by the things which were written in the books. [13] The sea gave up the dead who were in it, and Death and Hades delivered up the dead who were in them. And they were judged, each one according to his works. [14] Then Death and Hades were cast into the lake of fire. This is the second death. [15] And anyone not found written in the Book of Life was cast into the lake of fire.

These verses of Rev 20 describe the "Great White Throne Judgment". What a profound and gripping description of the final Judgment. According to Dispensationalism, this judgment of Revelation 20 is only for unbelievers, and is a different judgment from the Matthew 25 judgment. Let us examine this idea. The Great White Throne judgment description itself seems to preclude it. When it says "the dead", surely it is referring to all the dead? And if there were no saved and righteous people present why would the Book of Life be opened?

The description of the Judgment in Matthew 25, where we saw that "ALL the nations" will be gathered to Him, contradicts this theory as both sheep and goats are present. Similarly the Romans 2 description of the Judgment, in its differentiation between "those who by patient continuance in doing good seek for glory, honour, and immortality" and "those who are self-seeking and do not obey the truth, but obey unrighteousness", precludes a judgment where only sinners are present.

Furthermore, the notion common in Dispensationalism that there are several judgments, one for believers who were in the 'Pretrib' rapture, one for tribulation converts, one for Jews alive in the millennium, one for converts during the millennium, and a final one for unbelievers, as we have seen, seems counter-intuitive and anti-Biblical. We have examined several passages that inextricably link together the resurrection of the dead (righteous and unrighteous) with the Judgment. The expectation of all the Bible writers was always ONE Judgment and ONE resurrection, as we have seen. We will discuss some aspects of the judgment:

THE OPEN, PUBLIC NATURE OF THE JUDGMENT

The Judgment will be open and in public. Everyone will know the outcome:

"No one, when he has lit a lamp, covers it with a vessel or puts it under a bed, but sets it on a lampstand, that those who enter may see the light. For nothing is secret that will not be revealed, nor anything hidden that will not be known and come to light. Therefore, take heed how you hear. For whoever has, to him more will be given; and whoever does not have, even what he seems to have will be taken from him." Luke 8:16-18

THE JUDGMENT WILL BE FOR ALL PEOPLE OF ALL TIMES

The Old Testament Sodom and Gomorrah belonged to a completely different era from us. But Jesus tells us that their inhabitants will be present at the same judgment as us. Everyone who ever lived will be at this Judgment, as noted earlier.

Mat 10:15....... whoever will not receive you nor hear you, when you depart from there, shake off the dust under your feet as a testimony against them. Assuredly, I say to you, it will be more tolerable for Sodom and Gomorrah in the day of judgment than for that city!" [24]

THE SERIOUSNESS OF THE JUDGMENT

Jesus graphically emphasised the seriousness of the coming judgment. He urged people to go to any lengths to avoid eternal punishment.

Matt 18:8-9 "If your hand or foot causes you to sin, cut it off and cast it from you. It is better for you to enter into life lame or maimed, rather than having two hands or two feet, to be cast into the everlasting fire. 9 And if your eye causes you to sin, pluck it out and cast it from you. It is better for you to enter into life with one eye, rather than having two eyes, to be cast into hell fire.

Was He advocating self-mutilation? Of course not. He was emphasising the gravity of offences against God, using an extreme image to emphasise His point, just as He would later use many extreme images in the book of Revelation to make His points.

---

[24] Also Mark 6:10-11

THE CHARACTER AND QUALIFICATIONS
OF JESUS AS JUDGE - JESUS THE KING.

God started to teach mankind about the character of Jesus long before the Gospels were written, or He was born. The Holy Spirit said of Jesus:

> Psa 45:7 You love righteousness and hate wickedness;
> Therefore God, Your God, has anointed You
> With the oil of gladness more than Your companions.

So, we know Jesus will be a passionate but absolutely fair Judge on the Day of the Lord. Right from his first chapter Matthew sets the scene in his Gospel. The angel told Joseph that Jesus would save His people from their sins[25]. (This core function was inaugurated at the crucifixion and will finally be realised fully on the Day of the Lord.) Wise men told people in chapter 2 that Jesus will be King and Ruler[26] who will shepherd Israel. Miraculous signs accompany the birth – Jesus born to a virgin, into the line of David; angelic appearances; visit of the Wise Men[27]; His birthplace foretold[28]. All these events and signs build the picture of Jesus' immense stature and uniqueness, fitting for the One who will be the Judge at the end of time.

Mark opens with a fast-paced account of the call to repentance by John the Baptist, his recognition of the Messiah, and God's ringing endorsement of the Son. Jesus is then portrayed defeating Satan over the temptations and taking up the mission of calling the people to repentance.

Luke includes a different set of events bearing witness to Jesus' uniqueness: the angel visit to Mary[29]; the presence of the Holy Spirit[30]; the miracle of Zacharias' speech returning[31]; angels' appearance to the shepherds[32]; and prophetic revelation given to Simeon and Anna[33].

---

[25] Mat 1:21
[26] Mat 2:2,6,11
[27] Mat 1:23,25, 1-17,2:1
[28] Mat 2:5-6
[29] Luke 1:26-38
[30] Luke 1:40-42
[31] Luke 1:67-79
[32] Luke 2:8-20
[33] Luke 2:25-38

John introduces Jesus with his magnificent prologue, with details of some of Jesus' eternal attributes: His eternal co-existence with the Father as the Word[34]; His role as creator and as the Light of the world[35]; Saviour[36]; bringer of glory, grace and truth[37]; living in the presence of God[38]. So the four Gospel writers are careful to start right at the beginning by portraying Jesus as someone with the stature required to preside over the events of the Last Day.

CATHOLIC VIEW OF THE QUALIFICATIONS OF JESUS TO BE JUDGE

On this issue also it seems my findings are very much compatible with the modern-day Catholic emphasis. This from the Catechism:

679 Christ is Lord of eternal life. Full right to pass definitive judgement on the works and hearts of men belongs to him as redeemer of the world. He "acquired" this right by his cross. the Father has given "all judgement to the Son." Yet the Son did not come to judge, but to save and to give the life he has in himself. By rejecting grace in this life, one already judges oneself, receives according to one's works, and can even condemn oneself for all eternity by rejecting the Spirit of love. (Catechism of the Catholic Church, 1997)

WHAT ISSUES DETERMINE WHETHER AN INDIVIDUAL IS JUSTIFIED OR CONDEMNED AT THE JUDGMENT?

The whole of the New Testament bears witness to the fact that there is no other way to be found righteous at this Judgment than to believe in Jesus Christ. All of us have sinned and fallen short of what God wanted us to be. The whole world is guilty before God. The Law of God shows the standard and defines righteousness; the prophets in the Old Testament proclaim the standard and call people to repentance. This

---

[34] John 1:1-2
[35] John 1:3-10
[36] John 1:12-13
[37] John 1:14-17
[38] John 1:18

is the character of *this present evil age*[39]. But God has paid the price for us who put our faith in Jesus. He has given Jesus as a sacrifice for our sins. All the universe recognises that God's actions have been totally righteous and just. He passed over sins that were committed in former times to demonstrate in this time that He is prepared to pay the ultimate price for us to obtain forgiveness. Having paid the price, God becomes Himself our justifier, whether we be Jew or Gentile. This is precisely laid out in the very theological letter to the Romans:

Rom 3:19-31 Now we know that whatever the law says, it says to those who are under the law, that every mouth may be stopped, and all the world may become guilty before God. Therefore by the deeds of the law no flesh will be justified in His sight, for by the law is the knowledge of sin. But now the righteousness of God apart from the law is revealed, being witnessed by the Law and the Prophets, even the righteousness of God, through faith in Jesus Christ, to all and on all who believe. For there is no difference; for all have sinned and fall short of the glory of God, being justified freely by His grace through the redemption that is in Christ Jesus, whom God set forth as a propitiation by His blood, through faith, to demonstrate His righteousness, because in His forbearance God had passed over the sins that were previously committed, to demonstrate at the present time His righteousness, that He might be just and the justifier of the one who has faith in Jesus. Where is boasting then? It is excluded. By what law? Of works? No, but by the law of faith. Therefore we conclude that a man is justified by faith apart from the deeds of the law. Or is He the God of the Jews only? Is He not also the God of the Gentiles? Yes, of the Gentiles also, since there is one God who will justify the circumcised by faith and the uncircumcised through faith. Do we then make void the law through faith? Certainly not! On the contrary, we establish the law.

THE LAW NOT SET ASIDE

The law in all its perfection is not laid aside but established and fulfilled in Jesus. It is seen to be so much more than small regulations, but it is

---

[39] Gal 1:4

the expression of justice, mercy and faith. He has planted His law in our heart:

Ezekiel 36:26-28 I will give you a new heart and put a new spirit within you; I will take the heart of stone out of your flesh and give you a heart of flesh. I will put My Spirit within you and cause you to walk in My statutes, and you will keep My judgments and do them. Then you shall dwell in the land that I gave to your fathers; you shall be My people, and I will be your God.

Now we are saved through faith – but that faith must be tested for its genuineness. I was asking a group of fairly new Chinese believers how they could reconcile Romans 3 with James 2 (we had finished reading the two chapters together). One young man said with a smile, "It must be a living faith." I thought that was a good answer and told the group so. Even a new believer can understand that true faith must change our behaviour. Or as John Wesley put it, there is a huge difference between faith and mental assent. Many churchgoers give mental assent to the teaching, but this is far from heart-changing faith. Wesley himself acknowledged that in his early years of ministry he only gave mental assent to the doctrines of Christianity. Then one day he was at a meeting of Moravian Christians in Aldersgate, London and he felt his heart "strangely warmed". Forever after that experience he was a changed man. He travelled over 250,000 miles on a donkey, preaching up and down Britain, rejoiced in persecution, and has been credited by historians with founding a movement so influential it probably stopped a revolution like the French revolution happening in Britain.

TRUE FAITH MUST FIND ITS EXPRESSION IN GOOD WORKS

The letter of James discusses the relationship between faith and works:

James 2:14-26 What does it profit, my brethren, if someone says he has faith but does not have works? Can faith save him? If a brother or sister is naked and destitute of daily food, and one of you says to them, "Depart in peace, be warmed and filled," but you do not give them the things which are needed for the body, what does it profit? Thus also faith by itself, if it does not have works, is dead. But someone will say,

"You have faith, and I have works." Show me your faith without your works, and I will show you my faith by my works. You believe that there is one God. You do well. Even the demons believe—and tremble! But do you want to know, O foolish man, that faith without works is dead? Was not Abraham our father justified by works when he offered Isaac his son on the altar? Do you see that faith was working together with his works, and by works faith was made perfect? And the Scripture was fulfilled which says, "Abraham believed God, and it was accounted to him for righteousness." And he was called the friend of God. You see then that a man is justified by works, and not by faith only. Likewise, was not Rahab the harlot also justified by works when she received the messengers and sent them out another way? For as the body without the spirit is dead, so faith without works is dead also.

This passage from James is the counter-balance to Ephesians:

Eph 2:8-9 For by grace you have been saved through faith, and that not of yourselves; it is the gift of God, not of works, lest anyone should boast.

It is true that there is nothing we can do to bring about our salvation from God's righteous wrath. Romans pronounces all of us dead in sins against God. The blood of Jesus is the only thing which is an acceptable price to purchase us for eternal life. But having said all that, a genuine faith will produce good works. Abraham was saved by faith. Without faith he would not have been able to please God. But how can we tell that Abraham had faith? By observing his actions or *works*. He walked up the mountain to sacrifice Isaac. This showed that he really did believe that God had spoken to him about the sacrifice of his son. If he had not actually walked up the mountain and prepared for the sacrifice, we would know that he did not really believe God had spoken to him. Likewise, James tells us that if we do not have a genuine care for people, especially for fellow followers of Jesus, we cannot have a genuine faith. This agrees with Matthew 25 as we have seen.

GOD HAS A SPECIAL HEART FOR THE POOR

That God has a special care for the poor is often referred to in the Bible. This is to be practically lived out in the life of the church. We may not show "partiality" towards the rich. The judgment is the time when the poor will be compensated by receiving the kingdom, which is their inheritance. They will have to qualify on the other grounds mentioned in this chapter. But they are more likely to qualify because God has specially chosen the poor to be rich in faith.

James 2:5 Has God not chosen the poor of this world *to be* rich in faith and heirs of the kingdom which He promised to those who love Him?

Moreover, those who have not followed God's command to treat the poor well and be merciful will be punished at the judgment. James 2:9,13 echoes this point from Matthew 25.

THERE IS A CHOICE TO BE MADE, SOMETIMES A DAILY CHOICE:

It is true that Jesus will keep us and guard us until that final day. But it is also true that we must make a choice every day to follow Him and not just live for fleshly desires. The fact that Paul urged the believers to live by the Spirit presupposes that it is possible to make the wrong choice and end up not qualifying for life.

Romans 8:12-13 Therefore, brethren, we are debtors—not to the flesh, to live according to the flesh. For if you live according to the flesh you will die; but if by the Spirit you put to death the deeds of the body, you will live.

THE AMOUNT OF LIGHT PEOPLE HAVE RECEIVED WILL BE CONSIDERED.

The people of Chorazin, Bethsaida and Capurnaum had seen the mighty miracles of Jesus yet still didn't believe. They will be sentenced more severely than Tyre, Sidon and Sodom because they had so much more light of truth from the Lord Himself:

Mat 11:24 Then He began to rebuke the cities in which most of His mighty works had been done, because they did not repent: 21 "Woe to you, Chorazin! Woe to you, Bethsaida! For if the mighty works which were done in you had been done in Tyre and Sidon, they would have repented long ago in sackcloth and ashes. 22 But I say to you, it will be more tolerable for Tyre and Sidon in the day of judgment than for you. 23 And you, Capernaum, who are exalted to heaven, will be brought down to Hades; for if the mighty works which were done in you had been done in Sodom, it would have remained until this day. 24 But I say to you that it shall be more tolerable for the land of Sodom in the day of judgment than for you."

Jesus confirmed this principle in His words about the Pharisees:

John 15:22 "If I had not come and spoken to them, they would have no sin, but now they have no excuse for their sin."

REWARDS AT THE JUDGMENT – POSITION IN THE KINGDOM OF GOD

Of course, it is much more pleasant to contemplate the rewards given out at the judgment. John and James' mother understood God's kingdom was being established. She thought by speaking out for them she could influence Jesus to give them a better position in the new order. Of course her request was partisan and declined by Jesus. But she was correct in her understanding that there will be structure and differing positions of authority in the kingdom of God.

Matt 20:20-23 Then the mother of Zebedee's sons came to Him with her sons, kneeling down and asking something from Him. And He said to her, "What do you wish?" She said to Him, "Grant that these two sons of mine may sit, one on Your right hand and the other on the left, in Your kingdom". But Jesus answered and said, "You do not know what you ask. Are you able to drink the cup that I am about to drink, and be baptized with the baptism that I am baptized with?" They said to Him, "We are able." So He said to them, "You will indeed drink My cup, and be baptized with the baptism that I am baptized with; but to sit on My right hand and on My left is not Mine to give, but it is for those for whom it is prepared by My Father."

We see more of the structure in the next passage. Many whom men have looked down upon, or ignored and thought to be inferior, or persecuted mentally or physically, will come to the fore in the days of the kingdom, and will receive honour:

Mat 19:27 Then Peter answered and said to Him, "See, we have left all and followed You. Therefore what shall we have?" So Jesus said to them, "Assuredly I say to you, that in the regeneration, when the Son of Man sits on the throne of His glory, you who have followed Me will also sit on twelve thrones, judging the twelve tribes of Israel. And everyone who has left houses or brothers or sisters or father or mother or wife or children or lands, for My name's sake, shall receive a hundredfold, and inherit eternal life. But many who are first will be last, and the last first.

MORE REWARDS – THE CROWN OF LIFE

Those who have lived their lives for the kingdom of God will receive crowns of righteousness. God is not looking for a mere mental assent to the doctrines of the Bible. Jesus lays out to us in Matthew 22 God's greatest command, to love Him with all our heart, soul and mind. Notice in this extract from the letter to Timothy that only those who have "loved" His appearing will receive the crown:

2 Timothy 4:8 Finally, there is laid up for me the crown of righteousness, which the Lord, the righteous Judge, will give to me on that Day, and not to me only but also to all who have loved His appearing.

The gift of this crown of life is confirmed as being awarded to those who are "faithful unto death":

Be faithful until death, and I will give you the crown of life (Rev 2:10).

Most of the mystic Revelation gifts are said to be given to the "overcomers". By "overcomers" John means those who walked in victorious faith. It could be translated as "conquerors" and was paraphrased by one commentator as "...(those who have won) a victory over all kinds of evil that would harm the church or prevent the salvation of the contender." (Hinds, 1962) Lovers of Jesus' appearing, overcomers, and those "faithful unto death" will receive an incomparable reward!

MORE GIFTS DESCRIBED IN THE BOOK OF REVELATION

When the overcoming believer "eats of the tree of life" full restoration of everything lost at the fall of Adam is in view (Gen 2:9). In a sense the whole Bible is about the recovery of everything lost at that time:

I will give to eat from the tree of life, which is in the midst of the Paradise of God (Rev 2:7).

The overcomer will not be cast into the lake of fire after the judgment:

(He) shall not be hurt by the second death (Rev 2:11).

Some commentators think that all these images, such as the white stone, the hidden manna, and the white garments are merely symbols for eternal life. I prefer to think they denote some particular flavour or gift different believers are given when they enter the new heavens and earth (1 Cor 2:9). But eternal life is definitely the most important part of the package! For reasons of space, I will leave the reader to imagine what the remaining rewards look like. To study them in detail, Geoff Beale's work is authoritative and highly regarded (Beale, 1999).

Rev 2:17 I will give some of the hidden manna to eat. And I will give him a white stone, and on the stone a new name written which no one knows except him who receives *it*.

Rev 2:26-28 I will give power over the nations. [27] 'He shall rule them with a rod of iron;

They shall be dashed to pieces like the potter's vessels'— as I also have received from My Father; [28] and I will give him the morning star.

Rev 3:4-5 ...and they shall walk with Me in white, for they are worthy. [5] He who overcomes shall be clothed in white garments, and I will not blot out his name from the Book of Life; but I will confess his name before My Father and before His angels.

Rev 3:12 I will make him a pillar in the temple of My God, and he shall go out no more. I will write on him the name of My God and the name of the city of My God, the New Jerusalem, which comes down out of heaven from My God. And *I will write on him* My new name.

Rev 3:20 I will come in to him and dine with him, and he with Me.

Rev 3:21 I will grant to sit with Me on My throne, as I also overcame and sat down with My Father on His throne.

At the very least the Revelation rewards mean that we will have continued fellowship with our wonderful Lord, and we will be reigning with Him.

SERMON ON THE MOUNT WITH QUESTIONS ANSWERED IN THE LIGHT OF THE JUDGMENT

The understanding of the last judgment helps to make sense of the well-known and much-loved sermon on the mount (Mat 5-7). Here is some of the text, with my questions:

"Mat 5:1-11 Blessed are the poor in spirit,
   For theirs is the kingdom of heaven. When will they take possession?
4 Blessed are those who mourn,
   For they shall be comforted. When will they be comforted?
5 Blessed are the meek,
   For they shall inherit the earth. When?
6 Blessed are those who hunger and thirst for righteousness,
   For they shall be filled. When?
7 Blessed are the merciful,
   For they shall obtain mercy. When?
8 Blessed are the pure in heart,
   For they shall see God. When?
9 Blessed are the peacemakers,
   For they shall be called sons of God. When?
10 Blessed are those who are persecuted for righteousness' sake,
   For theirs is the kingdom of heaven. When will they receive it?
11 "Blessed are you when they revile and persecute you and say all kinds of evil against you falsely for My sake. 12 Rejoice and be exceedingly glad, for great is your reward in heaven, for so they persecuted the prophets who were before you. When will you receive this great reward?

WHEN INDEED?

The obvious answer to all these "when" questions is "at the universal Judgment"! This understanding makes sense of the Sermon on the Mount. I have always felt it to be a noble discourse with fine sentiments and language. But I did not feel I understood it until I realized its context in relation to the universal Judgment. The assumption running through the Sermon on the Mount is that all mankind will face the Judgement together, as we have discussed. Presumably, in the crowd He was addressing, there would have been at least some people who would ultimately believe in His message, and also some who would reject the Gospel and also our saviour. Rewards and punishments are given out at the same event. The notion that Jesus will come for the Church, then 3 ½ or 7 years later will bring us back to rule the earth, just does not square with the Sermon on the Mount. Nor does the teaching of Premil that there will be a period of 1000 years reign on earth before the universal judgment. In either of these scenarios there would need to be a "pre-judgment" on who would be in the rapture, or who would be part of the 1000-year government.

By contrast the notion of only one judgment is fair and just and glorifies God! It is the only satisfying answer to at least some of the individual "when" questions.

Q AND A

Q: When do the poor in spirit (humble praying people) and the persecuted, inherit the Kingdom of Heaven?
A: At the creation of the new heavens and new earth!

Q: When are they that mourn (in a righteous sense, which means for example grieve over the flouting of God's laws, or be moved by others' suffering) comforted?
A: It is certain that not all those who mourn are comforted during this life (though some are). At the universal Judgment they will be greatly comforted, as they see the operation of God's justice and mercy.

Q: When do those who have been ill-spoken of because they have taken the side of God's Kingdom obtain their great reward?

A: Of course, at the universal Judgment! That way they will be fully vindicated because everyone will see them get their reward. Loud will be the cheers of angels and men at that day! Justice will be served as all are judged according to the same standard in the sight of all. A rapture scenario where the unjust do not see the just being rewarded would not have been just; they might never realise that they could have inherited the promises, or how they could have responded to God and obtained an everlasting reward. They may feel unjustly treated for all eternity.

Other revealing "when" questions from the remainder of the Sermon might be:

Q: When will the unforgiving learn that our Father has finally decided to withhold forgiveness from them?[40]

A: At the universal Judgment. There must be a time when this is finally decided – this time can only be the Day of the Lord.

Q: When will we inherit the treasures we have laid up in Heaven?[41]

A: At the universal Judgment.

Q: When will those who have secretly done charitable acts, prayed, or fasted be rewarded openly?[42]

A: At the universal Judgment. This is an obvious one. It must be at the universal Judgment for it truly to be said that the Father rewards them openly. If it were at the ("secret") rapture as it is taught in many places today, our Father would not be rewarding them openly!

---

[40] Mat 6:15
[41] Mat 6:19-21
[42] Mat 6:4, 5, 18,

WHO IS DISQUALIFIED FROM ETERNAL LIFE WITH GOD?

Who will receive eternal life and who will be disqualified? The Bible has a lot more to say about this than merely stating that "Christians" will be saved. First of all those with glaring sin present in their lives will not receive eternal life no matter how much they protest that "nobody is perfect", "Jesus didn't come to judge but to forgive" and "God is a loving father and He doesn't condemn". Let's have a look at the following list:

1Cor 6:9-10 Do you not know that the unrighteous will not inherit the kingdom of God? Do not be deceived. Neither fornicators, nor idolaters, nor adulterers, nor homosexuals, nor sodomites, nor thieves, nor covetous, nor drunkards, nor revilers, nor extortioners will inherit the kingdom of God.

The exposure of senior church leaders who have consorted with prostitutes or had serial affairs with women in their congregations has never ceased to astonish me. They obviously did not believe the Bible they were preaching. Idolaters will not receive eternal life with God. As a follower of transcendental (Hindu) meditation, I was in this category of idolatry before Jesus mercifully revealed Himself to me. Adulterers – if we have an eye for someone else's husband or wife we had better repent, fast.

Homosexuals – the Bible here means active homosexual practice. Many sincere Christians, who have experienced same sex attraction, have become free of these feelings through prayer, or have learned to live a God-honouring, fulfilling life while abstaining from sexual activity.

FALSE TEACHERS

One category of people in big trouble at the judgment will be false teachers:

Jam 3:1 My brethren, let not many of you become teachers, knowing that we shall receive a stricter judgment.

Why is the Lord so opposed to false teachers? Surely it must be because they present the sheep with such danger. They can subvert whole churches and denominations,

There is no inevitability about anyone's conviction for sin "on that day". Even unto our last breath we will be able to repent. God will never leave anyone without a way of escape, if they are alive. There were former practising homosexuals, and people who had committed all kinds of sexual sin and other sins on this list in the congregation Paul was addressing. They were able to turn away from their old sins and be completely renewed, now in line to receive the richest rewards at the judgment.

(1 Cor 6:11) And such were some of you. But you were washed, but you were sanctified, but you were justified in the name of the Lord Jesus and by the Spirit of our God.

It may come as a shock to some in our materialistic society that 'covetousness' comes in the same category as homosexuality as a sin disqualifying us from eternal life. Indeed, any of these sins is enough to disqualify us from heaven. There are 124 sins listed in the New Testament altogether (Angelfire, 2020). Balanced against this, we are told that "love covers a multitude of sins", and enjoined to follow "the Spirit, and not the letter" of the law. Paul said we cannot possibly be saved by the law, but that the law was given to make us realize our need for Christ.

Jesus reserved His most caustic comments for religious hypocrites:

Mat 23:25-35 "Woe to you, scribes and Pharisees, hypocrites! For you are like whitewashed tombs which indeed appear beautiful outwardly, but inside are full of dead men's bones and all uncleanness. Even so you also outwardly appear righteous to men, but inside you are full of hypocrisy and lawlessness."

EIGHT SINS OF THE PHARISEES IDENTIFIED – MAT 23:1-36

1. Pride
2. Hypocritical religious leadership
3. Taking advantage of the vulnerable
4. Doing religious activities with a false motivation (to gain admiration of people)
5. Leading would-be disciples astray

6. Twisting spiritual teaching to gain personal advantage
7. Following minor rules but neglecting justice, mercy and faith, the important matters
8. Heart attitudes of extortion, self-indulgence, hypocrisy and lawlessness

OPPOSING AND KILLING TRUE SERVANTS OF GOD.

We have considered the next verse before, but let's look at it in a new context.

1 Thes 2:14-16.......the Judeans, who killed both the Lord Jesus and their own prophets, and have persecuted us; and they do not please God and are contrary to all men, forbidding us to speak to the Gentiles that they may be saved, so as always to fill up the measure of their sins; but wrath has come upon them to the uttermost.

Killing or opposing men or women appointed for a particular role by God is perilous territory to be in. And do not forget that everything hidden will be revealed at the judgment.

"I NEVER KNEW YOU"

The Israelites in the Old Testament were convinced they had the blessing of God, and therefore were invincible, because they had the temple and the promises of God to their ancestors. But Jeremiah prophesied to them essentially, "No! If you thoroughly amend your ways you will have the blessing of God and He will allow you to keep this temple and stay here in Jerusalem. But right now, He is angry with you because you haven't lived the kind of life He commanded" (Jeremiah chapters 7 and 26). Likewise, at the judgment "many" who know and have used His name will be excluded. The fact that they know and use His name shows they are in our churches today. Sadly, many will have to take the left hand path on that Day.

Mat 7:21 "Not everyone who says to Me, 'Lord, Lord,' shall enter the kingdom of heaven, but he who does the will of My Father in heaven." Many will say to Me in that day, 'Lord, Lord, have we not prophesied in Your name, cast out demons in Your name, and done many wonders in Your name?' And then I will declare to them, 'I never knew you; depart from Me, you who practice lawlessness!'

WE MUST ACKNOWLEDGE JESUS BEFORE PEOPLE

Mat 10:32-33 "Therefore whoever confesses Me before men, him I will also confess before My Father who is in heaven. But whoever denies Me before men, him I will also deny before My Father who is in heaven.

One obvious issue is whether we are prepared to acknowledge to others that we are followers of Jesus.

YOUR WORDS REVEAL THE STATE OF YOUR HEART

Mat 12:35-37 A good man out of the good treasure of his heart brings forth good things, and an evil man out of the evil treasure brings forth evil things. But I say to you that for every idle word men may speak, they will give account of it in the day of judgment. For by your words you will be justified, and by your words you will be condemned."

Our words may reveal us to be on-fire lovers of Jesus Christ, or indifferent clock-watchers waiting for life to pass us by. Be careful! Our words reveal our souls!

FOLLOW THE LORD WITH ALL YOUR HEART

Mat 10:37-39 He who loves father or mother more than Me is not worthy of Me. And he who loves son or daughter more than Me is not worthy of Me. 38 And he who does not take his cross and follow after Me is not worthy of Me. 39 He who finds his life will lose it, and he who loses his life for My sake will find it.

Following the Lord of Lords and King of Kings is not a light matter. The old saying "Jesus is either Lord of all, or not at all" has validity. Jesus has a right to our whole allegiance, and if we are going to follow Him, we had better make up our minds that it will be total commitment.

GIVE PLACE TO THE HOLY SPIRIT

Mat 12:32... but whoever speaks against the Holy Spirit, it will not be forgiven him, either in this age or in the age to come.

Cherish the Holy Spirit – Jesus sent Him for our benefit.

WOE TO THOSE WHO OFFEND AGAINST CHILDREN

Mat 18:6-7 Whoever causes one of these little ones who believe in Me to sin, it would be better for him if a millstone were hung around his neck, and he were drowned in the depth of the sea. Woe to the world because of offenses! For offenses must come, but woe to that man by whom the offense comes!

Children all have their angels. Don't act against a child!

FORGIVENESS IS ESSENTIAL

Matt 18:32-35 'You wicked servant! I forgave you all that debt because you begged me. 33 Should you not also have had compassion on your fellow servant, just as I had pity on you?' 34 And his master was angry, and delivered him to the torturers until he should pay all that was due to him. My heavenly Father also will do to you if each of you, from his heart, does not forgive his brother his trespasses."

Forgiveness is non-optional! We do not have the option to hang on to our grudges, or simmer in anger at some real or imagined offence. We ourselves are not righteous but saved only as a result of his grace and mercy. So how can we hold on to our grudges and bitter thoughts. We are commanded to forgive "from the heart".

Chapter Twenty

THE NEW HEAVENS
AND NEW EARTH

✠ ✠ ✠

LIFE IN THE RESURRECTION ACCORDING TO JOHN

In popular culture the place where eternal life is lived is termed "heaven", but in the Bible it is known as the new heaven and the new earth where the heavenly Jerusalem will also be found. Nobody will enter until the Day of the Lord. At that time Jesus will come to rescue the righteous. The armies of the enemy will be destroyed, and the devil thrown into the lake of fire. Last Judgment will begin, and the old heaven and earth will be done away with.

Rev 20:11 Then I saw a great white throne and Him who sat on it, from whose face the earth and the heaven fled away. And there was found no place for them.

Mat 24:35-36 Heaven and earth will pass away, but My words will by no means pass away. **36** "But of that day and hour no one knows, not even the angels of heaven, but My Father only.[43]

At the judgment those found righteous will enter their eternal

---

[43] Note the phrase "But of that day and hour no one knows" suggests the Day of the Lord

reward. This is the beginning of the wonderful experience of living with God in the new heavens and earth, having an all-embracing relationship with Him, and God Himself wiping away every tear:

Rev 21:1-4 Now I saw a new heaven and a new earth, for the first heaven and the first earth had passed away. Also, there was no more sea. Then I, John, saw the holy city, New Jerusalem, coming down out of heaven from God, prepared as a bride adorned for her husband. And I heard a loud voice from heaven saying, "Behold, the tabernacle of God is with men, and He will dwell with them, and they shall be His people. God Himself will be with them and be their God. And God will wipe away every tear from their eyes; there shall be no more death, nor sorrow, nor crying. There shall be no more pain, for the former things have passed away.[44]"

John emphasises that God will be living with His people. The relationship with Him will be intimate and He will take away all sorrow.

PETER LOOKS FORWARD TO THE NEW REALM

Peter agrees. John in his vision saw the new heavens and the new earth already created. Peter, however, looks forward to the new heavens and new earth. Under the inspiration of the Holy Spirit, he clarifies for us when they start:

2 Pet 3:11-15 Therefore, since all these things will be dissolved, what manner *of persons* ought you to be in holy conduct and godliness, [12] looking for and hastening the coming of the day of God, because of which the heavens will be dissolved, being on fire, and the elements will melt with fervent heat? [13] Nevertheless we, according to His promise, look for new heavens and a new earth in which righteousness dwells.

It is "on the day of God" that this new realm will be set up, and the old heavens replaced. Peter's description details how righteousness will dwell in the new realm. Both Peter's and John's descriptions have been partly drawn from Isaiah's description written about 700 years earlier:

---

[44] Jer 31:31-34 quoted and explained further in Heb 8:8-12

THE GLORIOUS NEW CREATION

Isaiah 65:17-25 "For behold, I create new heavens and a new earth;
And the former shall not be remembered or come to mind.
18 But be glad and rejoice forever in what I create;
For behold, I create Jerusalem *as* a rejoicing, and her people a joy.
19 I will rejoice in Jerusalem, and joy in My people;
The voice of weeping shall no longer be heard in her, nor the voice of crying.
20 "No more shall an infant from there *live but a few* days,
Nor an old man who has not fulfilled his days; for the child shall die one hundred years old,
But the sinner *being* one hundred years old shall be accursed.
21 They shall build houses and inhabit *them; t*hey shall plant vineyards and eat their fruit.
22 They shall not build and another inhabit; they shall not plant and another eat;
For as the days of a tree, *so shall be* the days of My people,
And My elect shall long enjoy the work of their hands.
23 They shall not labour in vain, nor bring forth children for trouble;
For they *shall be* the descendants of the blessed of the Lord, and their offspring with them.
24 "It shall come to pass that before they call, I will answer;
And while they are still speaking, I will hear.
25 The wolf and the lamb shall feed together, the lion shall eat straw like the ox,
And dust *shall be* the serpent's food. They shall not hurt nor destroy in all My holy mountain," says the Lord.

What a wonderful description of the life to come for the redeemed. All the sufferings, pains, fears, and frustrations, regarded as normal in our present life, will be over and forgotten. Jerusalem will be the new Jerusalem as described in Rev 21, filled with joy and the knowledge of God. And God Himself will delight in His people.

ARE THERE ANOMALIES IN THESE DESCRIPTIONS?

We have taken the future blessed and restored Israel, the kingdom to which the prophets refer, to be identical to the blessed hope of every Christian, whether ethnic Israelite or not, and the eternal life spoken of by Jesus. This has been the understanding of Amil commentators down the centuries, from the earliest church fathers, through Augustine, through Luther and Calvin, to Amil theologians of today.

But then, our Premil friends would say, what about, for example, the presence of death in Isaiah 65:20? We are told in Revelation 21 and elsewhere that there is no more death or sin in the eternal state. But both appear to exist still in this realm of the new heavens and the new earth (verse 20). "Therefore", contends Premil, "this and other scriptures must portray the millennial 1000-year reign of Christ on earth which is certainly blessed but nowhere near the eternal state of the saved."

Some of the answers to this objection would be:

- It is not stated anywhere in the Old Testament prophecies that a thousand year-reign is indicated.
- The language here is unequivocally the language of eternity, not of only 1000 years; "rejoice FOREVER: verse 18; "weeping shall NO LONGER be heard": verse 19.
- God is using Old Testament images to reveal His truths as far as possible to the people of Isaiah's day. Eternal life was beyond the conception of Isaiah and his people, so God gave them a metaphor they could relate to. He represents eternity by longevity, which was always counted a blessing in Israel, and not beyond their capacity to understand.
- Our Premil friend, insisting on Biblical literalism, does not appear to appreciate the metaphor.
- Isaiah, like the other Old Testament prophets, conveyed a wonderful picture of the life to come. But the understanding of his audience, and possibly that of himself, was limited to the Old Testament paradigm, and it would require the ministry of Jesus and the Apostles to bring the full truth of the nature of the end of the age and everlasting life (see Hebrews 11:39-40)

- Jesus was not at all a Biblical literalist. What about His parables? When talking about eating His body and drinking His blood, did He mean this literally? Of course, this touches on a centuries-old controversy. But surely everyone, whether Catholic or Protestant can see the metaphor in this. Jesus was speaking metaphorically when He said, "this is My body, broken for you"; "this is My blood, shed for you". However, the Church chooses to remember this action, all must surely see the metaphor in His statement. When people enquired about Elijah coming before the Messiah's appearance, Jesus stated that the coming of John the Baptist fulfilled Malachi's prophecy. The metaphorical, the mysterious and the symbolic made Jesus' teaching incisive and exciting.

IMAGES OF ETERNITY

We will bring this chapter to an end by considering three passages from the Old Testament prophets which poetically portray the wonderful nature of eternal life in "heaven" for the saved. Once again, they are all addressed to Israel but should not be thought of as only applying to ethnic Jews. They apply to anyone, Jew or gentile, who has repented and trusts with all their heart in our Lord and Saviour, Jesus Christ.

The first, from Jeremiah, speaks of the relationship we will have with God in that glorious time:

Jer 31:33-34 But this *is* the covenant that I will make with the house of Israel after those days, says the Lord: I will put My law in their minds, and write it on their hearts; and I will be their God, and they shall be My people. [34] No more shall every man teach his neighbour, and every man his brother, saying, 'Know the Lord,' for they all shall know Me, from the least of them to the greatest of them, says the Lord. For I will forgive their iniquity, and their sin I will remember no more."

Imagine a world where everyone knows God to such an extent that His words and thoughts are constantly in our hearts and minds. Even before we meet another person, we will know that person is devoted to God as we are. This means no manipulation, no fights, no depression, no boredom, no jealousies. It means complete saturation with wisdom, justice, creativity, purity and love. In our present life we may experience something akin to this when filled with the Holy Spirit. But what is described here is the full, completed reality, which will never diminish but will last for all eternity.

In our next passage from Amos, the prophet uses the image of mountains and hills dripping with sweet wine to capture the quality of life in that future existence:

> Amos 9:13-14 "Behold, the days are coming," says the Lord,
> "When the ploughman shall overtake the reaper,
> And the treader of grapes him who sows seed;
> The mountains shall drip with sweet wine,
> And all the hills shall flow with it.
> [14] I will bring back the captives of My people Israel;
> They shall build the waste cities and inhabit them;
> They shall plant vineyards and drink wine from them;
> They shall also make gardens and eat fruit from them.

We know this is not a literal passage by the imagery. The treader of grapes can never overtake the sower of seed. But the image is one of unimaginable abundance, joy, and rejoicing. The return of the captives of Israel, in addition to the literal return of Jewish people to the physical land, speaks of the turning away from sin and the restoration of our relationship with God of all the redeemed, both Jew and gentile. The separation from God, from the time of Adam, has caused untold suffering for all mankind, and the return surely speaks of this larger reality. This final passage from Isaiah must rank as one of the most sublime passages in the Bible. I will make some comments as we read through the passage.

> Isa 35:1-10 The wilderness and the wasteland shall be
> glad for them,
> And the desert shall rejoice and blossom as the rose;
> [2] It shall blossom abundantly and rejoice,
> Even with joy and singing.

Many commentators refer to this verse in the context of the modern-day development of the Israeli deserts by irrigation. This physical fulfilment of the prophecy is indeed remarkable and gives even more weight to the metaphoric meaning. The once-arid desert rejoicing and "blossoming as the rose" is a uniquely powerful image of the blossoming of redeemed humanity, and the beauty and delicacy of the new heavens and earth of the next age.

> The glory of Lebanon shall be given to it,
> The excellence of Carmel and Sharon.
> They shall see the glory of the Lord,
> The excellency of our God.

The glory will be everywhere, as we have seen in Matthew 13:43, Romans 8:18-21, Philippians 3:21 and other passages.

> ³ Strengthen the weak hands,
> And make firm the feeble knees.
> ⁴ Say to those *who are* fearful-hearted,
> "Be strong, do not fear!
> Behold, your God will come *with* vengeance,
> *With* the recompense of God;
> He will come and save you."

We have been weak in the past but the final revelation of heaven will turn our whole soul to strength, confidence and adoration of our almighty creator.

> ⁵ Then the eyes of the blind shall be opened,
> And the ears of the deaf shall be unstopped.
> ⁶ Then the lame shall leap like a deer,
> And the tongue of the dumb sing.
> For waters shall burst forth in the wilderness,
> And streams in the desert.
> ⁷ The parched ground shall become a pool,
> And the thirsty land springs of water;

In the habitation of jackals, where each lay,
There shall be grass with reeds and rushes.

We expect to see great healings of people and perhaps even ecology in this present age but these will be complete and perfect in the age to come. There will be no sickness and no pollution in heaven!

[8] A highway shall be there, and a road,
And it shall be called the Highway of Holiness.
The unclean shall not pass over it,
But it *shall be* for others.
Whoever walks the road, although a fool,
Shall not go astray.

We will enter this new reality by the Highway of Holiness, that is holiness which Jesus inaugurates in us and helps us to realise in our lives. There is no other way. Hebrews 12:14 commands us, Pursue peace with all *people,* and holiness, without which no one will see the Lord…

[9] No lion shall be there,
Nor shall *any* ravenous beast go up on it;
It shall not be found there.

No enemies, no devil, no demons nor any evil thing shall assail us there.

But the redeemed shall walk *there,*
[10] And the ransomed of the Lord shall return,
And come to Zion with singing,
With everlasting joy on their heads.
They shall obtain joy and gladness,
And sorrow and sighing shall flee away.

This promise stands for the "Israel of God", which includes all believers whether Jews or gentiles. Certainly, it includes those ethnic Jews, who it seems will collectively turn to the Lord in the last of the last days. But metaphorically "Zion" contains a much wider meaning than the geographical hill on the east side of Jerusalem. Zion was where the tabernacle, or ceremonial tent, of David was situated. As we have seen, this tabernacle, referred to by James in Acts 15, was where God Himself dwelt in the days of David. Prior to David's tabernacle, the seat of God on earth was the tabernacle of Moses, which was subject to rigid rules and practices. In the inmost recess of Moses' tabernacle's inmost recess was the Holy of Holies, where the presence of God was found. Only the High Priest was permitted to enter, and that once per year. But David's tabernacle was totally different. The Ark of the Covenant, the most holy item belonging to the Israelites, was housed there, and the king, who was barred from the Holy of Holies in Moses' tabernacle, was permitted to enter. In fact, we are told in the Psalms that David spent much time in there in adoring praise and worship to God, and probably wrote many of the Psalms there. So "Zion" speaks of jubilant freedom, of God's glorious presence being opened to all people, of any ethnicity, rank or location. Everlasting joy and gladness will permeate this new world, and in very truth sorrow and sighing shall flee away forever.

Chapter Twenty-One

"HOW SHALL WE THEN LIVE?"

✢ ✢ ✢

FROM ME TO YOU

In our study through this book, we started with some popular views of what the coming of Jesus will look like. Then we tested these views against the simple narrative of the Gospel of Matthew and found them wanting. As far as I can understand his Gospel, according to Matthew, there is no such thing as a rapture, followed by seven years of tribulation, followed by a 1000-year reign on earth, only then to be followed by the coming of Jesus in glory. Matthew gave us a simple chronology: Jesus will come in glory. To be sure, His saints will be lifted up to meet Him in the air – but they do not then vanish for a period of years. Matthew speaks of only one return, in the midst of a dreadful war, upon which the wicked are defeated, and the heavens and the earth are destroyed. The final judgement is then made, the evil committed to the lake of fire, and those made righteous by Jesus receive their final reward. They will live forever with God and Jesus.

It is a remarkably simple narrative. We looked at the sometimes-strange history of how various interpretations emerged. We found, however, that the rest of the New Testament supports the straightforward Gospel of Matthew best. And we found that, while still imparting precious revelation, some of the most complex prophecies of the Old and New Testaments, including the Book of Revelation, also fit this simple sequence of events. If I ever doubt where I have come, I go back to Matthew's simple Gospel account, as quoted, and commented on in Chapters 3-9 of this book. And I think, yes – this must be the truth.

How shall we then live? Surely the only satisfactory answer is to live the kind of life the Biblical Apostles did. Of course, I am not advocating a legalistic attempt to slavishly obey every sentence in the New Testament – we should apply the principles as led by the Holy Spirit. This chapter quotes several short passages where the New Testament writers gave their view on Jesus' second coming. They all spoke with one voice. None doubted that Jesus is coming. And they were of one mind in thinking He would come again ONCE! They gave out much simple instruction how we should live in the light of that truth.

THE LORD'S SUPPER – FOCUSSED ON THE RETURN

Even in the familiar context of the Lord's supper, for Protestant denominations, the focus is on "till He comes". In most forms of the Catholic Mass we find a prayer like this:

"We proclaim your Death, O Lord, and profess your Resurrection until you come again."

Are we ready? Will we be found by Him without spot and blameless when He comes?

1 Cor 11:26 For as often as you eat this bread and drink this cup, you proclaim the Lord's death till He comes.

FOCUS ON "THAT DAY" – THE CORINTHIANS

The first thing to notice is the huge focus the apostles had on "that Day". It is mentioned in almost every letter of the New Testament. There was no doubt on the part of anyone as to what "that Day" referred. It was universally recognised that it referred to "the Parousia", or "appearance" of Jesus Christ. As we have discussed, nowhere is there any suggestion that there would be two or more visitations of Jesus, or that the believers would be reigning on earth with Him for 1000 years and only then enter the eternal realm.

1 Cor 1:4 I thank my God always concerning you for the grace of God which was given to you by Christ Jesus, that you were enriched in everything by Him in all utterance and all knowledge, even as the testimony of Christ was confirmed in you, so that you come short in no gift, eagerly waiting for the revelation of our Lord Jesus Christ, who will also confirm you to the end, that you may be blameless in the day of our Lord Jesus Christ.

Paul's whole concern in the 1 Corinthians example above is that the believers should be "blameless in the day of our Lord". The phraseology supports our understanding gained from Matthew's Gospel that the judgment happens immediately on Christ's return, and we should be ready to face our Maker and give an account of our lives. Not only that but he addresses our attitude: we should be eagerly awaiting His coming.

FOCUS ON "THAT DAY" – THE ROMANS

To the Romans also, Paul emphasised the nearness of "the Day", and the importance of being ready at any time. There should be no drunken revelling, lustful or envious behaviour, or time wasted in arguments and fights.

Romans 13:11-14 And do this, knowing the time, that now it is high time to awake out of sleep; for now, our salvation is nearer than when we first believed. The night is far spent, the day is at hand. Therefore, let us cast off the works of darkness, and let us put on the armour of light. Let us walk properly, as in the day, not in revelry and drunkenness, not in lewdness and lust, not in strife and envy but put on the Lord Jesus Christ, and make no provision for the flesh, to fulfil its lusts.

He obviously felt the need to spell out some of the sins with potential to rob us of our inheritance, which he also did to the Corinthians elsewhere in his letter to them. His solution: "cast off the works of darkness" and "put on the Lord Jesus". Earlier in this letter to the Romans he had spoken of "not walking according to the flesh but according to the Spirit" (Rom 8).

FOCUS ON "THAT DAY – MODERN TIMES

Some would say "2000 years have now gone by – and now we don't believe in His coming." The great malady of our age in the West is that we cannot find anything to believe in. But belief in the return of Jesus Christ is not irrational. The disciples had no idea of the size of the world, and the huge effort of every kind, both individual and church-wide, needed to reach every people group with the Gospel. However, they believed in the imperative of the Great Commission, and set about it with such energy and determination that, except for John, every one of them was killed in the attempt to make disciples on foreign mission fields. The sense of the imminent return of Jesus gave them the necessary motivation. There is a hunger in every believer to live wholly for Jesus. If we genuinely believed in and set our priorities around Jesus' soon return, it would surely make wholly living for Jesus a much more attainable mindset. This could only be a most desirable development. After all we are accountable for our stewardship of what Christ has sown in our lives. And that accountability will be finally realised at the last judgment.

JUDGMENT OF WORKS

Many modern Christians are resistant to the idea that we will be judged for our works as Christians. And in churches where judgment of works is taught, it is made to seem less threatening. There is a commonly held teaching that the "judgment of works" is separate from the universal Judgment, and that believers do not have to appear before the universal Judgment, only this judgment of works. Paul disproves that theory in his letter to the Corinthians. Any reasonable interpretation of his words must surely draw the conclusion that the judgment of works is part of the universal Judgment:

1 Cor 3:11-15 For no other foundation can anyone lay than that which is laid, which is Jesus Christ. Now if anyone builds on this foundation with gold, silver, precious stones, wood, hay, straw, each one's work will become clear; **for the Day will declare it**, because it will be revealed by fire; and the fire will test each one's work, of what

sort it is. If anyone's work which he has built on it endures, he will receive a reward. If anyone's work is burned, he will suffer loss; but he himself will be saved, yet so as through fire.

"The Day will declare it" – it takes place on the Day of the Lord, along with the universal judgment, of which it is a part, the return of Jesus, and the general resurrection.

EVEN PAUL'S WORK WILL BE JUDGED

Obviously, we need to diligently get on with God's work. Some have summarised God's work as GC²: the Great Commission (Mat 28:18-20) and the Great Commandment (Mat 22:37-40). Faithfulness is the key. This scripture makes clear that in the final analysis we stand or fall before Jesus alone. It is to him alone we are responsible. And the works of every believer will be judged. Even Paul's work will be judged:

1 Cor 4:1-5 Let a man so consider us, as servants of Christ and stewards of the mysteries of God. Moreover, it is required in stewards that one be found faithful. But with me it is a very small thing that I should be judged by you or by a human court. In fact, I do not even judge myself. For I know of nothing against myself, yet I am not justified by this; but He who judges me is the Lord. **Therefore judge nothing before the time, until the Lord comes,** who will both bring to light the hidden things of darkness and reveal the counsels of the hearts. Then each one's praise will come from God.

Yet again we see that, at His coming, the hidden things will be revealed. It is "the" time – only one coming is spoken of. How have we ever come to a place where we believe that the believers will be raptured and hidden, the exact opposite of this very straightforward passage?

JUDGMENT IN THE CHURCH - EXPULSION FROM CHURCH FOR SIN?

Not many churches today have Paul's zeal and determination to see holy standards in the church. He commanded the Corinthian church to expel a member, so that that member will be shocked enough to repent, so that he may be saved "in the Day of the Lord". At that final call there will be people who only just get in by a slender margin, who perhaps got carried away through spending too much time "in the world".

1 Cor 5:3 For I indeed, as absent in body but present in spirit, have already judged (as though I were present) him who has so done this deed. In the name of our Lord Jesus Christ, when you are gathered together, along with my spirit, with the power of our Lord Jesus Christ, deliver such a one to Satan for the destruction of the flesh, that **his spirit may be saved in the day of the Lord Jesus.**

This is another example of Paul's focus on the reality of the day of the Lord, and the inevitable judgment to come with it. He was tenderly concerned lest this brother should be found wanting and was even prepared to expel the brother from the church in the hope that he would come to his senses, repent, and once more find a place of grace with the Lord. Paul's dealings with him reflect his concern for all the believers that they and we "be blameless **in the day of our Lord Jesus Christ"**.

JUDGE OURSELVES

Paul, in the following scripture, mentions two forms of judgment we experience in the Christian life. First we must judge ourselves and examine ourselves. Secondly God judges us and disciplines us, in order that we would be made ready for the final judgment.

1 Corinthians 11:31-2 For if we would judge ourselves, we would not be judged. But when we are judged, we are chastened by the Lord, that we may not be condemned with the world.

2 Corinthians 13:5: Examine yourselves as to whether you are in the faith. Test yourselves.

Paul was emphatic to the Corinthians that they should look at themselves and their lives to make sure they were really living out their faith. If we judge ourselves and take action on the things displeasing to God in our lives, we will not come under God's censure for those things.

JOHN EMPHASISES BEING OBEDIENT
TO GOD'S COMMANDS:

John 14:21 He who has My commandments and keeps them, it is he who loves Me. And he who loves Me will be loved by My Father, and I will love him and manifest Myself to him."

1 John 2:3-6 Now by this we know that we know Him, if we keep His commandments. He who says, "I know Him," and does not keep His commandments, is a liar, and the truth is not in him. But whoever keeps His word, truly the love of God is perfected in him. By this we know that we are in Him. He who says he abides in Him ought himself also to walk just as He walked.

John teaches that the true test of whether we know Him is whether we are following His commandments. He is not talking about "good deeds" done to try to merit God's favour. But if we have a true faith we will change and will naturally find ourselves following His commands. He will change us. We only need to co-operate with the work of the Holy Spirit in our lives.

REJOICING TOGETHER

Rejoicing in the day of Christ will be wholehearted, universal among those who have led a life of obedience to God's call, and far beyond what we consider to be happiness in this life.

Philippians 2:14-16 Do all things without complaining and disputing, that you may become blameless and harmless, children of God without fault in the midst of a crooked and perverse generation, among whom you shine as lights in the world, holding fast the word of life, so that I may rejoice in the day of Christ that I have not run in vain or laboured in vain.

A process of growing as a Christian believer is clearly implied by the words "you may become blameless and harmless..." Few Christians like to reflect on v 15 today – children of God in the midst of a crooked and perverse generation. But this is reality. Let us dare to believe God's word and see where it takes us. Obedience to Christ's call always leads in the end to joy. What great joy will greet the faithful believer "in the

Day of the Lord Jesus". Paul has given his all to shepherd the believers, and they will be his crowning achievement and boast in that Day. Why that day? Because that is the day everything will be revealed.

2 Cor 1:13 Now I trust you will understand, even to the end (as also you have understood us in part), that we are your boast as you also are ours, **in the day of the Lord Jesus**.

But note that not only will the Corinthian believers be his boast, but he will also be their boast. They must have ministered to him, prayed for him, given him hospitality and money – so they have assisted his ministry as he has theirs. It does not matter how inexperienced we are, we can minister to any man or woman of God – and they will be your boast in that Day.

THE HOLY SPIRIT AS A GUARANTEE FOR OUR FINAL SALVATION

Eph 4:30 And do not grieve the Holy Spirit of God, by whom **you were sealed for the day of redemption.**

After the day of redemption, it will be plain to all that we are redeemed – we will be living with the company of the redeemed, with God, in the light of His presence. Now, in the meantime, He has given us the Holy Spirit as a seal on that redemption – we can be confident in our redemption because it is sealed by God. This is one reason why we must all be filled with the Holy Spirit.

Paul's second letter to the Corinthians contains another verse which assures us of our inheritance in Christ. This time the Holy Spirit is described as a guarantee. It was customary for a Roman wine merchant to give a sample of the wine he had supplied as security for the whole consignment. In a similar way the Holy Spirit does this for us. He is a security, guaranteeing us the whole consignment of God's promises. The Greek word is arrhabon, pronounced *ar-hrab-ohn*. We must cherish the Holy Spirit and receive Him.

2 Cor 21-22 Now He who establishes us with you in Christ and has anointed us is God, who also has sealed us and given us the **Spirit in our hearts as a guarantee.**

We need the Holy Spirit in the times to come, however we

understand Him. And we must be sure that we are filled with the Holy Spirit. It is easy to have made a commitment to Jesus, and even to have been baptised, without being filled with the Spirit. The next passage illustrates this. The Samarians had been born again, filled with joy, and healed from many diseases but the Word says:

Acts 8:15-16 "…(the apostles) prayed for them, that they might receive the Holy Spirit. For as yet He had fallen upon none of them. They had only been baptised in the name of the Lord Jesus."

They had experienced the other blessings, but not the filling of the Holy Spirit. The non-Pentecostal line of Bible teaching has maintained for over a century that there is no experience of being filled with the Holy Spirit separate from the experience of being saved, but this passage makes it obvious that being filled with the Holy Spirit is a separate experience. Jesus said it is vital to a powerful witness.[45]

BE STEADFAST

2 Peter 3:10-18 But the day of the Lord will come as a thief in the night, in which the heavens will pass away with a great noise, and the elements will melt with fervent heat; both the earth and the works that are in it will be burned up. Therefore, since all these things will be dissolved, what manner of persons ought you to be in holy conduct and godliness, looking for and hastening the coming of the day of God, because of which the heavens will be dissolved, being on fire, and the elements will melt with fervent heat.

I have heard something like the following from many a modern pastor. "Come to the cross just as you are. God loves you unconditionally. It doesn't matter what you have done or what kind of life you are leading." It is true that Jesus is more than willing to forgive our sin, whatever it may be. But it doesn't stop there. The life from there onward needs to be one of discipleship and holiness, pondering and obeying the scriptures, and being filled with and guided by the Holy Spirit. This is true freedom.

1 Cor 15:57-58 But thanks be to God, who gives us the victory through our Lord Jesus Christ. Therefore, my beloved brethren, be

---

[45] See Acts 1:8, Luke 24:49

steadfast, immovable, always abounding in the work of the Lord, knowing that your labour is not in vain in the Lord[46].

THE WORK OF THE LORD

The work of the Lord above all is the Great Commission of Mat 28:18-20, which, in different words concludes each of the four Gospels. We start by reaching out to the people we know and have associations within our local area. In time there is no knowing where the Lord may lead us!

Heb 10:24-25 And let us consider one another in order to stir up love and good works, not forsaking the assembling of ourselves together, as is the manner of some, but exhorting one another, and so much the more as you see the Day approaching.

It is a great help to have Christian friends urging us on, and we can make a huge difference by urging them on "to stir up love and good works". This is normal Christian living. Note this should be happening more and more "as we see the Day approaching". We should be excitedly watching world events and see the evidence of His soon return. Also we should spend quality time increasing our knowledge of the scriptures and making sure we have a firm grasp of what the Bible describes of the end times.

THIS WORLD IS NOT OUR HOME; WE ARE PILGRIMS...

Hebrews 11:13-16, 39-40 These all died in faith, not having received the promises, but having seen them afar off were assured of them, embraced them and confessed that they were strangers and pilgrims on the earth. For those who say such things declare plainly that they seek a homeland. And truly if they had called to mind that country from which they had come out, they would have had opportunity to return. But now they desire a better, that is, a heavenly country. Therefore, God is not ashamed to be called their God, for He has prepared a city for them...

---

[46] 1 Cor 15:50-58

39 And all these, having obtained a good testimony through faith, did not receive the promise, God having provided something better for us, that they should not be made perfect apart from us.

What an utter privilege, that the knowledge and gifts these saints need for completion of their lives have been entrusted to us. The appropriate attitude for a Christian is surely to consider ourselves strangers and pilgrims with them until the great Day of the Lord and the appearance of the heavenly city.

SET OUR HEARTS ON THE HEAVENLY CITY TO COME, AND NOT ON THE THINGS OF THIS WORLD!

Hebrews 12:25-29 See that you do not refuse Him who speaks. For if they did not escape who refused Him who spoke on earth, much more shall we not escape if we turn away from Him who speaks from heaven, whose voice then shook the earth; but now He has promised, saying, "Yet once more I shake not only the earth, but also heaven." Now this, "Yet once more," indicates the removal of those things that are being shaken, as of things that are made, that the things which cannot be shaken may remain. Therefore, since we are receiving a kingdom which cannot be shaken, let us have grace, by which we may serve God acceptably with reverence and godly fear. For our God is a consuming fire.

When everything has been shaken that can be shaken, we will still be here, because we are rooted in Him

GOD WILL PRESERVE US AND PERFECT OUR FAITH AS THE DAY APPROACHES

Phi 1:6......being confident of this very thing, that He who has begun a good work in you will complete it until the day of Jesus Christ.

Phi 1:9-11 And this I pray, that your love may abound still more and more in knowledge and all discernment, that you may approve the things that are excellent, that you may be sincere and without offense till the day of Christ, being filled with the fruits of righteousness which are by Jesus Christ, to the glory and praise of God.

Paul prayed earnestly that the Philippians would be sincere and without offense "till the day of Christ." Do we hear this sort of prayer for a brother or a sister in Christ in our churches today? Surely if it were not necessary to pray like this, Paul would not have done it.

Jud 24 Now to Him who can keep you from stumbling, and to present you faultless before the presence of His glory with exceeding joy

He can keep us until the Great Day! There is a delicate balance between two realities. The first reality is the necessity for diligence to make sure we are obeying His commands and walking in His ways. The second reality is Him, holding us in the palm of His hand and sovereignly completing the work He has begun in us.

THE PERFECTION OF LOVE

We will not escape the judgment. But we will have confidence in that Day:

1 John 4:17 Love has been perfected among us in this: that we may have boldness in the day of judgment; because as He is, so are we in this world.

John tells us that the Day of the Lord, which is also the Day of Judgment, is surely coming. But those who are in Christ Jesus need have no fear of it. In the following passage, Peter tells us there is one thing we should do above everything else:

1Peter 4:7-11 But the end of all things is at hand; therefore, be serious and watchful in your prayers. [8] And above all things have fervent love for one another, for "love will cover a multitude of sins".

Above all things have fervent love for one another! How fervent is our love for the saints of God? Whether we are pre-, post-, or a-millennial, let us love one another, and look forward to the near return of our Lord. We can hang on to the many prophecies of the *Parousia* of Jesus Christ, knowing that the prophecies are genuine, complementing each other, and simple to understand.

Amen
Robin Corner

EPILOGUE

✠ ✠ ✠

THE "GREAT RESET"

This book has been four years in the writing, and the world is a different place now than it was when I started. At the time of writing, COVID-19 is rampaging around the globe, while I sit in a very privileged little bubble called New Zealand. The virus has provided a whole new massive opportunity for globalists to launch the "Great Reset" project. The best way to get the flavour of it is to examine the thoughts of its founder, Klaus Schwab, also founder of the World Economic Forum based in Switzerland:

"COVID-19 lockdowns may be gradually easing, but anxiety about the world's social and economic prospects is only intensifying. There is good reason to worry: a sharp economic downturn has already begun, and we could be facing the worst depression since the 1930s. But, while this outcome is likely, it is not unavoidable.

"To achieve a better outcome, the world must act jointly and swiftly to revamp all aspects of our societies and economies, from education to social contracts and working conditions. Every country, from the United States to China, must participate, and every industry, from oil and gas to tech, must be transformed. In short, we need a 'Great Reset' of capitalism."

"Left unaddressed, these crises, together with COVID-19, will deepen and leave the world even less sustainable, less equal, and more fragile. Incremental measures and *ad hoc* fixes will not suffice to prevent this scenario. We must build entirely new foundations for our economic and social systems."

"….. the pandemic represents a rare but narrow window of opportunity to reflect, reimagine, and reset our world …." (Schwab, 2020)

ATTACK ON CAPITALISM

Let us consider Schwab's words. He introduces the problem, the sharp economic downturn, which he then alleges will be ameliorated by his solution, the "Great Reset". His first target in his article is capitalism. Is he promoting communism? Here is what he says: "We must build entirely new foundations for our economic and social systems." And what are these "new foundations"? He wants to go as far as "reimagining and resetting the entire world". Is this a new communism, with all its old features of centralised control, and redistribution of wealth? The scope of these people's goal is breath-taking: control of the whole world. Could this itself be a confirmation we are in the end times, and the way is opening for the final Antichrist?

GLOBALISTS IN NEW ZEALAND

Some senior politicians are promoting the "Reset" in my own country of New Zealand and are aligning with an anti-Christian legislation agenda. I find attitude to abortion serves well as an instant "litmus test" of a MP's or a government's alignment or non-alignment with God's laws. Prior to 2020, New Zealand did have a very liberal abortion law, which effectively meant that anyone could get an abortion. But under our current government we have a new Act which has gone even further and removed abortion altogether from the jurisdiction of the Ministry of Justice to that of the Ministry of Health, which is equivalent to a declaration that abortion is not even a moral issue. In the thinking of today it is just a health matter for a woman to discuss with her doctor. On other moral issues such as "gay" marriage, legalisation of cannabis, and euthanasia, parliamentarians with some notable exceptions tend to take the liberal side. The traditional institution of marriage is challenged by the examples of some of those in power who have children but are not married. What sort of model is this setting for the younger generation?

These then are the type of values which would likely to come to the fore in any "Reset". As Christians we must be careful here to maintain a godly, charitable, attitude. We do not want the kind of demonisation of opponents we have seen in US politics of late. We must pray that our politicians gain a greater understanding of the Christian perspective. But we must also take heed of their atheistic values taking an ever increasing hold on the reins of government.

IDEAS GIVE RISE TO ACTIONS

In history, when we see societal change on the scale envisaged by the "resetters", the sincere idealists tend to lead initially, but soon get replaced by power-hungry individuals with their own agendas. Examples include Napoleon, Hitler, Stalin, Mao, and many others. Some of the worst African dictators started as the trusted subordinates of kinder men. Revolutions begin with ideas such as Marx's *Das Kapital*, or Hitler's *Mein Kampf*, but these ideas become the basis of action. The concern is about control of the world by the global elite.

And what more can we say about the spirit of this movement? It is summed up by these words quoted from the Rockefeller Foundation-Lancet Commission on Planetary Health. According to them, "human health and the health of the planet are inextricably linked, and that civilisation depends on human health, flourishing natural systems, and the wise care of natural resources." (Sadler, 2021)

PREPARING THE WAY FOR THE ANTICHRIST

Civilisation does not depend on these things. Civilisation depends on God and His Christ! These globalists take upon themselves the power to control the lives of billions. The way is opened for spirits like that of the Antichrist described in 2 Thessalonians 2: 4, "who opposes and exalts himself above all that is called God or that is worshiped, so that he sits as God in the temple of God, showing himself that he is God".

The stage is being set for the appearance of this personage. It is a time as never before to focus on our obedience to the commands of God. The coming scenario is laid out in some detail in 2 Thessalonians 2:1-12. If you are not familiar with this Bible chapter, I do commend it to you as vital information for survival in these times.

"GRASS ROOTS" MOVEMENT NEEDED

What is needed is a "grass roots", transformational, global Christian movement which will generate an avalanche of prayer and sharing of the Gospel. Not that we can halt the chain of events outlined in the scriptures, but we can be instrumental in the saving of many souls. And we can, God helping us, maintain our own salvation. As I have said throughout this book, there are many Christians of all persuasions who believe we are in the end times. The more I research the issue, the more I find credible witnesses who are convinced of the reality of the soon second coming of Christ.

CATHOLICS IN THE END TIMES

As I mentioned in the preface, my wife Margaret and I worship at our local Catholic Church. Catholics who believe in the end times have the support of the current Pope Francis. During one homily, referring to Luke 21:5-19, he said, "Of course they (the disciples) asked him: When will this happen? What will the signs be? But Jesus moves the focus from these secondary aspects — i.e. when will it be? What will it be like? — to the truly important questions. Firstly, not to let oneself be fooled by false prophets nor to be paralyzed by fear. Secondly, to live this time of expectation as a time of witness and perseverance. We are in this time of waiting, in expectation of the coming of the Lord." (Pope_Francis, 2013).

YOUNG PEOPLE ASKED TO BE
WATCHMEN AND WOMEN

Pope John Paul II believed in the approaching return of Jesus. He addressed this message to the youth:

"Dear young people, it is up to you to be the *watchmen* of the morning who announce the coming of the sun who is the Risen Christ!" —ST. JOHN PAUL II, *Message of the Holy Father to the Youth of the World*, XVII World Youth Day, n. 3; (cf. Is 21:11-12) (Mallett, 2020)

"I did not hesitate to ask them to make a radical choice of faith and life and present them with a stupendous task: to become "morning watchmen" at the dawn of the new millennium." —POPE JOHN PAUL II, *Novo Millennio Inuente*, n.9 (Mallett, 2020)

THE EXHORTATION OF FATIMA

Past and modern-day Catholic prophets, or seers as they tend to be called in Catholicism, have added weight to the expectation of His coming. Perhaps the best known prophecies are those given to three children, Lucia dos Santos, and her cousins, Jacinta and Francisco Marto at Fatima, Portugal. They went to a certain spring in the countryside six times in 1917 to meet with an apparition of the Virgin Mary and were accompanied by larger and larger crowds who heard rumours of the apparitions.

In a May visit, the children described receiving a vision of hell. They said that Mary asked all to earnestly pray and make sacrifices for the saving of souls. She told them to read the Book of Revelation in the Bible. She said World War I could rage because of mankind's sin and indifference to God. If there was a change in attitude there would be peace, but if not, there would be another more terrible war still. We know the outcome: humanity didn't change. World War I continued for another year, but only 22 years later, World War II started. History tells us that World War I cost 20 million lives, but that during World War II some 50 million lives were lost. The majority do not think the prophetic warning will be realised, because they do not make the causal connection between our sin and prayerlessness and the outbreak of war. But here, for those who can see, is the terrible outcome of ignoring God. And has mankind heeded?

70,000 SEE A MIRACLE

About 70,000 people gathered for the last vision on October 16th, 1917, when there was a significant miracle in the sky, the sun emitting many colours, then appearing to hurtle towards earth. Many repented and turned to Jesus, amazed by the miraculous sign. The media was present in force, many with an intention to discredit the by now famous apparitions. But as events turned out, incredulous and positive reports went out all round the world.

LUCIA LIVES TO BEAR WITNESS TO THE WORLD

The children asked Mary if she would take them to heaven. Her reply was that she would take Jacinta and Francisco quite soon, but that Lucia would remain longer in the world, to tell people of these teachings. Francisco died in 1919, aged 10, and Jacinta in 1920, aged 9, both from the influenza epidemic that took so many lives at that time. However, Lucia lived until 2005. She clarified some of the messages in the 1940's by setting them out in writing for the Vatican. (Wikipaedia, undated)

WARNING ABOUT RUSSIA

Another message was given to the children about Russia, which Lucia confirmed in writing in 1941:

"God… is about to punish the world for its crimes, by means of war, famine, and persecutions of the Church and of the Holy Father. To prevent this, I shall come to ask for the consecration of Russia to my Immaculate Heart, and the Communion of reparation on the First Saturdays. If my requests are heeded, Russia will be converted, and there will be peace; if not, she will spread her errors throughout the world, causing wars and persecutions of the Church. The good will be martyred; the Holy Father will have much to suffer; various nations will be annihilated. In the end, my Immaculate Heart will triumph. The Holy Father will consecrate Russia to me, and she shall be converted, and a period of peace will be granted to the world." —Message of Fatima, (Sister_Lucia, 1941)

Most Protestant Christians do not believe in apparitions of the Virgin Mary, but any fair-minded person would have to agree that there is evidence of the authenticity of these messages. The children's lives were very credible, and the accuracy of the prophecies, especially regarding Russia and World War II, remarkable. It was in 1917, the year when Lenin and the Communists took Moscow, that the children were told that Russia would "spread her errors throughout the world, causing wars and persecutions of the Church" if people would not turn to God in repentance and prayer. Of course, that is exactly what happened over the last 100 years, and some would say that the "Great Reset" could be the ultimate fulfilment of that prophecy.

ARE THE FATIMA MESSAGES AUTHENTIC?

"Consecration to the Immaculate Heart of Mary" in Catholic thinking means to have the same attitude of surrender and consecration to God as Mary did in her bringing up of Jesus. Aid is sought from Mary by prayers such as the Rosary to bring about this state of surrender to Jesus. Unacceptable to much Protestant theology, but could it be that these messages from Mary, the mother of Jesus, are authentic?

The only three alternatives seem to be: 1. Human fraud? 2. Satanic manifestation? Or 3. Authentic? Human fraud seems unlikely as 70,000 people were there, and there were many eye-witness accounts, including some from initially sceptical journalists, though sceptics have claimed that the accounts differ. The message itself, to fast, pray, and read the Book of Revelation, seems to exclude the possibility that it was a Satanic manifestation, though we know the devil can appear as an angel of light. Why would the devil want Christians to fast, pray and read the Book of Revelation? Does that leave the third alternative as the most likely?

PERIOD OF PEACE

In some modern Catholic eschatological thinking, the "period of peace granted to the world" spoken of by the Lady of Fatima is equated with the millennial reign (Mallett_and_O'Connor, 2020). According to Mallett and O'Connor, the millennium, which will be a period only symbolized by '1000 years', will be characterised by an unseen spiritual reign of Jesus in the future. They have some very persuasive teaching on Revelation 6, describing the seals as: 1. Time of mercy; 2. War; 3. Economic collapse; 4. Social collapse; 5. Persecution; 6: Universal warning; 7. The eye of the storm (explaining how Christians can find shelter in the troublesome times ahead). However, the timing is different from the Amil model, and the millennium is assumed to be lived here on earth. Their concept is similar to the scenario as conceived by Postmil, described in chapter 12. I find their presentation stimulating, but my own findings from Revelation 20 make me prefer the Amil interpretation. I am convinced especially by the fact that the battle of Revelation 20:7-10 seems to be a recapitulation of the same battle described in Revelation 19:11-21, and Ezekiel 37 and 38. Equally importantly, I believe strongly that the binding of Satan was at the crucifixion of Christ (or between the crucifixion and resurrection).

MAINSTREAM CATHOLIC TEACHING

Mainstream Catholic teaching is that Revelation 20:1-10 is a picture of the present time, and is in fact an Amillennialist position, though most Catholics would not recognise the term, and many would be unaware of the doctrine. The following is quoted from the Catholic Answers website:

"Early in the Christian age, Satan was bound (20:1-2) for "a thousand years," signifying a long but indefinite period (just as the assertion that God owns "the cattle on a thousand hills" means he owns the cattle on *all* the hills—a large but indeterminate number).

"Jesus himself had promised the binding of the devil—the "strong man"—as a precondition for the spreading of the gospel (Mt 12:29 in context). In Revelation, the devil is depicted as shut up and sealed in the abyss (v. 3a). Incorporeal spirits such as the devil do not actually occupy space and cannot be "shut up" in spatial regions, so the meaning of this is that he can no more deceive the "nations" (or "gentiles"—the word is the same in Greek) until the thousand years is over." (Akin, undated)

CATHOLIC TEACHING IS AMIL

Akin's view is close to my analysis of Revelation 20 in Chapter 16, except that he too does not address the non-chronological nature of the events in John's visions. Catholic doctrine on the end times allows for different interpretations but excludes certain positions. Catholicism explicitly rejects Premillennialism, again supporting the argument in this book. Catholic teaching holds that the rapture and the return of Jesus in Person will not happen until the end of the world and the universal judgment.

EASTERN ORTHODOX CHRISTIANS

To complete the overview, we should also look at the Eastern Orthodox view. I have taken the Greek Orthodox as an example. The following is a statement of this church's belief on end times:

"The Church accepts that upon the return of Christ the general resurrection will take place. Saint Paul tells us, "We who are alive who are left until the coming of the Lord shall not precede those who have fallen asleep. For the Lord Himself shall descend from heaven with a cry of command, with the archangel's call, and with the sound of the trumpet of God. And the dead in Christ shall rise first; then those who are alive, who are left, shall be caught up together with them in the clouds to meet the Lord in the air; and so we shall always be with the Lord (1 Thessalonians 4:15-18)."

"With these words of Paul the Church teaches that all people who were ever born shall receive their resurrection bodies, including those who will not enter the Kingdom, since Christ states in John's Gospel that all who are in the tombs will come forth, they who have done good into the resurrection of life, and they who have done evil into the resurrection of judgment (John 5:29). At every funeral service of the Church this particular reading from First Thessalonians is read, again as a reminder of Christ's return.

"The earth shall then be transformed as Saint Peter says; for he speaks of the transformation of the present elements by fire (2 Peter 3:7) into new heavens and a new earth (2 Peter 3:10).

"Death will be put to death, as Holy Scripture teaches. Death will be no more, and every person who was ever born will live forever, either in the glorious presence of Christ, the eternal Sun of Righteousness, or forever away from the presence of Christ in the outer darkness."

(Greek Orthodox Archdiocese of America, 2003)

AND ON THE ANTICHRIST:

"An oligarchy of power and control has begun. Technology has already made phenomenal advances wherein microchips are not only placed in inanimate objects, such as vehicles, for their immediate known location, but also in the bodies of children for fear of their being kidnapped or disappearing somehow.

"Many Orthodox Christians, especially monks with great insight, see these achievements as the preparation for a one-government world, ultimately with a one world ruler. This bespeaks of the coming anti-Christ. Before this occurs Saint John the Theologian speaks of many anti-Christs, saying, "It is the last hour (1 John 2:18)." Orthodoxy believes that many anti-Christs have already arrived and some have already gone. Although there are differing opinions by those who attempt to discern the signs of the times, one thing is certain and that is that the anti-Christ shall be embraced by many as the Messiah. His reign shall last seven long years according to the prophecies.

"Obviously, the time is not now for the anti-Christ to make his appearance. There is too much turmoil in the world and too many wars being fought, although this is also one of the signs of the final days. The world powers will ultimately bring about peace throughout the world. The Apostle Paul gives a prophetic insight to us. He writes to the people of Thessaloniki in his first epistle, "When people say 'There is peace and security,' then sudden destruction will come upon them as travail comes upon a woman with child, and there will be no escape (Thessalonians 5:3)." We know from the Lord's own words in Saint Matthew's Gospel that "there will be great tribulation, such as has not been seen since the beginning of the world until now, no, and never will be (Matthew 24:21)." Referring to the ones who will be saved He continues to say that "if those days had not been shortened, no human being would be saved; but for the sake of the elect those days will be shortened (Matthew 24:22)." Basically, all the Gospel readings, such as these which speak of the end of the age, are read in the various services of Great Lent and Holy Week in the Orthodox churches, as a preparation for the end."

(Greek Orthodox Archdiocese of America, 2003)

The alert reader will have noticed that what the Greek Orthodox Church holds is almost the same as this book has concluded. The coming Parousia (appearing of Christ) is seen as the time of the general resurrection of the dead, both righteous and wicked at the same time, and the judgment. This is the time when the old heavens and earth are done away with and replaced with the new. Death will have been defeated forever, and the saved will live for all eternity with our beloved Saviour and our God. When I started researching for this book, I had no idea that I would end up with the same conclusions as the Greek Orthodox church. I could have opted not to study, but just go and ask them! But then I would not have known whether the Greek Orthodox view was tenable. And I would have missed the most exciting journey of study I have ever undertaken.

PROTESTANTS AND EVANGELICALS

Many prophecies, videos and books on the end time have come out of the evangelical / charismatic wing of the Protestant church, as we have seen. But it seems that prophecies about politics have left this wing of the US church in absolute disarray. There must surely be a prophetic significance to the incredible and unanticipated chains of recent events in 2020-2021 in the USA that have captured the attention of the whole world.

However, much good material has been written by Premil, Postmil and Amil writers, and useful observations on our time and its correspondence with Bible prophecy have been made by writers of all millennial opinions. We need to recognise that there is a rich heritage of theology and experience coming from both sides of the Reformation divide. Mother Teresa has made Christian compassion known and valued all over the World. Another Catholic nun who captured the attention of the world's press recently was Sister Ann Rose Nu Tawng in Myanmar. Kneeling in the dust in front of a group of heavily armed police officers enforcing military rule, she begged them to spare children in the vicinity and take her life instead. She won much respect for Christianity in the Buddhist nation. Literally millions of Christian converts in the world's newer mission fields such as China and India are being won to Christ through church planting and discipleship movements. I have a friend who, for security purposes I cannot name, who founded a movement which, in the last 7 years, has seen 48,000 Muslims and over 150,000 Buddhists get baptised as Christ followers. Let us pray that there would be renewal and revival in all genuine expressions of Christianity, and a true working together of Catholic, Protestant, and Orthodox.

THE LOOMING LAST BATTLE

We as Christendom must choose our battlefields with care. Our battle with the coming Antichrist is not the world's political stage. Again and again the Bible tells us we shall lose that battle at the end of the world, at least from the perspective of political control of the world. Today's battlefield is the battle for the hearts and minds of men and women. What is our weapon? Our weapon is the Gospel.

Revelation 11 pictures the times we are coming into. The passage Rev 11:3 to 11:18 begins with an image of the church[47]. John portrayed it as two witnesses, perhaps Jews and Gentiles, or New Testament believers and Old Testament believers.

---

[47] Reasons why the witnesses should be interpreted as the whole community of God's people and not two individuals such as Moses and Elijah (according to Beale). 1. The witnesses are called "two lampstands". Lampstands were identified as churches in Rev 1:20. Symbolism is normally consistent through one book.

2. The beast attacking them in v7 is based on the beast of Daniel 7, who attacks the nation of Israel, not an individual. 3. All the nations will see the bodies of the witnesses, indicating that the witnesses are a community throughout the world. 4. The woman of Rev 12 stands for the community of God's people, and the woman of Rev 17 for the community of the ungodly. It is quite consistent for the two witnesses to represent a whole community. 5. Often in Revelation the whole community of believers is identified as the ones who testify about Jesus. 6. The two have the same powers. They are not pictured as independent individuals. (Beale, 1999)

Rev 11:3 And I will give *power* to my two witnesses, and they will prophesy one thousand two hundred and sixty days, clothed in sackcloth."

Interestingly, for a long time there have always been "two witnesses", depending on our perspective in time and geography. The "Great Schism", formally enacted in 1054AD but the result of a split going back much earlier, left the Eastern Orthodox and Roman Catholic Churches as "two witnesses". The Reformation left the Catholic and Protestant Churches as two witnesses. Twentieth century debates over spiritual gifts resulted in evangelicals and charismatics as "two witnesses". There have been doctrinal differences between the witnesses. However, God, over the centuries, has providentially ensured that each witness has retained enough of the Gospel to bring salvation to those who would receive it from the heart. Of course, John, in his writing of Revelation, could not have foreseen these instances of "two witnesses", but he wrote under the inspiration of the Holy Spirit, who knows all the things to come.

The Gospel itself is power, as we learn from Romans 1:16, quoted below. This is why the witnesses are described by John as "prophesying". This has nothing to do with whether the churches believe in the gift of prophecy. True "prophecy" is always a message from God to people, so the witnesses are bringing God's message to the world. The "1260 days" is a symbol representing a long period of time. This of course has been fulfilled in history. So far, the church has been proclaiming the message for 2000 years but has not finished yet. The witnesses are "clothed in sackcloth": the wearing of sackcloth perhaps reflects the gravity, mourning and sadness of the witnesses because they know their message will ultimately be rejected by the majority.

Rev 11:4 These are the two olive trees and the two lampstands standing before the God of the earth.

The witnesses, the olive trees and the lampstands represent the church proclaiming the Gospel.

Rev 11:5-6 And if anyone wants to harm them, fire proceeds from their mouth and devours their enemies. And if anyone wants to harm them, he must be killed in this manner. [6] These have power to shut heaven, so that no rain falls in the days of their prophecy; and they have power over waters to turn them to blood, and to strike the earth with all plagues, as often as they desire.

The fire, the drought, the waters turning to blood and the plagues all reflect the wrath of God directed at those who resist His word and His servants. The images give power to the total picture. The witnesses have great power, God-given authority and protection. John alludes to the ministries of Moses and Elijah to bring this out. The power to withhold rain was given to Elijah to rebuke the evil Ahab (1 Kings 11) and Moses turned the waters into blood (Exodus 7:17-25). John, in Revelation, uses these images to bring out the spiritual realities now prevailing. If we consider, for example, the fire coming from the witnesses (v 5), in the Book of Kings account, Elijah literally caused fire to burn his opponents. During the Gospel era that is not the character of the ministry to be exercised, as Jesus firmly impressed on John and James in Luke 9:51-56. However, the fire comes from the mouths of the witnesses in Revelation, and represents the powerful Gospel messages proclaimed by men and women of God over the centuries of the church era. This metaphor would have been familiar to John's audience, many of whom would have been well instructed in the scriptures. God told Jeremiah,

> Jer 5:14 "Because you speak this word,
> Behold, I will make My words in your mouth fire,
> And this people wood,
> And it shall devour them."

Jeremiah's metaphor is of a type common in the whole Bible, not just in John's Book of Revelation. In v7 we move to the apparent defeat of the church:

Rev 11:7 When they finish their testimony, the beast that ascends out of the bottomless pit will make war against them, overcome them, and kill them.

At the end of history, as confirmed elsewhere in the Bible[48], God will allow the apparent defeat of the church, which is symbolised

---

[48] See also Dan 7:21, 8:24, Mat 24:15, Mark 13:14, Luke 21:21, 2Thes 2:3-4, Rev 20:3b, 7-8

here by the killing of the witnesses by the beast (Antichrist). Beale writes "The picture of the witnesses' bodies lying on the 'street of the great city' probably does not indicate that the entire church will be exterminated so that it cannot bear witness any longer. Rather... that the true church will seem defeated...will appear small and insignificant, and will be treated with indignity...At the time thus portrayed the church's public influence will not be felt as formally because persecution will have grown more severe and the church will have been reduced to a remnant - not being completely annihilated but driven underground. Though parts of the church's voice throughout history may be temporarily silenced, a universal silence will fall on the church at the very end of history and just as small groups of believers continued to exist throughout earlier temporary silencings, so a small remnant of witnesses remain in the future scenario of verses 8 onwards. The continued existence of a small church is pointed to by other references in Revelation to a small community of believers undergoing persecution in the period immediately preceding the final judgement. In fact, the parallels in Revelation and the Gospels indicate that if God did not defeat the church's persecutors at this point, the church would actually be wiped out entirely[49]." (Beale, 1999, pp 590-591)

Rev 11:8 And their dead bodies *will lie* in the street of the great city which spiritually is called Sodom and Egypt, where also our Lord was crucified.

The great city is Babylon. The addition of Sodom and Egypt extends the meaning to include the whole ungodly world in general. The image of the dead bodies represents the apparent defeat and humiliation of the church.

Rev 11:9-10 Then *those* from the peoples, tribes, tongues, and nations will see their dead bodies three-and-a-half days, and not allow their dead bodies to be put into graves. [10] And those who dwell on the earth will rejoice over them, make merry, and send gifts to one another, because these two prophets tormented those who dwell on the earth.

---

[49] Rev 17:8, 20:7-8, Mat 24:15-22, 37-39

Non-believers generally have a massive aversion to resolute and righteous people who bring God's message of repentance and salvation. Here they are rejoicing at the defeat of the church and resultant freedom from constraint. The exhortation to holiness is torment for the people of the world. The bodies of the witnesses will only be around for a short time, symbolised by the three and a half days, which contrasts with the 1260 days the church was proclaiming the Gospel. God will only allow the apparent defeat of the righteous to last a very short time. The people of the world are drawn from "the peoples, tribes, tongues and nations" and the witnesses tormented "those who dwell on the earth". This use of universal language is further proof that John is writing about the universal church and the whole world, not just the Jews.

Rev 11:11-13 Now after the three-and-a-half days the breath of life from God entered them, and they stood on their feet, and great fear fell on those who saw them. [12] And they heard a loud voice from heaven saying to them, "Come up here." And they ascended to heaven in a cloud, and their enemies saw them. [13] In the same hour there was a great earthquake, and a tenth of the city fell. In the earthquake seven thousand people were killed, and the rest were afraid and gave glory to the God of heaven.

The breath of life entering the witnesses is an exact quote from Ezekiel 37:5, where the subject is the restoration of the twelve tribes of Israel. The restoration has never happened in the natural – the identity and abode of the northern tribes of Israel is still disputed or not known. Certainly, there has never been a reunion of the twelve tribes on the scale described in Ezekiel and Jeremiah[50]. Whatever the possible future natural fulfilment of the prophecy, it is clear that the reunion of the tribes symbolizes the gathering together of the saved of all regions of the earth and all times. This gathering takes place in the sky, as described in 1 Thes 4:16-18 (see also 1 Cor 15, 2 Thes 2:1, Mat 13:30, 48, Mat 25:32). Vindication and victory are the keynotes.

In our Revelation passage, it is not clear whether "the rest who were afraid and gave glory to the God of heaven" will experience genuine saving faith, or merely a forced and reluctant recognition of the power

---

[50] Jeremiah 31 and 32; Ezekiel 37

of God. If the former, they will have left their cry to God very late. Isaiah's[51] exhortation, "Seek the Lord while He may be found, Call upon Him while He is near" is surely applicable to all people. But sadly the latter outcome seems more likely in the context.

Rev 11:14 The second woe is past. Behold, the third woe is coming quickly.

For those who do not heed the warnings, the third woe, retribution from God, will follow swiftly.

Rev 11:15 Then the seventh angel sounded: And there were loud voices in heaven, saying, "The kingdoms of this world have become *the kingdoms* of our Lord and of His Christ, and He shall reign forever and ever!"

Glorious victory to our God! Once again we have arrived at the climactic moment and the heavens are open to our view. The 24 elders from chapters four and five are pictured again in the verse following. Beale (Beale, 1999) argues persuasively they are representative of all the servants of God of all ages. They can be seen as twelve Apostles and twelve Patriarchs of the tribes of Israel, representing New and Old Covenant saints together. John goes on to recap the end of the age again, the culmination of history. He recalls again the anger of the unbelieving nations, the wrath of God, the universal judgment, punishment of the wicked and reward of the righteous at the end of these verses:

Rev 11:16-18 And the twenty-four elders who sat before God on their thrones fell on their faces and worshiped God, [17] saying:

"We give You thanks, O Lord God Almighty,
The One who is and who was and who is to come,
Because You have taken Your great power and reigned.
[18] The nations were angry, and Your wrath has come,
And the time of the dead, that they should be judged,
And that You should reward Your servants the prophets
and the saints,
And those who fear Your name, small and great,
And should destroy those who destroy the earth."

---

[51] Isaiah 55:6

Joel addressed this period of history. We know he was talking about the end of the age, because the time is pinpointed by the sun, moon and stars going dark:

> Joel 3:14-15 Multitudes, multitudes in the valley of decision!
> For the day of the Lord *is* near in the valley of decision.
> ¹⁵ The sun and moon will grow dark,
> And the stars will diminish their brightness.

Multitudes in the valley of decision pictures ever restless humanity, facing the choice of accepting God's infinitely gracious offer of entire forgiveness, or eternal punishment for our sin. Every person must make their own decision. Paul's didactic teaching on the power of the Gospel is found in the first chapter of Romans:

Rom 1:16-18 "For I am not ashamed of the Gospel of Christ, for it is the power of God to salvation for everyone who believes, for the Jew first and also for the Greek. ¹⁷ For in it the righteousness of God is revealed from faith to faith; as it is written, "The just shall live by faith." ¹⁸ For the wrath of God is revealed from heaven against all ungodliness and unrighteousness of men, who suppress the truth in unrighteousness......"

I quoted Daniel 12 in chapter 6 and cannot resist recalling his wonderful words. Of course, as we have learned, he is addressing the same time in history as Joel in Joel 3 and John in Revelation 11.

> Dan 12:1-3 ......there shall be a time of trouble,
> Such as never was since there was a nation,
> *Even* to that time.
> And at that time your people shall be delivered,
> Everyone who is found written in the book.
> ² And many of those who sleep in the dust of the earth shall awake,
> Some to everlasting life,
> Some to shame *and* everlasting contempt.
> ³ Those who are wise shall shine

Like the brightness of the firmament,
And those who turn many to righteousness
Like the stars forever and ever.

We could be living at the climax of history. We yearn to "turn many to righteousness" as foretold by Daniel. However, we cannot say definitely this is the final time. Jesus made it quite clear that no-one knows the time or the hour. This is deliberate on God's part. All His servants should be always fully alert. Even if it turns out we are not at the end of the age, it is right that we should be living as if we were. In any case for all of us, the end of the age is only a heartbeat away. Any of us could have a car crash, or a heart attack at any time, and suddenly find we have run our race. Eternity suddenly envelops us. Are we ready?

We have discussed many doctrines during our time together It is important we have clear and Biblical thinking. Whether Dispensationalists, classical Premils, Amils, or Postmils, Protestants, Catholics, or Orthodox, let's by all means vigorously debate our doctrines. Paul wrote to Timothy:

2 Tim 4:2-4 Preach the word! Be ready in season *and* out of season. Convince, rebuke, exhort, with all longsuffering and teaching. [3] For the time will come when they will not endure sound doctrine, but according to their own desires, *because* they have itching ears, they will heap up for themselves teachers; [4] and they will turn *their* ears away from the truth and be turned aside to fables.

We must be well versed in scripture – of all things this will help us avoid fables and hold to solid Biblical truth.

However, some issues will probably never be resolved until Jesus comes personally to correct our thinking. Paul wrote:

1 Cor 11:19 For there must also be factions among you, that those who are approved may be recognized among you.

Let us hold our views with enthusiasm and become strong in our convictions. But let us also share them in charity, making a distinction between essential truths, and allowable differences. We need truth as never before. But we also need each other as never before.

Let's do this together!

REFERENCES

✠ ✠ ✠

Specifically Amil writers included in this list of references: Beale; Coffman; Davis; Hendriksen; Hoekema; Kercheville; Riddlebarger; and Storms.

Akin, Jimmy. undated. Does the Church teach that the prophecy of Revelation 20:1-10 is being fulfilled now? *Catholic Answers.* [Online] undated. [Cited: 27 May 2021.] https://www.catholic.com/qa/does-the-church-teach-that-the-prophecy-of-revelation-201-10-is-being-fulfilled-now.

Angelfire. 2020. The Official List of Sins (New Testament). *Angelfire.* [Online] 2020. http://www.angelfire.com/empire2/psuclass0/sinlist.html.

Bahnsen and Gentry. 1989. *House Divided.* 1989. www.kennethgentry.com/house-divided-bahnsen-gentry-limited-stock.

Balcombe, Dennis. 2021. *Zoom missions conference hosted by Victor Choudhrie, Nagpur, India. 2021.* s.l. : Unpublished, 2021.

Beale, GK. 1999. *The Book of Revelation, The New International Greek Commentary.* Grand Rapids, Michigan : Eerdmans Publisdhing Co, 1999. ISBN 978-0-8028-7107-7.

Bennett, David Malcolm. 2014. Edward Irving. *Edward Irving and John Nelson Darby.* [Online] 2014. [Cited: 24 3 2017.] https://www.edwardirving.org/untitled.

Berkhof, Louis. 1932. *Systematic Theology.* s.l. : Eerdmans, 1932.

Bible Study Tools. 2019. 11.4 Summary of the millennial kingdom. *Bible Study Tools.com.* [Online] 2019. [Cited: 09 09 2019.] https://www.biblestudytools. com/commentaries/revelation/related-topics/summary-of-the-millennial-kingdom.html.

Brown, Robert. 2015. The Coming of the Lord. *Theologue.* [Online] Providence Baptist Ministries, March 2015. [Cited: 22 September 2020.] https://theologue. files.wordpress.com/2015/03/thecomingofthelorde28093robertbrown.pdf.

Catechism of the Catholic Church. 1997. He will come again in glory to judge the living and the dead. *Catechism of the Catholic Church.* [Online] 7 9 1997. [Cited: 27 5 2021.] https://www.vatican.va/archive/ENG0015/ P1.HTM.

Christianity.com. 2020. Church history. *Christianity.com.* [Online] 2020. [Cited: 30th July 2020.] https://www.christianity.com/church/church-history/timeline/1-300/the-spread-of-the-early-church-11629561.html.

Coffman, James Burton. 1992. Commentary on Matthew 25. *Studylight.org/ commentaries.* [Online] 1992. https://www.studylight.org/commentaries/bcc/ matthew-25.html.

Coffman, James. 1992. Coffman's Commentaries on the Bible - Ezekiel. *Studylight.org.* [Online] 1992. [Cited: 18 09 2017.] https://www.studylight. org/commentaries/bcc/ezekiel-38.html.

Davis, Dean. 2014. *The High King of Heaven.* Enumclaw : Redemption Press, 2014. ISBN 978-1-63232-024-7.

Delitzsch, and Keil. 1861. *Commentary on the Old Testament.* https://www. studylight.org/commentaries/kdo/malachi-3.html : Studylight, 1861.

DeMar, Gary. 2013. Gary DeMar - Preterist interpretation of Revelation. *American Vision.* [Online] 2013. [Cited: 6 Jul 2017.] https://americanvision.org/7289/ was-the-preterist-interpretation-of-revelation-invented-by-the-jesuits/.

Dressler, Bob. 2014. Premillennial Dispensationalism. *Mount Carmel Outreach www.CONTENDER.org.* [Online] 2014. [Cited: 24 Aug 2017.] https://www. youtube.com/watch?v=V7fv9EJB23g.

dw.com. 2010. Lutherans reconcile with mennonites 500 years after bloody persecution. *dw.com.* [Online] 2010. [Cited: 29 May 2021.] https://www.

dw.com/en/lutherans-reconcile-with-mennonites-500-years-after-bloody-persecution.

Episcopal Church. 1979. An outline of the Faith commonly called the Catechism . [Online] 1979. http://justus.anglican.org/resources/bcp/catechism.pdf.

Eusebius. c250AD. *The History of the Church, Book VII, Chapter 24.* Alexandria : s.n., c250AD.

Fee and Stuart, Gordon and Douglas. 2002. *How to read the Bible book by book.* Grand Rapids, Michigan : Zondervan, 2002. ISBN 0-310-21118-2.

Greek Orthodox Archdiocese of America. 2003. The End Times; The Othodox Christian Perspective. *Greek Orthodox Archdiocese of America; Metropolis of Denver.* [Online] Sept 2003. [Cited: 12 February 2021.] https://www.denver.goarch.org/understanding-the-parousia.

Haynes, Joe. 1999. Interpreting Daniel. *Historicism.com.* [Online] (website founded) 1999 . [Cited: 24 9 2017.] historicism.com/Haynes/interpretingdaniel.htm.

Hendee, Caitlin. 2015. Federal-report-finds-major-increase-in-earthquake. *Denver Business Journal.* [Online] 23 April 2015. [Cited: 119 February 2017.] http://www.bizjournals.com/denver/news/2015/04/23/federal-report-finds-major-increase-in-earthquake.html.

Hendriksen, William. 1940. *More than Conquerors.* Grand Rapids : Baker Books, 1940.

Hickey, Stephen. 2013. Recognition Theology: America, Israel, the Lost Tribes and now Glenn Beck. *The Green Stick.* [Online] 30 Aug 2013. [Cited: 29 Jul 2017.] https://stevehickey.wordpress.com/tag/steven-m-collins/.

Hill, Napoleon. 1937. *Think and Grow Rich.* 1937.

Hinds, John T. 1962. cited by Coffman in "Commentary" on Rev 2:7. [Online] John T. Hinds, A Commentary of Revelation (Nashville: Gospel Advocate Company, 1962), p. 34., 1962. https://www.studylight.org/commentaries/bcc/revelation-2.html.

Hoekema, Anthony. 1977. Amillennialism. *The Highway.* [Online] 1977. [Cited: 10 Jul 2017.] https://www.the-highway.com/amila Hoekema.html.

Ice, Thomas. 2016. http://www.pre-trib.org/articles/view/rapture-in-pseudo-ephraem. *http://www.pre-trib.org.* [Online] 2016. [Cited: 19 March 2017.]

—. **1996.** Study Resources; Text Commentaries; Thomas Ice; An interpretation of Mat 24 - 25. *Blue Letter Bible.* [Online] 1996. [Cited: 5 9 2019.] https://www. blueletterbible.org/Comm/ice thomas/Mat24-25/Mat24-25 Part01.cfm.

Ingersol, Julie. 2011. C Peter Wagner: Dominion Theology and Postmillennialism on NPR. *Huffington Post.* [Online] 7 Dec 2011. [Cited: 17 June 2017.] http://www.huffingtonpost.com/julie-ingersoll/c-peter-wagner-dominion-theology-and-postmillennialism-on-npr b 996000.html.

Jeffrey, Grant R. 1998. *The Signature of God.* Nashville : Word Publishing, 1998. cited on website: http://revelationrevolution.org/matthew-24-commentary-that-generation-shall-not-pass/.

Josephus. *The Wars of the Jews 5.10.5.*

Kercheville, Brent. Undated. Unveiling the future. *Revelation made clear.* [Online] Undated. [Cited: 17 11 2020.] https://thebookofrevelationmadeclear.com/.

Kirkus. The-Spanish-Inquisition. Henry Kamen: The Spanish Inquisition. *Kirkus.* [Online] The-Spanish-Inquisition. [Cited: 29 May 2021.] https://www. kirkusreviews.com/book-reviews/henry-kamen/the-spanish-inquisition/.

Koesta, Helmut. Undated. The Great Appeal. *Frontline.* [Online] Undated. [Cited: 28 5 2021.] https://www.pbs.org/wgbh/pages/frontline/shows/religion/why/appeal.html.

Kroll, Paul. 2016. The Millennium of Revelation 20. *Grace Communion International.* [Online] 2016. [Cited: 12 Jul 2017.] https://www.gci.org/bible/rev/millenn.

Larkin, Clarence. Undated. The Resurrections. *Blue Letter Bible.* [Online] Undated. [Cited: 9 Jan 2021.] https://www.blueletterbible.org/study/larkin/dt/16.cfm.

LeBrun, Ken. undated. The Commandment to Restore and to Build Jerusalem. *The Patmos Papers.* [Online] undated. [Cited: 24 9 2017.] http://www.patmospapers.com/daniel/457.htm.

Leupold, H.C. 1969. Exposition of Daniel; Baker

Lim, David PhD. 2018. A Missiology of Philippine Roman Catholicism on Overcoming Nominal Christianity. 2018.

Lindsey, Hal. 1970. *The Late Great Planet Earth.* s.l. : Zondervan, 1970.

Luther, Martin. 1528. *Concerning Rebaptism: A Letter to Two Pastors, 1528, Luther's Works, Vol. 40, 225-262; translated by Conrad Bergendoff.* s.l. : Cited in http://www.patheos.com/blogs/davearmstrong/2013/06/exchange-with-anti-catholic-calvinist.html#ySliyzs0vdAHWoXW.99, 1528.

MacPherson, Dave. 1975. http://www.preteristarchive.com/dEmEnTiA/1975 macpherson incredible-coverup.html. *http://www.preteristarchive.com.* [Online] 1975.

Mallett, Mark. 2020. Jesus is coming. *The Now Word.* [Online] 23 November 2020. [Cited: 11 February 2021.] https://www.markmallett.com/blog/jesus-is-coming/.

Mallett and O'Connor, Mark and Daniel. 2020. *Countdown to the Kingdom; The Time of Fatima is here.* [Video] s.l. : Queen of Peace Media, 2020. https://www.youtube.com/results?search query=mark+mallett+and+daniel+o%27connor+youtube.

Mandryk, Jason and Wall, Molly. 2016. *Third Lausanne Younger Leaders Gathering (YLG2016) held in Jakarta, Indonesia, from 3-10 August 2016.* Jakarta : https://www.lausanne.org/content/state-world-jason-mandryk-molly-wall-ylg2016, 2016.

McArthur, John. 1969. *Grace to you.* [Online] 1969. [Cited: 09 09 2019.] https://www.gty.org/library/sermons-library/1329/israel-in-the-tribulation.

Missions Conference. **Balcombe, Dennis. 2021.** Nagpur : Hosted by Victor Choudhrie, unpublished, 2021.

Muehlenberg. 2017. Theological liberalism and progressive Christianity. *CultureWatch.* [Online] 15 07 2017. [Cited: 16 Oct 2020.]

Orthodox Catachism, Bishop Sotirios Athanassoulas. 2017. *Orthodox-Catechism-Basic-Teachings-of-the-Orthodox-Faith.pdf.* [Online] 2017. https://www.gometropolis.org/wp-content/uploads/2017/01/Orthodox-Catechism-Basic-Teachings-of-the-Orthodox-Faith.pdf.

Pavao, Paul. 2014. rule-of-faith. *christian-history.org.* [Online] Christian History for Everyman. Greatest Stories Ever Told. 2014, 2014. [Cited: 20 September 2020.] https://www.christian-history.org/rule-of-faith.html.

Pope Francis. 2013. Pope Francis 17.11.13 Angelus, St Peter's Square 33rd Sunday of Ordinary Time Year C Luke 21: 5-19 . *Pope Francis homilies.*

[Online] 17 November 2013. [Cited: 11 February 2021.] http://www.popefrancishomilies.com/end-of-the-world.

Pseudo-Ephraim. Est 9th century. *"Sermon of Pseudo-Ephraim on the End of the World" (Syriac version); "On the Last Times, the Anti-Christ, and the End of the World A Sermon by Pseudo-Ephraem" (Latin version).* s.l. : Text available http://www.bible.ca/rapture-pseudo-ephraem-latin-syraic-texts.htm, Est 9th century.

Riddlebarger, Kim. 2018. The Man of Lawlessness. *The Riddleblog.* [Online] 25 7 2018. http://links.christreformed.org/realaudio/20070928a.mp3.

Romanism and the Reformation. **Grattan-Guiness, Henry. 1887.** London : Protestant Educational Institute, 1887.

Ryrie, Charles C. 1953. *The Basis of the Premillennial Faith.* Neptune NJ : Loiseaux Brothers, 1953. ISBN 0-87213-741-4.

Sadler, Rachel. 2021. Coronavirus pandemic a chance to 'build back better', ensure there's future 'pandemic readiness' - Helen Clark. *News Hub.* [Online] 2 February 2021. [Cited: 11 February 2021.] https://www.newshub.co.nz/home/new-zealand/2021/02/coronavirus-pandemic-a-chance-to-build-back-better-ensure-there-s-future-pandemic-readiness-helen-clark.html.

Schaff, Philip. 1893. Fathers of the Third century; Julius Africanus p235 Fragments: On the seventy weeks of Daniel. *Ante-Nicene-Fathers vol 6.* [Online] 1893. [Cited: 10 Jan 2021.] https://www.ccel.org/ccel/schaff/anf06.v.v.xvi.html?highlight=daniel,seventy,weeks#highlight.

Schwab, Klaus. 2020. Now is the time for a great reset. *World Economic Forum.* [Online] 3 June 2020. [Cited: 11 February 2021.] https://www.weforum.org/agenda/2020/06/now-is-the-time-for-a-great-reset/.

Scott, James W. undated. How many resurrections are there? *The Orthodox Presbyterian Church.* [Online] undated. [Cited: 9 Jan 2021.] https://opc.org/new horizons/NH98/04c.html.

Sheeran, Josette. 2017. hunger-in-the-21st-century-the-need-to-feed-smarter/. *ideas4development - Agence Francaise de Development.* [Online] 19 February 2017. http://ideas4development.org/en/hunger-in-the-21st-century-the-need-to-feed-smarter/.

Sister Lucia. 1941. The message of Fatimah. *Congregation of the Doctrine of the Faith.* [Online] 8 December 1941. [Cited: 11 February 2021.] http://www.

vatican.va/roman curia/congregations/cfaith/documents/rc con cfaith doc 20000626 message-fatima en.html.

Sizer, Steven. 2000. http://www.informationclearinghouse.info/article4531. htm# edn111. *http://www.informationclearinghouse.info.* [Online] 12 Dec 2000. [Cited: 26 Mar 2017.] http://www.informationclearinghouse.info/ article4531.htm# edn111.

Sproule, R C. 1998. *The Last Days According to Jesus, pp.156-157).* s.l. : Amazon, 1998.

Storms, Sam. 2014. I am an amillennialist because of revelation 20. *Sam Storms enjoying God.* [Online] 19 05 2014. [Cited: 26 02 2021.] https:// www.samstorms.org/enjoying-god-blog/post/i-am-an-amillennialist- -because-of--revelation-20.

Tacitus. *Annals 15.44.4.* s.l. : Cited by http://revelationrevolution.org/matthew-24-commentary-that-generation-shall-not-pass/#easy-footnote-bottom-11.

The Interactive Bible. 2012. The interactive Bible. *Bible.ca.* [Online] 2012. [Cited: 12 Jul 2017.] http://www.bible.ca/pre-date-setters.htm.

The International Bible Encyclopaedia. 2001. What is the significance of numbers in scripture? *Bible.org.* [Online] 1 Jan 2001. [Cited: 12 Jul 2017.] https://bible.org/question/what-significance-numbers-scripture.

Twenge, Jean. 2014. *Generation Me.* s.l. : Amazon, 2014.

UCG. undated. Bible Commentary: The decree of Artaxerxes, Ezra 7. *United Church of God.* [Online] undated. [Cited: 24 9 2017.] http://bible.ucg.org/ bible-commentary/Ezra/Ezra-sent-to-Jerusalem-by-Artaxerxes'-decree/.

Wikipaedia. undated. Three Secrets of Fatimah. *Wikipaedia.* [Online] undated. [Cited: 12 February 2021.] https://en.wikipedia.org/wiki/Three Secrets of F%C3%A1timaaedia.

Wikipedia. undated. Catholic missions. *Wikipedia.* [Online] undated. [Cited: 25 May 2021.] https://en.wikipedia.org/wiki/Catholic missions.

—. Historical-revision-of-the-Inquisition. https://en.wikipedia.org/wiki/ Historical revision of the Inquisition. *Wikipedia.* [Online] Historical-revision-of-the-Inquisition. [Cited: 29 May 2021.] https://en.wikipedia.org/ wiki/Historical revision of the Inquisition.

—. Left Behind (2014 film). *Wikipedia.org.* [Online] [Cited: 28 October 2017.] https://en.wikipedia.org/wiki/Left Behind (2014 film).

—. **Undated.** Timeline of Christian Missions. *Wikipedia.* [Online] Undated. [Cited: 26 May 2021.] https://en.wikipedia.org/wiki/Timeline of Christian missions#cite note-180.

Williams, Dr Dave. 2017. What do you do if you miss the rapture? *Charisma Magazine.* [Online] 04 02 2017. http://www.charismanews.com/opinion/64002whattodoifyoumisstherapture?.

Yosippon, Sepher. *A Mediaeval History of Ancient Israel translated from the Hebrew by Steven B. Bowman. Excerpts from Chapter 87 "Burning of the Temple")* .

INDEX

✠ ✠ ✠

PUT IT INTO PRACTICE! E-LETTER AND COURSES FROM 222 FOUNDATION[52]

✝ ✝ ✝

NEW TESTAMENT END TIME STUDY GUIDE

Check it out for yourself! The only way to really know what the Bible teaches on the end times is to study the scriptures yourself! All the main NT scriptures are compiled with brief commentary and study / discussion questions. Guidelines for the Book of Revelation help you understand it. Plus Daniel's 70 "sevens" in depth. Available on https://222foundation.net

"THE WORLD CHANGER" – E-LETTER ON PUTTING BIBLE PROPHECY INTO PRACTICE

On-going commentary on Bible prophecy and world events by Robin Corner and others, along with Biblical teaching and practical suggestions for mission. You can subscribe through our website, or by email. https://222foundation.net/world-changers-resources/

---

[52] Robin started the 222 Foundation in 2007, to provide training and motivation for discipleship movements. The name is drawn from 2 Timothy 2:2 "And the things that you have heard from me among many witnesses, commit these to faithful men who will be able to teach others also."

WORLD CHANGERS COURSE

"World Changers Course" – discipleship course equipping us all to be led by the Holy Spirit, effective in mission, able to endure hardship, and experiencing Christ's richness and love. Taught by WhatsApp and other media. Includes discussion on Bible prophecy, meeting with Christian disciples from different nations and mentoring by successful CPM practitioners. Ecumenical. Available as a complete course, or individual modules, to churches, other Christian communities or groups, and individuals – all welcome. More information on our website and/or by email. https://222foundation.net/events/

222 INTERNATIONAL CHRISTIAN NETWORK

✠ ✠ ✠

A world-wide network of Christians dedicated to be authentic Christian disciples and to complete the Great Commission. See website for details – https://222foundation.net/prayer-168/

Website: https://222foundation.net
Email: info@222foundation.net
Robin Corner personal email: robinc@222foundation.net

Printed in the United States
by Baker & Taylor Publisher Services